WITHDRAWN

Teaching Death and Dying

AMERICAN ACADEMY OF RELIGION

TEACHING RELIGIOUS STUDIES SERIES

SERIES EDITOR
Susan Henking, Hobart and William Smith Colleges

A Publication Series of
The American Academy of Religion
and
Oxford University Press

TEACHING LEVI-STRAUSS
Edited by Hans H. Penner

TEACHING ISLAM
Edited by Brannon M. Wheeler

TEACHING FREUD
Edited by Diane Jonte-Pace

TEACHING DURKHEIM
Edited by Terry F. Godlove, Jr.

TEACHING AFRICAN AMERICAN RELIGIONS
Edited by Carolyn M. Jones and Theodore Louis Trost

TEACHING RELIGION AND HEALING
Edited by Linda L. Barnes and Inés Talamantez

TEACHING NEW RELIGIOUS MOVEMENTS
Edited by David G. Bromley

TEACHING RITUAL
Edited by Catherine Bell

TEACHING CONFUCIANISM
Edited by Jeffrey L. Richey

TEACHING RELIGION AND FILM
Edited by Gregory Watkins

AMERICAN ACADEMY OF RELIGION

Teaching Death and Dying

EDITED BY

CHRISTOPHER M. MOREMAN

OXFORD
UNIVERSITY PRESS

2008

OXFORD
UNIVERSITY PRESS

Oxford University Press, Inc., publishes works that further
Oxford University's objective of excellence
in research, scholarship, and education.

Oxford   New York
Auckland   Cape Town   Dar es Salaam   Hong Kong   Karachi
Kuala Lumpur   Madrid   Melbourne   Mexico City   Nairobi
New Delhi   Shanghai   Taipei   Toronto

With offices in
Argentina   Austria   Brazil   Chile   Czech Republic   France   Greece
Guatemala   Hungary   Italy   Japan   Poland   Portugal   Singapore
South Korea   Switzerland   Thailand   Turkey   Ukraine   Vietnam

Copyright © 2008 by The American Academy of Religion

Published by Oxford University Press, Inc.
198 Madison Avenue, New York, New York 10016

www.oup.com

Oxford is a registered trademark of Oxford University Press

Library of Congress Cataloging-in-Publication Data
Teaching death and dying / edited by Christopher M. Moreman.
    p. cm.
Includes bibliographical references and index.
ISBN 978-0-19-533522-4
1. Death–Religious aspects–Study and teaching.
I. Moreman, Christopher M., 1974–
BL504.T43 2008
202'.3–dc22   2008014442

9 8 7 6 5 4 3 2 1

Printed in the United States of America
on acid-free paper

For Carol Leger
Who learned more about death
than any one person should ever have to

Acknowledgments

This collection has traveled a long road to finally arrive at the point it is now. Along this road, a number of people have provided much needed assistance, and as ever, I must express thanks where thanks are due.

Obviously, as a collection of essays, I must thank all of the contributors to this volume. Everyone involved has been patient throughout the process and has willingly taken my advice where it was worthwhile. I am very thankful for all of the great effort and energy that went into crafting each of the chapters that constitute this volume.

I want to express considerable thanks to the AAR's Susan Henking, who is editor for the Series on Teaching in Religion and who encouraged me throughout the earliest (and most difficult) stages of making this collection a reality. Dr. Henking recognized the importance of this particular subject for the series and persevered through rounds of proposals, reviews, revisions, and organization. This volume would not have come to light without her dedication to it. Likewise, I must express thanks to Cynthia Read, the editor at OUP, for also recognizing the value of this contribution and for assisting in the final stages of getting the text to print. Thanks are also due to Krishna Mukerji, and the rest of the staff at OUP, who worked diligently to see this project through. Thanks also to Josh Hayne for assistance in some details.

I must express thanks to Jim Strathdee for allowing the lyrics to his song, "Listen to the Dark," to be used in Amir Hussain's chapter, titled after the song. Also, thanks to Dr. Jeremy Hall, editor of *Dialogue: A Journal of Religion and Philosophy*, for providing permission to reprint Paul Badham's essay, "Life after Death." I would also like to acknowledge gratitude to the Organization of American Historians for providing permission to reprint Dr. Albert N. Hamscher's article, "Talking Tombstones: History in the Cemetery," from the *OAH Magazine of History*, as a part of his chapter in the present volume.

Finally, I'd like to express thanks to Deena Rymhs, whose example I cannot hope to achieve but is enough to spur me on to greater heights of my own.

Contents

Contributors

Paul Badham is Professor of Theology and Religious Studies at the University of Wales, Lampeter, and the Director of the Alister Hardy Religious Experience Research Centre also housed there. He is also a Senior Research Fellow of the Ian Ramsey Centre for Science and Religion at Oxford University, a Patron of Dignity in Dying, and he teaches for an MA in "Death and Immortality." His publications include *Christian Beliefs about Life after Death* (1976); *Immortality or Extinction?* (1982); *Facing Death* (1996); *The Contemporary Challenge of Modernist Theology* (1998); *Religious Experience in Contemporary China* (2008); and "Concepts of Heaven and Hell in the Modern Era," in Peter Jupp (ed.), *Death our Future* (2008).

David E. Balk is Professor at Brooklyn College where he directs Graduate Studies in Thanatology. His research has examined adolescent bereavement over the death of family members and friends. He is collaborating with colleagues at different universities to establish the prevalence and severity of college student bereavement. With department colleagues and a Brooklyn physician, Balk is examining the psychological impact of early pregnancy losses. Balk is Associate Editor and Book Review Editor of the peer-reviewed journal *Death Studies*, and Editor-in-Chief of the 2007 publication *Handbook of Thanatology: The Essential Body of Knowledge for the Study of Death, Dying, and Bereavement*.

L. Stafford Betty is Professor of Religious Studies at California State University, Bakersfield. His interests include Asian religions and philosophies, philosophy of religion, mysticism, literature, and death and afterlife. Recently published papers focus on a new argument for God's existence, Jung's attempt to accommodate his theory of synchronicity to the near-death experience, the implausibility of materialism in the face of paranormal evidence, and the implications of "possession phenomena" for psychiatry. He is presently marketing his book *Faith of a Skeptic*. He also writes fiction with religious and paranormal themes. His novel *Thomas* (1998) is a research-based saga of Thomas the Apostle's travels through India.

Lucy Bregman is Professor of Religion at Temple University, Philadelphia, Pennsylvania. She received her Ph.D. from the University of Chicago Divinity School. She has written *Death in the Midst of Life* (1992), *Beyond Silence and Denial: Death and Dying Reconsidered* (1999), and *Death and Dying, Spirituality and Religions* (2003) and other publications on contemporary perspectives on death and religion. She has taught an undergraduate death and dying class for decades and has mentored teaching assistants and adjuncts who also teach sections of this course. She has been active in American Academy of Religion and is a member of Association for Death Education and Counseling.

Kathleen Garces-Foley is Assistant Professor of Religious Studies at Marymount University and received her doctorate in religious studies from the University of California at Santa Barbara. Garces-Foley has published articles on the hospice movement and funerals and is the editor *of Death and Religion in a Changing World* (2006). She teaches courses on religious approaches to death and religious pluralism in America. Garces-Foley is also presently co-chair for the AAR's consultation on Death, Dying, and Beyond. She also studies multiracial churches and is the author of *Crossing the Ethnic Divide: The Multiethnic Church on a Mission* (Oxford University Press, 2007).

John Graham-Pole graduated from St Bartholomew's Medical School, London University, and since 1976 has been on the faculty of London University, Case Western University, and University of Florida. He is now Emeritus Professor of Paediatrics and Palliative Care at the University of Florida. Most of his working life has been spent in oncology; his primary clinical, research, and teaching interests and expertise are in art, palliative care, and spirituality and health. He has authored or edited six books, including three poetry anthologies, and about 250 peer-reviewed articles and chapters. He has given invited talks in North and South America, Europe, and Asia.

Albert N. Hamscher is Kenneth S. Davis Professor of History at Kansas State University and the author of two books as well as scholarly articles that examine judicial administration and politics in seventeenth-century France. He teaches the course Death and Dying in History and under the auspices of the Kansas Humanities Council, regularly gives presentations about cemeteries in towns across Kansas. In recent years, he has also published articles on U.S. cemeteries in *Kansas History* (2002), the OAH *Magazine of History* (2003), and *Markers: Annual Journal of The Association for Gravestone Studies* (2006). His edited collection of scholarly articles, *Kansas Cemeteries in History*, appeared in 2005.

Estelle Hopmeyer is an Associate Professor of Social Work at McGill University. She presently teaches an undergraduate course in Social Work Practice with Groups and a graduate course on Life Threatening Illness, Bereavement, and Loss. A telephone call, close to 20 years ago, from a suicide survivor seeking a support group led Hopmeyer, and a colleague, to develop a graduate level course on bereavement. That area of specialization has evolved to include issues related to chronic and terminal illness and non-bereavement loss.

Amir Hussain is Associate Professor in the Department of Theological Studies at Loyola Marymount University in Los Angeles, where he teaches courses on world religions. His own particular specialty is the study of Islam, focusing on contemporary Muslim societies in North America. His most recent book is *Oil and Water: Two Faiths, One God* (2006).

Dorothy Lander is Senior Research Professor in Adult Education at St. Francis Xavier University, Nova Scotia, and a recently bereaved spouse. She received her Ph.D. from Nottingham University, England. Her research, teaching interests, and expertise span art, palliative care, women's social movements, popular education, and arts-based qualitative research. She has presented and published in peer-reviewed journals and practitioner conferences on her arts-based qualitative research and organizational studies; and, with John Graham-Pole, on art, palliative care, and love medicine.

Michael McKenzie is an Associate Professor of Philosophy and Religion at Keuka College in the Finger Lakes region of New York. He has written books in the disciplines of ethics and religion, and numerous articles and essays on the religious geographies of upstate New York and the West Coast of the United States. Currently he is working on a book that examines the growth of Methodism in the nineteenth-century, specifically looking at how this denomination fared in the diverse environments of the Pacific Northwest.

Christopher M. Moreman is Assistant Professor in the Department of Philosophy at California State University, East Bay. He completed a Master's degree in the Study of Mysticism and Religious Experience from the University of Kent at Canterbury and a Ph.D. in Religious Studies from the University of Wales, Lampeter. His interests are in mystical and religious experience, especially as these relate to death and the afterlife, as well as popular culture and new religions. He recently founded the program unit, Death, Dying, and Beyond at the American Academy of Religion and is the author of a comparative study of beliefs and experiences relating to the afterlife, *Beyond the Threshold: Afterlife Beliefs and Experiences in World Religions* (2008).

Diana Walsh Pasulka is a junior faculty member and Assistant Professor in Religion at the University of North Carolina, Wilmington. Her research focuses on representations of the afterlife in the nineteenth-century United States, as well as representations of immortality and the immortal in contemporary popular culture. She also has written and presented on Catholic iconography and themes in popular fiction and movies.

Christian Perring is Associate Professor of Philosophy at Dowling College, Long Island, New York. He has a B.A. in Physics and Philosophy from Oxford University, an M.Sc. in History and Philosophy of Science from King's College, London, and a Ph.D. in Philosophy from Princeton University. He is editor of *Metapsychology Online Reviews* and has published a number of papers in medical ethics and philosophy of psychiatry. He has a broad range of interests in philosophy, including moral psychology, personal identity, philosophy of education, applied ethics, philosophical counseling, metaphysics of morality, and philosophy of law.

Sarah K. Pinnock is Associate Professor of contemporary religious thought at Trinity University in San Antonio, Texas. She received her Ph.D. in Religious Studies at Yale University specializing in the philosophy of religion. Her major publications include *Beyond Theodicy: Jewish and Christian Continental Responses to the Holocaust*, an edited book entitled *The Theology of Dorothee Soelle*, and "Atrocity and Ambiguity: Recent Developments in Christian Holocaust Responses" published in the *Journal of the American Academy of Religion*. In 2006–2007 she held a Fulbright grant in the Theology Faculty at Latvia University. Currently, she is conducting research on mystical selfhood in the writings of French philosophers Simone Weil and Luce Irigaray.

G. Lee Ramsey Jr. holds the position of Professor of Pastoral Theology and Homiletics at Memphis Theological Seminary in Memphis, Tennessee. A Ph.D. in Religion from Emory and Vanderbilt Universities, he is an ordained United Methodist minister and frequently teaches courses in pastoral care at times of grief and loss. His current research interests include the use of fiction and film to instruct students on the arts of Christian ministry.

Vanessa Rebecca Sasson has been teaching at Marianopolis College since 1999 and is Professor of Comparative Religion in the Liberal Arts Department. She is also a Research Fellow in the Department of Biblical and Religious Studies at the University of the Free State, Bloemfontein, South Africa, and Adjunct Professor of Comparative Religion at McGill University. Sasson is the author of *The Birth of Moses and the Buddha: A Paradigm for the Comparative Study of Religions* (2007) and co-editor of *Imagining the Fetus: Embryology and Mythology from around the World* (forthcoming).

Teaching Death and Dying

I

Introduction

Christopher M. Moreman

Death is, of course, a topic of concern for every person, eventually affecting each of us. From the dawn of humankind, death has been an important issue in the lives of thinking beings, as archaeological evidence indicates a religious attitude toward the treatment of the dead from the time of the earliest humans. Religions have attempted to answer the ultimate questions of life and death and what lies beyond. Many of the major world religions, from Hinduism to Christianity, have considered matters of antemortem theology of prime importance. Others, like Judaism and Confucianism, have largely focused on this life here and now, though always acknowledging the mystery of death in their teachings. The fact of death is the greatest philosophical problem facing every human today.

Death is an unavoidable fact of life that is entirely unknown and effectively unknowable. The certainty of death does not bring with it the comfort of expectation; the fear of the unknown overpowers any such possible comfort and produces naught but fear and avoidance. The West has been described as a death-denying culture for some time, and though the meaning of this description may be debated, the fact of death's uncertainty likely invokes a certain reaction of fear or avoidance in every person regardless of cultural heritage. "Death denial" might more aptly be described as "death avoidance," "death ignoring," or perhaps euphemistically as "life affirming." The inevitable cessation of life as we know is, perhaps understandably, an unsettling thought to consider. Much more comfortable is to simply ignore the inevitable and live as if death is something that happens only to others.

Ignoring the reality of death has some very serious consequences, however, for the individual and for society as a whole. In efforts to deny their own mortality, many have supported the progressive compartmentalization of death and the dying to the extent that one need not witness the death of the other and so not be reminded of mortality at all. Instead, the dying have had to pass through this final rite of passage away from the comforts of home and family and instead die under the bright lights of the hospital surrounded by strangers. Outside the new halls of death, most people continue to live on without thought to the grander meaning of life thrust to the fore by a consideration of one's mortality. Even among health professionals who have been increasingly trained to deal sympathetically with the dying and their families, the denial of death carries on. Hannelore Wass points out how new euphemisms are simply replacing old ones in an Orwellian newspeak of death denial masked as acceptance and empathy. "We are taking the 'D' words out of new death education programs, calling them education for 'end-of-life care,' or time-efficiently, 'EOL,' 'EPEC [Education in Palliative and End-of-Life Care].' 'Hospice' care is becoming 'palliative,' 'palliative' is taking the place of 'terminal,' and dying patients are merely 'life-threatened.' "[1] It is apparent that death education has much more work to do.

The death education movement has been a relative newcomer to academia, but is one that is seeing a general increase in interest and attention as the wave of the baby-boomer generation crests and an increasingly large percentage of the population collectively nears that unavoidable end. David E. Balk points to studies indicating the widespread interest among undergraduates as well in courses on death, emphasizing that a good number of students also express some anxiety over death, even at their young age (see chapter 7). Indications are that such courses hold more than simply an academic interest for students, many of whom realize the universality of the experiential side of death itself.

Often, courses in death and dying have been aimed at professionals who might have to deal directly with the grieving or the dying, and so the methods and intentions of education have been of a practical nature. There is a wide body of students in other disciplines, however, interested in such courses for a variety of reasons. Courses on some aspect of death and dying can be found at most institutions of higher learning, though these courses are scattered over several departments. Courses entitled Death and Dying or something similar can be found taught in departments of psychology, anthropology, sociology, and social work, as well as religious studies. The Web site for King's University

College at the University of Western Ontario lists over 100 institutions that offer specific courses in the study of death, though this number does not include the thousands of others that offer service courses within nonspecialist departments.[2]

Problematically, when one department offers a course on death, it generally restricts the availability of related courses in other departments, so limiting the disciplinary perspectives present within said course. Most of the courses being so designed will lean toward the psychosocial elements of grief and bereavement, ignoring the variety of religious elements inherent in death itself. This particular complaint has been raised by more than one scholar of religious studies engaged in the study of death-related material. I, for one, from first-hand experience of this very problem, can attest to the lack of cross-disciplinary communication. While I was teaching at one university, the department chair of religious studies lamented to me that the psychology department had "got" the death and dying course, and so our department could not offer a similar course. Under the rubric of a "special topics" course, however, I was able to teach a course dealing with concepts of the afterlife across religions. Unfortunately, as a special topics course, its availability would be severely limited so as not to encroach upon the terrain of the psychology department. I was, however, able to cooperate with the psychology professor who was teaching Death and Dying. We exchanged guest lectures, and through this cooperation, it became obvious that the established course on death and dying, as offered by the psychology department, was completely ignorant of concerns raised in religious studies. Certainly, further communication between those offering such courses should be important to providing students with a balance. *Teaching Death and Dying* aims to meet this need, at least to some small degree, from both the perspective of those in religious studies as well as those in psychology and other fields engaged in the teaching of death and dying. The present volume aims to meet a more interdisciplinary need addressing issues relating to the teaching of death-related material, in ways that not only have practical professional applications (though these are addressed) but also might have implications for the more fundamental questions of meaning in life that are probed in a more general education.

Teaching Death and Dying brings together a range of scholars who have taught death-related courses. These scholars not only represent a range of disciplines but also bring distinct perspectives to their courses. The chapters that form this volume present the reader with differing perspectives without judgment as to the value of one over another. It is hoped that readers will draw from each chapter some value that might aid in their own teaching or simply in their own considerations of death. Christina M. Gillis correctly states that "while death may be the vanishing point of medical knowledge and representation, it is also a point of mediation. Neither doctors nor humanists, nor artists nor policy makers, can provide answers where death is concerned; any inquiry into its cultural, scientific, and perhaps even spiritual contours must be a plural one."[3]

On one hand, the present volume addresses the need for plurality in including voices from across disciplines in an attempt to encourage conversation across departmental boundaries that might not otherwise be crossed. The universality of death as a part of human experience necessitates a cross-disciplinary conversation. Represented disciplines include philosophy (Christian Perring), theology (G. Lee Ramsey), psychology (David E. Balk), social work (Estelle Hopmeyer), education (Dorothy Lander), history (Albert N. Hamscher), and medicine (John Graham-Pole). As a volume within the American Academy of Religion's Series on Teaching in Religious Studies, it will not be surprising that scholars of religious studies make up the balance of the contributors. Religious studies might seem to be a natural home for courses on death given the general tendency to associate established religion with consolations for human mortality, but religious studies is itself a relatively young field and it has been slow to integrate with death studies. Aside from a short-lived experiment in the 1970s, the American Academy of Religion (the largest community of scholars in religious studies in North America) did not have a program unit devoted to the study of death until I founded one in 2001.[4] The present volume thus adds to the newly emergent coordination of religious studies scholars involved in the study of death.

Even within the realm of religious studies, this volume offers widely divergent perspectives. For instance, readers will encounter religious studies scholars working in areas including the psychology of religion, comparative religion, cultural studies, paranormal and religious experience, and ethics. In addition to the broad range of perspectives from which contributors in the present volume view death, these scholars offer a breadth of methodologies from which the reader might draw inspiration. Readers are encouraged to approach this collection as if one is entering into a conversation. The tone of the papers presented herein is a conversational one, with many of the contributors offering very personal anecdotes. Indeed, the need to be personal in discussion of the subject of death and its teaching is noted by several of the authors. Some incorporate personal experience very deeply into pedagogical methodology to great effect, while most others recognize the importance of the experiential aspect of death and grief as they relate to such courses. S. Brent Plate elsewhere relates his own experience of discovering his partner's cancer while teaching about death, forcing him to a realization: "It wasn't until my personal confrontation with death that I realized just how much the two different approaches toward death—one theorizing about it, one living in its midst—are deeply connected."[5] The fact of death faces every one of us, both teacher and student, and so a course on death takes on a very personal tone by necessity. This situation presents very unique opportunities for learning as well.

A recent issue of the *Chronicle of Higher Education* included an article titled "A Professor's Own Grief Informs a Course on Mourning in Literature" that described a course offered by Jeffrey Berman, who became interested in teaching a course on death after the unexpected passing of his wife from pancreatic cancer.[6] The article points out that Berman "decided to share his grief with students in the classroom," and in his own words, Berman states: "Teaching courses on dying and death not only helps me deal with my own grief, but it helps my students when they write about their feelings of grief." Berman's statement raises some important questions about what ought to be going on in a course on death. For one thing, is it at all appropriate for a professor to be using the classroom to work out his or her own personal issues? For another, should students be expected to "write about their feelings" in a university classroom? The article further describes Berman's classes as "emotionally charged," with students occasionally excusing themselves, and mentions one student even exploding in anger. The issue of death is one that will evoke many emotions, and managing such emotional responses will, to some extent, fall upon the professor. It is important, therefore, for a professor teaching such a course to be as well prepared as possible. The article ends by citing a student in Berman's class, who says, "Mr. Berman taught the class less as an authority and more as a student himself. It was his own experience with death . . . not his position as professor, that gave him authority." One fundamental premise in the collecting of the essays in the present volume is that one should most certainly have some measure of authority in the classroom, and that this authority comes in large part from the knowledge of how best to approach the subject at hand. First-hand experience with death will have an impact on how one handles the material of such a course, but there is much more that is needed than simply experience in order to be considered an authority on the subject. Further, being that the subject of death is such a sensitive and universally important one, it requires particular attention to how it will be taught.

The first section of this volume presents three approaches to answering the question of what ought a course on death accomplish. Lucy Bregman brings her wealth of experience to bear upon the question from within the framework of the evolving death-education movement and attempts to relate the field to religious studies. Recognizing the monopolization of death studies by groups outside of religious studies, such as psychology or social work, Bregman attempts to reconcile the philosophies brought to the subject by these disciplines with an approach more clearly suited to religious studies. She makes clear the difficulties inherent in subjecting an area that is as deeply personal as death to objective academic scrutiny, and poses questions directly relevant to the kinds of teaching described by not only Berman above but many of the authors in the present volume. That later chapters will come into direct philosophical conflict with Bregman's conclusions is the very heart of academic debate, and in this context will hopefully ignite further discussion of these and other issues in the teaching of death.

Christian Perring takes on the issue from an entirely different angle, breaking the issues down in philosophical detail. Perring eruditely describes the "standard approach" to teaching a death-related course and points out some serious deficiencies, especially in regard to the variation that exists in the outcomes expected of such courses. He ponders conceptions of teaching that are aimed at skill development and wonders what kinds of skills might be inculcated by a course on death, if such should be the aim in the first place. When held up to scrutiny, Perring wonders how these kinds of courses prepare students to make moral decisions regarding death, or whether this should even be an aim of such courses.

Vanessa R. Sasson offers a discussion of how the typical survey course in world religions might be constructed thematically around the subject of death and dying. She describes being thrust into the position of offering a broadly comparative introductory course and electing to focus it on death as a means of making the material more manageable for both instructor and students. Sasson had great success with this model, and describes how she sees death as the perfect pivot for a survey of world religions. Not only do the world's religions all encounter death in their own particular ways, but students can be engaged by the concept of death in a number of ways that they may otherwise miss.

The second section of this volume follows from the first in presenting some practical approaches to the teaching of death-related material. The contributors presented here all come from disciplines that aim to train professionals in how to deal with the dying and the bereaved. G. Lee Ramsey begins this section by detailing the ramifications of death-related material from the Christian ministerial perspective. His chapter actually deals with two distinct issues. There is on one hand the matter of adequately training professionals who might be sensitive to the dying and bereaved while also understanding their condition, which is a concern for the subsequent two chapters as well.

On the other hand, Ramsey as a seminarian is also concerned with maintaining a distinctly Christian vision, and so confronts the issue of promoting faith in the face of suffering and death. Ramsey's chapter is unique in this regard as the rest of the chapters included in this volume speak from within a secular academic framework. Regardless, Ramsey deals with issues that will be relevant beyond religious boundaries.

It is worth recognizing, while on the subject, that the present volume does privilege a Western secular perspective on teaching. Bregman's chapter, for instance, refers directly to efforts to distinguish religious studies as a secular academic discipline from other faith-based kinds of education, such as that presented by Ramsey. While the essays in this volume all speak specifically about teaching death-related matter, questions remain regarding the overarching framework of secular versus faith-based education, not to mention culturally influenced conditions that might result in different requirements for teaching. For instance, the present volume includes only Western scholars from the United States, Canada, and the United Kingdom. I recently had the opportunity to participate in an international conference on death, dying, and spirituality, held at Sogang University in Seoul, South Korea. Korean scholars at this conference expressed a genuine openness to expanding internationally the cooperation on the study of death. A future volume might offer perspectives from other cultures and educational contexts in order to see where there may be similarities shared or differences that need to be met.

Estelle Hopmeyer, coming from the area of social work, continues examining the practical needs for a death-based education. Hopmeyer presents pedagogy as it is offered to students preparing for a career in counseling, especially as it relates to the bereaved. She has been involved in the foundation and development of a center for bereavement counseling in Montreal, Canada, aside from her teaching in the Department of Social Work at McGill University. Following from the first section, this chapter again presents an alternative perspective on what a course on death should accomplish. Here, Hopmeyer examines the practical needs of students preparing for an extremely hands-on form of counseling, as social workers are apt to find themselves dealing with the most disenfranchised grievers. Hopmeyer and Ramsey share some distinct similarities in purpose as they both endeavor to train professionals to deal directly with the bereaved. Still, major differences appear even apart from the specifically religious framework, given that both of these professionals will expect to deal with very different groups of people and so have distinctly different methods and aims. While the debate over what a course on death should accomplish is important, it must always bear in mind the possibility that there may be varying valid answers to this question.

David E. Balk finishes out this section with a chapter dealing with the psychology of grief, specifically relating to students in a course on death. With a long-standing interest in thanatology and pedagogy, Balk offers his expertise in psychology in the context of creating an atmosphere that encourages student learning, while at the same time maintaining an awareness of grief and the reality, and potential proximity, of death to students. Despite his personal focus in psychology, Balk incorporates a discussion of pedagogy that generally opens itself to conversation with other disciplinary approaches. Balk explicitly reaches out for an ongoing dialogue on issues relating to teaching death; it is my hope also that this volume will assist in sparking just such dialogue.

The third section of this volume moves to an explicit examination of teaching methods, one that orients itself towards the uses of media as teachers and in teaching. Today's students are increasingly media savvy and the introduction of various media in the classroom has become a staple of the professor's repertoire. Diana Walsh Pasulka begins this section with a thought-provoking analysis of the media-influenced context from which students approach death. Pasulka discusses the difficulties that arise when trying to discuss the relevance of life's one true certainty with an audience that has been raised in the postmodern media-drenched environment of the hyper-real. While one may question some of Pasulka's examples in her comparison of the real to the hyper-real (for instance, her denial that Jediism is a religion as compared to Judaism, on the grounds that the latter relates to a specific divine Creator, where the former does not), the issue of knowing one's audience is a critical one. Again, such discussion has much wider relevance than to the issue of death alone, but the undeniable fact of death makes an interesting starting point when examining the uncertainties inherent in the postmodern mind. Professors need to be aware of their audience as much as of the material they present.

Michael McKenzie follows with a detailed discussion of how one might use media in the classroom, here focusing on Hollywood films as the means by which to get a message across. The use of films as teaching aids is mentioned by several contributors to this volume, particularly Hopmeyer and Hussain, illustrating how widely this medium is already being employed in the classroom. McKenzie presents pedagogical theory germane to the use of film as a teaching aid, and then embarks on a description of his own experiences with specific films and how they worked and why. In light of Pasulka's chapter, the use of media would seem to be increasingly important as a means by which to reach students minds. McKenzie makes clear the usefulness of this medium in the classroom.

Moving on to section 4, the volume switches focus from popular depictions of death and their presentation in the classroom to discussions of how one might take the students out of their comfort zones and situate them in such a way that brings death into focus for them. Albert N. Hamscher, a historian, offers his insights derived from teaching courses on death from a historical perspective. Expanding upon a previously published essay, Hamscher emphasizes the need for a hands-on student experience of history, and in this case, death. To get this hands-on experience, Hamscher has developed a cemetery-based exercise that allows his students an opportunity to get out of the classroom and read history from the markings of the cemetery.

Kathleen Garces-Foley follows from this chapter with her own suggestions for escaping the classroom and providing the student with hands-on experience. Garces-Foley also discusses the options presented by taking a class to the cemetery, and adds some ideas for bringing students to a funeral home as well. The experience of witnessing the inside of the death industry is an invaluable and normally unavailable one to most. Garces-Foley also includes several caveats and warnings for conducting successful site visits. Such caveats are essential in order to avoid causing distress in students, professors, or anyone else that might be involved. Again, it is worth keeping in mind both Bregman's observations at the outset of this volume as well as the questions raised by the example of Berman given above. Garces-Foley is among those contributors who make an attempt to walk the line between these two positions.

Part 5 examines the importance of written narrative in the classroom. Sarah Pinnock begins this section with a detailed literature review and a discussion of the appropriateness of certain texts for a course on death. Pinnock makes the case for the use of literature as a means of reaching the student and making the facts of death more relevant, an argument that runs along similar lines to that urging the use of visual media in the classroom. Pinnock goes further, however, in disavowing the usefulness of formal textbooks and preferring the engagement that students can experience with a work of literature. In her chapter, Pinnock provides a brief literature review in defense of her case that no suitable textbook exists and that literature is a more useful tool for teaching. As anyone who has offered a survey course on death in religious studies knows, it is apparent that no single text is suitable. Most texts relevant to teaching such courses are geared toward disciplines other than religious studies, usually psychology. Further, those surveys of religious beliefs concerning death and the afterlife are generally culturally biased or neglect major world religions.[7]

Amir Hussain takes up the issue of alternative media in teaching with his very personal account of his own experience with the death of his wife, and how this life-altering event affected his ideas of teaching about death. To some extent, Hussain appears in a similar vein to Berman and Plate mentioned earlier, but Hussain's approach to his own experience is unique. For one thing, he brings a specifically Muslim perspective to his own personal loss, as re-flected in his finding solace in the Qur'an. On the other hand, Hussain also realizes the very personal nature of death and grief, and so has developed methods that aim at bringing this personal component home to students in ways that give the students complete control. Hussain brings his own expe-rience with death openly into the classroom, but he does not derive his au-thority from this experience. Further, Hussain invites students to discover personal connections with death that come from everyday experience, such as listening to a particular song or watching a certain television program. Through discussing these various examples, Hussain provides a learning environment for both students and teacher alike. As he mentions in his essay "Shannon's Song," a first-person account of his experience of the loss of his wife, his grief at loss was transformed into a joy at having had. In connection with his own teaching experience, Hussain offers brief outlines of how he has succeeded with certain types of media, namely video, literature, and music. The first two have been covered in greater depth by other contributors (McKenzie and Pinnock), but Hussain's use of music lyrics and poetry lies at the heart of his chapter. Hussain's approach is one that allows the students to offer media of their own choosing that relates the course material to each of them individu-ally. By example, Hussain offers "Shannon's Song." He ends the chapter by including that essay, as well as the lyrics to a song, both of which help to bring the fact of death to the level of the real in a way that generally connects with students. Hussain encourages interfaith dialogue, and his teaching of a course on death accomplishes something along similar lines; he found solace per-sonally in the Qur'an, and he allows students to discuss and discover a variety of other personal responses and reactions to death.

This fifth section ends with another very personal account from Dorothy Lander and John Graham-Pole. In this very experimental chapter, they ex-amine the potential that might be found in using autoethnography, combining a personal (often therapeutic) elegiac letter-writing to the dead with a conver-sational dialectic analysis of these same writings. With Lander and Graham-Pole, the individual becomes the producer of the literature which can then be analyzed along with a partner or group. Hussain's use of "Shannon's Song" is similar here in that he uses an elegy that he himself has written, and then develops the meaning behind this with his class. Lander and Graham-Pole diverge from Hussain in two important ways. For one, they address their writings directly to the dead. But more important, they create a learning situation by entering into a dialogue about the writings. As a kind of experiment in pedagogy, it appears to be very successful on a personal level, and may have applications in a broader context. Much as Hussain attempts when inviting students to choose material that is personally relevant, Lander and Graham-Pole encourage each other to actually produce the relevant material. This approach obviously has limitations in as far as a typical university course might go, but the applications of the basic outline are more broad, and one can see how this approach might even work in situations where the goal is to overcome grief. Were one to introduce such methods into a general classroom on death, however, one would be treading on dangerous emotional ground and would certainly have to take great care.

Lander and Graham-Pole's continuing bonds with the dead provide a bridge to the last section of this collection. Closing out the collection of essays, there are two chapters dealing specifically with the afterlife. It is in this area that religious studies has perhaps more to offer than any other single discipline. Paul Badham begins this section offering a chapter that has been previously published and is now regularly used as a guide for teachers at the preuniversity A-level, and also as an introduction for students entering the master's program, Death and Immortality, at the University of Wales, Lampeter. In this short chapter, Badham provides a brief summary of beliefs and some attendant experiences while making the case for the importance of keeping both in mind when considering issues relating to death for use in the classroom.

L. Stafford Betty follows by presenting the case for why a discussion of the evidence for an afterlife is crucial to a course on death. Many courses of death, especially in religious studies, provide a survey of beliefs in the afterlife, but Betty urges readers to consider the history of human experience associated with these beliefs. Reports of contact with the dead have been common across cultures and throughout history, but have been sorely under investigated. Especially for scholars of religious studies, questions of the relationship between experience and belief are fundamental. Whether occurrences such as a near-death experience or a death-bed apparition are the product of wishful thinking associated with culture-specific beliefs or whether the experiences themselves predate and so influence the beliefs, the fact that such experiences have been recorded by cultures throughout history deserves closer attention. Betty points to some of the basic literature on the study of experiences relating to an afterlife. This material requires further study and ultimately has implications related both to death and to life itself.

Many of the ideas presented in the following chapters can work when combined with one another, while others may be diametrically opposed. All these ideas share the fact of having already influenced the way courses on death have been taught. By bringing these ideas together, we can critically evaluate them for their merit, and it is hoped that where they be deemed successful, their influence may spread. The International Work Group on Death, Dying and, Bereavement has recommended several criteria for death-education: that it (1) incorporate an interdisciplinary body of knowledge; (2) integrate theory and practice; (3) promote sensitivity to the personal nature of its subject; and (4) provide emotional support for its students.[8] The essays found in this volume when taken collectively cover each of these criteria in detail. If the essays in this collection serve to spark further dialogue on issues relating to teaching death, or provide insight to inspire other teachers in this area, then the volume has succeeded.

NOTES

1. Hannelore Wass, "A Perspective on the Current State of Death Education," *Death Studies* 28: 4 (2004): 303.

2. King's College Centre for Education about Grief and Bereavement, "Where to Study about Death, Dying, and Bereavement," http://www.uwo.ca/kings/academic _programs/centres/deathed/courses-death.html (accessed October 25, 2007).

3. Christina M. Gillis, ed., *Seeing the Difference: Conversations on Death and Dying*, Occasional Papers of the Doreen B. Townsend Center for the Humanities, nos. 24–25 (Berkley: University of California and the Doreen B. Townsend Center for the Humanities, 2001), vi (preface).

4. It is through the founding of this program unit—Death, Dying, and Beyond— that the present volume gained inspiration.

5. S. Brent Plate, "Bringing Ideas about Life and Death to the Classroom," *Chronicle of Higher Education* 49, no. 26, March 7, 2003, B5.

6. Erik Vance, "A Professor's Own Grief Informs a Course on Mourning in Literature," *Chronicle of Higher Education* 53, no. 36, May 11, 2007, A22.

7. My own forthcoming volume, *Beyond the Threshold* (Lanham, MD: Rowman & Littlefield, 2008), aims to address this last problem.

8. C. A. Corr, J. D. Morgan, and H. Wass, *International Work Group on Death, Dying, and Bereavement: Statements on Death, Dying, and Bereavement* (London, ON: King's College, 1994), 236.

BIBLIOGRAPHY

Corr, C. A., J. D. Morgan, and H. Wass. *International Work Group on Death, Dying, and Bereavement: Statements on Death, Dying, and Bereavement*. London, ON: King's College, 1994.

Gillis, Christina M., ed. *Seeing the Difference: Conversations on Death and Dying.* Occasional Papers of the Doreen B. Townsend Center for the Humanities, nos. 24–25. Berkley: University of California and the Doreen B. Townsend Center for the Humanities, 2001.

Moreman, Christopher M. *Beyond the Threshold.* Lanham, MD: Rowman & Littlefield, 2008.

Plate, S. Brent. "Bringing Ideas about Life and Death to the Classroom." *Chronicle of Higher Education* 49, no. 26, March 7, 2003, B5.

Vance, Erik. "A Professor's Own Grief Informs a Course on Mourning in Literature." *Chronicle of Higher Education* 53, no. 36, May 11, 2007, A22.

Wass, Hannelore. "A Perspective on the Current State of Death Education." *Death Studies* 28: 4 (2004): 289–308.

PART I

What Ought a Course on Death Accomplish?

2

What Should a Course on Death and Dying Accomplish? "Death Education" in an Undergraduate Religion Course

Lucy Bregman

Death Education

From the beginning of the modern death awareness movement, "death education" has been a part of its mission. It is still part of the title for a leading professional organization, Association for Death Education and Counseling (ADEC). But what is meant by "death education"? What is its meaning within the context of the "death and dying" movement, which encompasses healthcare workers, funeral directors, therapists, chaplains, and social workers, as well as professional educators at all levels? And, after we have answered these questions, how does this vision of "death education" coexist with the goals of a religion course in an academic department at the college or university level? This essay explores these two very different enterprises, which come together in the course Death and Dying taught by the Temple University Religion Department and in many similar courses at other schools. Although such courses were established during the early flowering of the death awareness movement in the 1970s, they no longer necessarily reflect that ethos, nor has the death awareness movement remained unchanged. Yet over the decades since that post-Vietnam era, the popularity of REL 343 Death and

Dying has never waned, nor is it likely to do so even if there are drastic changes in the curriculum requirements for undergraduates.

The blend of death education and the academic study of religion in this course is not obvious, or without potential conflicts. Certainly there is a need for some reflection on what can or ought to be happening in this mix of two different enterprises. This essay draws on my long-term experience teaching this class and mentoring the many teaching assistants and adjuncts who also teach sections of it. I can truthfully say that during two-and-a-half decades of this work, the philosophy behind the course and its basic aims have never been a problem. Instead, problems include finding suitable textbooks and sufficient staffing. Since the course currently runs approximately fourteen sections of thirty-five students each semester, and about five sections in the summer, we are talking of a large-scale endeavor. Perhaps the reason for the lack of faculty debate over the aims of the course is because it is so successful, so well enrolled semester after semester. Even those who might otherwise question its intellectual foundations can't argue with the boost it gives to departmental enrollment figures. As for students' perceptions of what goes on in the course, the issues discussed in this paper have never been a source of wonder, questioning, or complaint. Perhaps I should consider us all fortunate, and leave this enviable situation alone. In contrast, a course on women in Islam, for instance, is likely to provoke complaint and controversy from both faculty and students, no matter who teaches it and what her/his relation to Islamic tradition may be.

The modern death awareness movement can be dated back to the early work of Herman Feifel, and even more to that of Elisabeth Kübler-Ross, particularly her 1969 book *On Death and Dying*. This book opened the door to public discussions about hospital care for the dying, the experience of "being dying" in America, and the accompanying experiences of the families. Dying and bereavement, rather than death per se, were the foci of this movement, yet the book title gave its name to the entire area, which soon flourished in the wake of Kübler-Ross's popularity. From this start, there has always been a mix of clinical and research goals, an interdisciplinary focus, and a distinctive moral vision. The pioneers all discovered that death in American society was taboo—silence and denial reigned. In a climate where doctors were told, "The one thing you never do is to discuss death with a patient," the movement aimed to overcome this repression. "The notion that patients could offer important lessons for health care professionals was viewed as radical," recalls one reviewer of the movement's foundations.[1] We could learn from the dying and bereaved how to live in the face of death, rather than flee from it. The movement hoped to change not only the training and practice of doctors and nurses but also the societal attitudes that made death and dying taboo. Thus, death education included the following goals: "to promote discourse about death; integrate the dying with the living; explain the developmental processes of death understanding and grief; heighten sensitivity about cultural variations in dying, death and grief; and appreciate the universal and individual course of the grief experience."[2] To use a term developed later by researchers in the field, Americans' grief and suffering was "disenfranchised,"[3] and the role of the death educator was to overcome silence and denial.

Such a model of education exceeded the boundaries of the traditional classroom. Death educators could seize "teachable moments," such as the death of a pet, a classmate, or a co-worker, to model newer, more open attitudes toward the topic. But they also used a variety of planned venues and strategies to get the message across, that discourse about death was better than silence and that it was possible to integrate the dying with the living, death with life. Some of these venues were workshops open to the public, with speakers such as Kübler-Ross or others well known in the field. The openness of the movement toward "expertise" of the dying and bereaved meant that speakers' formal credentials were often less important than hands-on experience. In the countercultural ethos of the early 1970s, suspicion of "head-trip" knowledge bolstered this. For instance, the workshops of Stephen Levine had intentionally little cognitive content and were scornful toward anyone who intellectualized or tried to turn death into an academic exercise. But as the movement matured, concern for credentialing, certification, and standards of expertise gradually triumphed, so that virtually all the conferences I have attended since the mid-1990s have offered continuing education credits for those who wanted them or needed them for employment.

In addition to workshops and open-to-the-public conferences, the National Hospice Organization began in 1971, the aforementioned ADEC professional organization was established in 1976, and other professional organizations began to take an interest in the field. For some, the label "thanatology" helped define the field as the scientific empirical study of death and dying. For others, this misleadingly played into the hands of those who wished to keep death "medicalized" and its study a branch of psychiatry. Maybe the field wasn't "science," or wasn't exclusively science. It was an enterprise where counselors, social workers, and chaplains probably played a larger role than those who focused on research. Moreover, the presence of chaplains right from the earliest days of Kübler-Ross shows that hostility to religion was never part of its agenda; to recognize dying and loss as human experiences rather than medical problems was an aim shared by the religious and the secular alike. The relation of this movement to religions is complex[4] but unthematized and ignored in contrast to the relation to the medical profession and the healthcare establishment.

Another area of death education was the filming of subjects focused on death and dying, in a manner aimed at breaking through Hollywood visions. A plethora of television specials tried to do this, sometimes failing because the actors themselves had too much life and liveliness to accurately portray a desperately sick hospital patient (for example, Maureen Stapleton did not look like someone seeking active euthanasia—she looked about ready to get up and dance at an all-night party—in the film version of Betty Rollin's *Last Wish*). More "realistic" documentary treatments included *Walk Me to the Water*, a series of black and white still shots of hospice patients.[5] Other contributors to this anthology will focus on the use of films in the college classroom, but it appears that the American media were receptive at this level to the message of the death awareness movement. As the above example indicates, a source of film plots were the many autobiographies that appeared in print to support the death awareness movement with personal examples and testimonies. Silence was replaced by storytelling, and a large number of books whose plots charted terminal illness or bereavement overwhelmingly endorsed the basic moral vision of death integrated into life.[6] Many of the authors/autobiographers were not professional writers; they felt it important to let the world know what suffering from cancer, liver failure, and later, AIDS, was really like. These books were also memorial tributes to the dead individuals, written by those who had loved and cared for them. They continue to appear, and continue to be justified by appeal to their function as death education.

But the death awareness movement also developed college-level courses on death and dying, taught in a variety of departments and programs.[7] There seemed no necessary reason why a course on death and dying could not be offered by psychology, health education, nursing, philosophy, social work, medical humanities, or religious studies departments. Recent reviews of such courses by ADEC officers and committees has led to new calls for standards of professional knowledge,[8] but not for housing them in any one specific department or program.

Moreover, even with the most academic, research-oriented approach to classroom instruction, the moral agenda intrinsic to all death education endures. Death and life could be integrated, and participants will be better able to encounter and interpret their own experiences with death and dying and bereavement. Therefore, at a personal level, a course on death and dying could help overcome American society's denial of death. College-course instructors, conference speakers, and workshop-leaders were expected to have done this for themselves. Teaching about death should not become just another way to intellectualize and repress its emotional significance, and instructors could continuously appropriate their own message and recognize its helpfulness.[9]

I believe this goal lies at the heart of the modern death and dying, or death awareness, movement. We do not just study neutrally *about* death, we face it in our own lives and model this stance for our students. This is the ideal behind all death education, even when the research aims and specialized professional goals are stressed in the syllabus. It is apparent on the first class day, when the instructor resolutely refuses to use euphemisms and talks about "death" directly. This pattern of personal involvement and modeling may parallel activities such as "music education" and "health education." It is one reason why selecting appropriate adjuncts to teach a religion department death and dying course can be tricky. They are not future pastors, chaplains, or counselors, they are graduate students in religion who need to teach part-time to continue their studies of the Qur'an or Japanese Buddhism or Derrida. But as an aim, it has not been publicly problematic, and no one has ever turned down the chance to teach "Death and Dying" because they disagreed with the basic aims of "death education," as we have defined it.

Religious Studies

How does this ideal of death education fit within the aims of a religion department, especially at a public state university? It is immediately obvious that the trajectory and history of religion study is very, very different from that of death education. The aim of instructors who teach religion at an institution of higher learning cannot be defined as providing a way for students to "deepen one's faith," or experience "personal religious growth," even if that happens as a side-effect for some students. Our aim is to broaden the students' understanding of the important roles religion has played and continues to play in the lives of the world's peoples. It is to convey how the world's religions have handled universal and fundamental questions of life and meaning, including the roles for death and dying in an ultimate and transcendent environment. It is a goal congruent with liberal arts education, and it is guided by the 1963 Supreme Court decision *Abington v. Schempp*, which distinguishes teaching *about* religion (legal) from religious instruction in the classroom (unconstitutional). It is a goal intentionally severed from the personal religiousness of the instructor and of the students. In the words of a colleague, "Just as studying math does not turn you into a triangle, studying religion does not make you religious."[10] Or, in response to the suggestion that personal religion was indeed a prerequisite for work in the academic field, one young instructor fired back, "Do all oncologists have cancer?"[11] Even for those who find both these statements extreme, there is a real difference between the aims of a religion department at a university and the model of death education sketched above.

How different can be seen by a close look at the contributions to *The Chicago Forum on Pedagogy and the Study of Religion,* from which the latter quote was drawn. The essays in this collection focus on religion courses within the context of humanities education in liberal arts, and assume that there is indeed a moral dimension. Religion is viewed as an object of study, and occasionally an obstacle to proper engagement with humanistic education. Students' religious beliefs are part of what they bring to the classroom, but the dominant focus is on severing the close connection between personal belief and how one studies anything. The disruptive nature of religious beliefs, whether from the "Satanist in the classroom" or in the subtler form of Christian biases in the theories about religion developed by founders of the field, is a pervading theme. Even the contributor who wants to speak more intentionally and directly about theology actually finds that relatively high levels of religious affiliation among students go along with massive and all but universal ignorance about their own traditions (let alone anyone else's).[12] The major themes, again and again, are that education unsettles, and this is its legitimate moral agenda. Students' religiousness is not a resource in this enterprise but an impediment, an unexamined and yet-uncriticized baggage some of them bring to their college work. These essays may reflect the atmosphere of the University of Chicago, but I believe they express pervasive attitudes in the field as it has flourished since the 1960s.

I believe the actuality of religion study in colleges is more double-edged than the Chicago authors manage to convey. Religiousness can motivate students to study about their own traditions, and personal dissatisfaction with their religion of origin can point them toward exploring other, exotic traditions. In this engagement, "obstruction" and "ignorance"—let alone the analogy to cancer!—are far from the best images to employ. For example, within the framework of "studying about religion," a student has a chance to pit his/her personal experiences with Hinduism against what Huston Smith and other textbook authors think Hinduism is "really about." Maybe the idealized philosophically oriented portrait in the textbook is a product of its author's hidden Protestant bias, or maybe he simply overlooked the range of religious phenomena for other reasons. But the discrepancy cannot be laid down to "student ignorance" and a lived experience within a Hindu family *is* a resource for reflecting on the many dimensions and levels within which a religious tradition operates.

Intrinsic to our aims for the study of religion are visits to sites of worship for our basic introductory courses. These visits are possible because, as Clifford Geertz noted, most religions do have occasions when they are "on display," when the public performance of the religion is available to engage visitors and insiders alike.[13] This kind of assignment isn't mentioned by any of the Chicago contributors, yet I suspect it is pretty standard for urban campuses if not everywhere. Sometimes what students notice helps them reflect back on what they are used to, or onto their preconceptions, and see differently, which is exactly one of the Chicago contributors' goals for religion study. But the results of this process can be marvelously unpredictable. My favorite example of this was the group visit of a class to a local mosque. The male students all wrote about how sexist Islam is because the women have to stand in the back. The female students wrote how welcomed they felt, how they found the ceremonial ablutions really meaningful, and how they liked praying around other women. These visits also portray religion as a living activity, important to recognize as a present, contemporary feature of the culture, rather than as a remnant or leftover from the past. Not just the cultural past; every student raised religious was probably exposed to the "kid version" of their tradition, and to recognize that an "adult version" is more normative and sometimes radically different from what they know, is part of the process. Here, too, I'm not sure if "ignorance" covers the situation. The greedy Hindu child who hears his parents warn him, "Don't eat so much, or you'll be reborn as a pig!" is learning *something*, even if it sounds nothing like Huston Smith.

But do we require that all our students confront questions such as Who is God for you personally? What does your faith mean to you now, in contrast to when you were a child? and How has your faith been tested by your life-experiences as a college student? No. No. No. The Chicago contributors would take all such questions as confusions over cancer versus oncology. Even if I suspect that a religion course at a religiously based institution might well find some of these appropriate questions to guide syllabus construction and class time, the atmosphere within which university-based "religious studies" arose and grew post-1963 was filled with suspicion of such goals. They smacked of pious indoctrination, "religious education" as Sunday school would practice it. It did not help that sometimes university trustees were confused about this and hoped that the presence of a religious studies department on campus would reduce student rowdiness and drunkenness. (No, I am not kidding about this!) Residual resistance to religion programs on the part of faculty of other departments undoubtedly includes this issue, and the Chicago contributors all would admit that their enthusiasm for "teaching about" religion (even using the dubious theories of *Religionswissenschaft*) includes reaction against this model of religious education.

From the students' side, those who wish to write reflection papers on their religious experiences quickly learn that personal testimonies in and of themselves do not work, and that critical reflection is what we as college instructors are after. An autobiographical narrative such as "How *chi* energy changed my life" is not what studying Asian religions should be about. Not that this is necessarily the disruptive "Satanist in the classroom," but it needs to become raw material for class discussion and critical analysis, rather than personal witnessing. From the instructor's side, this means that those who wish to directly promote devotional or meditative practice in the classroom are doing something that is not only unconstitutional, but ill advised educationally, given our basic aims. (The Chicago contributors did not even bother to mention this, but I must, given the topic of this essay). At a multi-religious but basically secular university supported by public funds, we have to be clearer and more hard-nosed about this than at other kinds of schools. Moreover, an older generation of faculty, some refugees from wartime Europe, may have been particularly attuned to the potential abuse of the classroom for religious indoctrination. (Others were egregious violators of this norm, however; it is not neatly a generational problem.) While the issue of religious advocacy has been clearly defined legally, it is not always clear that other kinds of advocacy are ruled out, or what guidelines should be followed. Student complaints often reveal their perceptions of misuse of instructor's power for special advocacy ("He turned the class into a vote for the Kerry campaign!") and my sense is that some kinds of advocacy are less than successful. But nothing in the religious studies model supports the inclusion of personal and existential goals so intrinsic to death education. In truth, the issues seem so different on the surface that advocacy for hospice (of which I am surely guilty) will never be noticed as advocacy, nor will it be the subject of student complaints.

Death Education within a Religion Course: "Honoring" Experiences

And, what might these personal and existential goals be for a class on death and dying? It has long been recognized that students come to such courses for all sorts of personal reasons; they often seek an opportunity to come to terms with family deaths or other traumas within the context of the course. The list of death education goals neither rules this out nor makes it primary. A presupposition in favor of using the death education class to challenge the silence and denial of death in the society at large makes it likely that the course can serve as a safe space to discuss these personal concerns. Yet suppose a student wants to write on the death of her brother by gang violence? Or on taking care of a grandmother who died at home of cancer the year before? Unequivocally, death education norms require that we "honor" these experiences, and consider them potentially part of the students' education. I put the word "honor" in quotes because it has become part of therapists' jargon, frequently appearing in death education presentations, while *never* in the essays on pedagogy in religious studies. To "honor" experiences means to respect that we are meeting a person with a narrative of personal identity, a story that includes suffering and sometimes traumatic events. For this student, these experiences help define who he or she is, they are not just "beliefs" that ought to be challenged and critiqued in a liberal arts class. To honor experiences does not mean to gush over the recital of this narrative, or to give the student course credit or a higher grade simply for having a dramatic narrative to tell. This theme of honoring experience strongly counteracts the stress of the Chicago contributors on the ignorance and unreflective and occasionally obstructive nature of students' religion, which presumably means that their religious experiences must be overcome or set entirely aside before real education can begin.

How do we include this sense of "honoring" in ways that will fit within liberal arts education, especially when few if any of the persons teaching our death and dying course are trained counselors or therapists? I am always happy to recommend the University Counseling Center and its grief support groups to students who want them, but an academic course is very different from grief support. (This should be made clear from day one, and perhaps included on the syllabus.) Nevertheless, the course is an opportunity to place these personal nonacademic experiences in a context of reflection, theoretical frameworks, and historical and philosophical study. Many of us have found ways to achieve this goal without sacrificing the academic credibility of the course or indirectly undercutting the norms of religious studies courses in a university context. In the process, we have made some accommodations that perhaps depart from the Chicago ideal of liberal arts education, or at least challenge its idealized picture of higher education in humanities.

One such accommodation is to shift away from the "traditional term paper" to more innovative and course-specific kinds of writing assignments. This has been a major movement at Temple anyway, and I suspect at other schools too. Partly it is in response to plagiarism from the Internet, but there has also been a long-term push to make course assignments more "life-like," and so offer better preparation for workplace tasks. We have long known that we do not replicate ourselves, that few of our students will be heading toward academic careers. There is pressure against making the undergraduate curriculum into a dumbed-down version of graduate training (a concern also noted by Jonathan Smith, one of the Chicago contributors).[14] This goes beyond the situation of being a "service department," for it affects every program to one degree or another. In the case of the death and dying course, substitution of interview projects for term papers has been a success. An interview project gives the student a chance to think through issues of personal interest, relating these back to materials studied in the course. It must be planned out in advance, and it requires a well-defined topic or issue. So, not "My brother's funeral," but "How does the Roman Catholic Church now celebrate the funerals of sui- cides?" will work. Projects that cover personal experiences include "How does the death of a father affect the life of his teenaged son?" and "For women who have had abortions, is their experience something like mourning a dead child, or is it a bad surgery experience, or something else?" This latter topic works really well to avoid the slogans of the abortion debate, which is itself a plus. Others match "textbook" accounts of religions against the actual appropriation of these. "Do Baptists really believe in Hell, and if so, how does this get applied in the cases of problematic deaths?" and "Do the Jewish mourning practices help heal grief for nonreligious as well as religious Jews?" are samples.

But this kind of assignment takes coaching and planning on the instruc- tor's part. It is not as easy as assigning a term paper, and it requires a more activist stance than simply reading student journals. (There are other problems with student journals, especially given our students' need for feedback on their writing.) But it can work to help find academic space for even the most hor- rendous personal traumatic events, linking study with life and deaths already experienced. This is one way that the basic aim of death education can be fulfilled, while preserving the goal of critical reflection and analysis of theo- retical material. And, because this assignment is so "course specific," the very few examples of plagiarized interview projects stand out like sore thumbs.

However, such a strategy assumes that students are already having plenty of nonacademic experiences with death and dying, even before they set foot in class. Sadly, in my experience, this is a very safe assumption. "Ignorance" in this area is not the norm. I guess there are a few students who know no one who has died, have had no friends killed in car wrecks or by drug overdoses. But that is just not the case for most. I do try to alert students that if they have experienced very recent losses, they should postpone taking the course and consider other resources (such as those of the Counseling Center). I some- times urge students to drop the course mid-semester when they have over- estimated their emotional resiliency (or their capacity to do well in four to five courses plus a part-time job). Many Temple students come from the Philadelphia inner city, and with depressing frequency they write of brothers and other relatives shot in gang wars or dying of AIDS. But my stereotypes can get upset as well; a sweet-looking white girl from rural Pennsylvania wrote a paper in which she mentioned how she witnessed a family murder. Have students faked such tales, to get sympathy or even just to have something exciting to write about? I doubt it. Indeed, the number of "pre-exam grand-mother deaths" in this course is ironically miniscule compared to that in any other course. When family deaths are reported, they are almost invariably con-vincing, and students bring in funeral directors' notes, Mass cards, and so on to document the event. Surrounded by fellow-students whose tragedies are often mentioned in class discussion, those tempted to fake traumas seem to be dis-couraged from doing so.

Recall that the death awareness movement assumes that persons are probably already suffering from unvoiced experiences of this sort, which in America are "disenfranchised." There was no need whatsoever to manufacture such experiences; they were already present, albeit made invisible and inau-dible. They cast shadows over the students' abilities to face the new situation and friendships of college, let alone complete assignments on time. The task of breaking silence and denial about such traumas and losses was what the death awareness movement took on, and still considers its basic moral agenda. A death and dying class had better be safe space for discussing such other-wise closed-off areas of experience. The truly obstructive "Satanist in the class-room" would be the instructor who insists that in an academic course such personal experiences are entirely off limits. Here, then, the difference between "having cancer" and "oncology" seems to get blurred, for we wouldn't all be doing this course if we did not share some of the concerns over dying, end-of-life-care, and grief. Indeed, ironically for the religion instructor who used the analogy, the experiences of future oncologists with cancer (in themselves or their families) are probably very relevant to shaping their aims as doctors; see the discussion of Sandra Bertman below.

Personal Experiences in the Classroom

But there is another side to this matter. If students already have nonacademic, deeply emotional experiences to bring to the course, that is one thing. For me or any instructor to intentionally produce these is quite another matter. That would indeed be a practice parallel to training the class in contemplative prayer, which would violate the norms of our religion curriculum. Here, I am absolutely adamant that just as I do not make prayer or meditation a required class activity, I do not engage in the kind of classroom guided exercises whose sole purpose is to provoke personal experiencing of inner emotional issues regarding death. I am old enough to recall participation in the "touchy-feely" exercises of the Human Potential Movement; I do not think these have stood the test of time as pedagogy, at least in the setting I work in. This means I do not ask students to write their own obituaries or imagine themselves lying dead in their coffins. Perhaps these leftovers from the 1970s, however they were intended, are a kind of denial of death's destructive and disruptive power. They are ways to bring death near and make it controllable and spookily comfortable; my students, most of them, already know better. This was never, really, what death education was meant to be about, although in the enthusiasm of the early death awareness movement it sometimes took these forms.

There may be some contexts, however, in which sensitizing future professionals to their own attitudes and expectations does call for something closer to this. Medical humanities arose explicitly to supplement the scientific model of training for doctors which left them ill-equipped to practice medicine as a human "art" and to understand the patients' perspectives on the experience of illness. Here, death education is one important element of this endeavor, and indeed the need for medical humanities is closely tied to the complaints against doctors' impersonal and denial-ridden attitudes towards dying voiced so frequently within the death awareness movement. As already hinted, that cancer/oncology analogy so inappropriate for religion study *is* worth pursuing here, since the personal history of illness and emotional attitudes toward it definitely shape the identities of those who work in the healthcare field. Silently and half-consciously such inner personal factors remain, even as the dominant scientific paradigm of medical education holds sway and discourages exactly this kind of introspective awareness of personal motives.

For an excellent example of the challenge to this paradigm, and as an example of death education which intentionally induces emotional experiences, we may take Sandra Bertman's fascinating use of artwork in her medical humanities classes. (This is found in *Facing Death: Images, Insights, and Interventions*, significantly subtitled *A Handbook for Educators, Healthcare Professionals and Counselors*). Bertman displays and juxtaposes artwork so as to provoke and jar—to evoke memories and feelings of anxiety and helplessness, for example. The purpose of her course is not to study art history, nor to increase art appreciation (though it probably does accomplish this for some) but to prepare future doctors for encounters and experiences they will surely undergo.

Images from the visual and literary arts . . . can stimulate insight, dialogue, solace and even resolution. Employed with patience and sensitivity, these images can elicit responses and attitudes toward death heretofore unspoken or acknowledged even to ourselves. The very act of naming our worst fears is a step toward mastery. . . . Often simply articulating such unmentionables is enough to initiate the painful but necessary work of grief.[15]

Does this model fit with "religious studies"? Absolutely not, as the Chicago contributors would all agree. I believe at this point I am with them; it certainly seems much more appropriate for specific professional education, and presumes a much more narrowly self-selected group of students than does the undergraduate humanities class. Yet it is intriguing to imagine how religious studies might have developed had it been promoted as a vehicle for stimulating solace and insight, or to initiate the necessary work of grief or recovery of religious sensibilities. Even assuming the Constitutional questions could have been resolved, such aims as these were extraordinarily far from the ethos of the 1960s when the push to establish "study about religion" in state-supported universities was strongest. Love/hate, loss and yearning for the liberal Protestant tradition may have been an undercurrent in the field's favorite theories, and among those who first staffed religion departments, but the stance toward this has been very different from Bertman's.

However, even without this goal of explicitly and intentionally inducing death-related emotionally loaded experience in the classroom, I can guarantee that some will happen. They will happen because of the nature of the topic. But there is also a very special niche for them in the space given to non- or extra-academic voices. For this is where guest speakers can do what official faculty instructors cannot. A guest speaker is usually an advocate, or a representative of some group or profession. It is understood that they are "guests," and what they say (while it may appear in some form on the exam!) is said *by them*, and not by me the instructor. Some of their class presentations will inevitably evoke deep anxieties and conflicts. Two examples suffice. For many years, I invited a local hospital pathologist to come as a guest speaker to talk about his work. Dr. K. was a rather boring speaker, but he brought a slide show of memorable autopsies he had performed. An emaciated child, an immensely fat man, a tiny fetus, a woman with her breast eaten away by cancer: these images were a powerful reminder of the bodily side of death. I justified their presentation as a way to balance the psychological and philosophical and world-religions perspectives stressed through the semester, with very concrete focus on embodiment and mortality. No one could doubt that these people were all dead, what we were viewing made clear the messiness of death, especially in the face of students' enthusiasm for "acceptance" and "closure" as goals. Over the years, I watched this slide show time after time, and found it salutary. It became more poignant as I realized that eventually the only earthly survival of these people would be as images of their dead mangled bodies in the autopsy slide show. While the students saw the slides only once, their responses were subdued and thoughtful, just the opposite of fake ghoulishness or bravura in the face of death.

The second example involved "advocacy" in a more direct fashion, as I invited a team from a local group called Action AIDS to give a class presentation on illness, dying, and bereavement as related to AIDS. Inevitably, during the late 1980s and early 1990s, this turned into a practical question-and-answer session, which included telephone numbers to call for anonymous HIV testing. This was classic "health education," relevant to the academic content of the course but clearly more authoritative coming from these guest speakers (most of whom were themselves HIV+). I remember vividly one session where the speaker, in response to a student question, gave some explicit instructions for "safe oral sex." At the time, I felt grateful that questions like this were being answered honestly, and even more grateful that *I* was not the one to do it. (Just in case anyone wonders, I never heard any complaints from students; I paid the honorarium out of my own pocket—except when a dean heard of the organization's visit and offered to find university money to pay for this.) A course cannot realistically be built around guest speakers, for many reasons. But as these cases indicate, there is a role for them which can tip an undergraduate religion course on death and dying temporarily toward the kind of death education that the death awareness movement uses as its model. The overall tenor of the college death and dying course need not be of this type of death education in order to put in doubt some of the assurances that run through the contributions to *The Chicago Forum on Pedagogy and the Study of Religion*. Both religion study and study about death and dying are situated in contemporary life, where religion continues as an element in persons' lives, even as do concerns (and occasionally public debate) over dying and mourning. If death is "repressed" from American society, in spite of far more public discussion of it than when the death awareness movement began, there is also evidence that the academic environment "represses" and "disenfranchises" religion, eliminates its presence from serious consideration. This problem is recognized by Paul Griffiths, one of the Chicago contributors,[16] but so overwhelmingly has this situation taken hold of us in the field, that it seems almost natural to treat students' religiousness as an odd and unwelcome intrusion into the serious business of liberal arts education. As already stated, no language equivalent to "honoring" appears in relation to students' own religious lives and experiences.

I am convinced that careful and truthful recognition of the differences between death education and religion study will help greatly in preparing a death-and-dying course within a humanities model of liberal arts education. But it may not leave this model entirely untouched, unexamined or unchanged. Nonetheless, it is possible to design and teach a course which will enrich students intellectually, as well as in other ways, and remain congruent with the basic aims of religion departments.

NOTES

Those who teach in seminaries and divinity schools where students are assumed to be preparing for the professional ministry may wonder if the strongly secularist tone and suspicion of "religious indoctrination" reflects the universal ethos of religious studies (as with the Chicago contributors), the specific atmosphere at Temple University, or merely the author's personal stance. In response to this, I can report that I taught a version of Death and Dying at a theological seminary, intentionally focusing on material I believed would be resources for students' later work in congregations or as hospital chaplains. I did not attempt to do what CPE (continuing professional education) training would accomplish, nor what Sandra Bertman does. I gave students the same interview project assignment and let them decide if they wanted to cover issues exclusively from the pastoral perspective (and not more than one-third did). I did do some things which could never be done at Temple. Very intentionally, I opened the class with prayer, and invited student prayers for the sick and the bereaved by naming those prayed for. I gathered these names together into a "class prayer list," and distributed it. This was in part a deliberate attempt to model intercessory prayer for those who were going to make it a regular public vocational activity. Ironically, I discovered that this practice was actually unusual at this school, although it met with no criticism or resistance. It seems my long-term affiliation with a secular teaching setting had increased my awareness of what opportunities were open at a religious school, while those used to that environment took it for granted and saw prayer at the start of class as an optional activity, entirely dependent on instructor preference.

1. L. DeSpelder, "So Much to Know: The Foundations of Death Studies," *Forum ADEC Newsletter* 24 (January/February 1998): 1.

2. R. A. Kalish, cited in I. Noppe, "Death Education and the Scholarship of Teaching: A Meta-Educational Experience," *Forum ADEC Newsletter* 30 (January/February/March 2004): 1.

3. K. Doka, ed., *Disenfranchised Grief: Recognizing Hidden Sorrow* (New York: Lexington Books, 1989).

4. See L. Bregman, *Death and Dying, Spirituality and Religion* (New York: Peter Lang, 2003).

5. *Walk Me to the Water: Three People in Their Time of Dying*, a film by John Seakwood (Lebanon, NY: John Seakwood Photography, 1981).

6. L. Bregman and S. Thierman, *First Person Mortal: Personal Narratives of Illness, Dying and Grief* (New York: Paragon Press, 1995).

7. Noppe, "Death Education," 3.

8. Note, for instance, M. Lambrecht, "Death Education Revisited," *Forum ADEC Newsletter* 31 (January/February/March 2005): 13; and also DeSpelder, "So Much to Know."

9. See Noppe, "Death Education," 4.

10. Kalman Bland, personal communication.

11. C. Tolton, in *The Chicago Forum on Pedagogy and the Study of Religion* (Chicago: Martin Marty Center, University of Chicago Divinity School, 2005), 15, http://marty-center.uchicago.edu/fellows/chicagoforum.shtml. Other contributors are J. Smith, J. Hawley, D. Clairmont, P. Griffiths, and D. Simmons.

12. Griffiths, in *Chicago Forum*, 47.

13. C. Geertz, *The Interpretation of Cultures* (New York: Basic Books, 1973), p. 113.

14. Smith, in *Chicago Forum*, 11.

15. S. Bertman, *Facing Death: Images, Insights and Interventions* (New York: Taylor & Francis, 1991), 6.

16. Griffiths, in *Chicago Forum*, 44–45.

BIBLIOGRAPHY

Bertman, S. *Facing Death: Images, Insights and Interventions.* Washington, DC: Taylor & Francis, 1991.

Bregman, L. *Death and Dying, Spirituality and Religions.* New York: Peter Lang, 2003.
———, and S. Thiermann. *First Person Mortal: Personal Narratives of Illness, Dying and Grief.* New York: Paragon House, 1995.

The Chicago Forum on Pedagogy and the Study of Religion. *The Chicago Forum on Pedagogy and the Study of Religion.* Contributors are J. Smith, C. Tolton, J. Hawley, D. Clairmont, P. Griffiths, and D. Simmons. Chicago: Martin Marty Center, University of Chicago Divinity School, 2005. Available online at http://marty-center.uchicago.edu/fellows/chicagoforum.shtml.

DeSpelder, L. "So Much to Know: The Foundations of Death Studies." *Forum ADEC Newsletter* 24 (January/February 1998): 1, 15.

Doka, K., ed. *Disenfranchised Grief: Recognizing Hidden Sorrow.* New York: Lexington Books, 1989.

Geertz, C. *The Interpretation of Cultures.* New York: Basic Books, 1973.

Kübler-Ross, E. *On Death and Dying.* New York: Macmillan, 1969.

Lambrecht, M. "Death Education Revisited." *Forum ADEC Newsletter* 31 (January/February/March 2005): 13.

Noppe, I. "Death Education and the Scholarship of Teaching: A Meta-Educational Experience." *Forum ADEC Newsletter* 30 (January/February/March 2004): 1, 3–4.

3

Ethical Issues in Teaching Death and Dying: Pedagogical Aims in End-of-Life Ethics

Christian Perring

Nearly all ethical issues in teaching can be formulated in terms of what it takes to be a good teacher and the nature of the teacher-student relationship. The ethical issues that arise in teaching a course in death and dying to undergraduates at the college level are mostly issues about how to teach well. For example, consider the following questions:

What academic expertise should a teacher of an interdisciplinary course such as death and dying have?

What personal experience of death and dying should a teacher of such a course have, if any?

Can teachers of such courses be too personally invested in death and dying to be able to teach the topics objectively?

Should teachers of such courses make special allowances for students who themselves are dying, who are currently grieving, or who are currently caring for someone who is dying?

Should a teacher attempt any valuation or assessment of the practices surrounding death or dying in other cultures, or should the tone remain as neutral as possible?

Often textbooks and experts argue that Western Anglo culture of the last fifty years has put the reality of death at one remove, and is impoverished compared to other cultures that face death more squarely. Should teachers endorse this criticism of modern trends or invite students to question it?

Often students complain that a course in death and dying is depressing.
Should teachers try to make the course less depressing?

These are all important questions, but I will not attempt to answer them. My
focus will be on the ethical issues in death and dying, especially as they overlap
with end-of-life issues in medical ethics. I will ask what should be the pedagogical aims in teaching these topics to undergraduates. This is an ethical issue
as much as the other questions above raise ethical issues, in addressing the
stance of the teacher toward the students and what it means to be a good
teacher of the topic of death and dying.

The standard approach to the philosophical discussion of end-of-life issues, which is mirrored in most textbooks for courses in death and dying, is to
present important legal precedents (Quinlan, Cruzan, and undoubtedly in the
future, Shaivo), and to describe and analyze the reasoning of the various parties
involved. Often ethical issues will be presented through the frameworks of
Aristotelian, Utilitarian, and Kantian moral theories. The views of different
religions will be surveyed and compared. Occasionally, issues of personal
identity and the nature of personhood will be raised in connection with debates
over the definition of death.

I will raise the question whether this sort of approach to end-of-life questions is particularly useful to students—and what alternatives might be available if we should want to help students who will face the end of lives of their
friends and family—and even to future health professionals who will face death
and dying in their careers. The current trend in educational assessment is
to focus on the outcomes of the educational experience, and this is generally
couched in terms of the skills that students gain. Clearly, the ability to write
scholarly papers and get high scores in exams will in itself be of little use
outside of college for nonscholars, and we have little evidence that these abilities help to improve decision making of people in "real-life" situations.

Most people will not personally have to be part of drawn-out legal cases
over decisions about whether to remove life-support systems for people who
need them, but they are quite likely to have to make decisions about when to
turn off life-support systems for family members or make other decisions
about how loved ones should end their days. This will often involve talking
with doctors, other professionals who care for the dying, and family members.
The skills of consulting with others in the emotionally-charged time of a
person facing death and making good decisions are rarely if ever covered in
death and dying.

Thus it seems a case could be made for focusing far more on communication and decision-making skills in death and dying courses if the aim of such

courses is to be useful. There would also need to be much more focus on how to integrate the general philosophical/ethical/religious debate into the personal decision faced by a family. Indeed, this could be extended to other areas of competence, such as how to face one's own death with dignity, what kind of funeral to have, and how to help others who are facing death.

It is clear that should courses be given such a practical focus, teachers would also need different trainings in order to be able to successfully teach the skills to students. Currently, nearly all teachers in humanities and social sciences are given an academic training and are taught to instill academic skills in their students. Most teachers have only a hazy conception of how to go about teaching practical skills to students that will be directly applicable outside of the academic sphere.

Once we have clarified what it would be to consciously make a death and dying course useful in the ways outlined above, we can return to the question of whether it is appropriate for a college course to have such aims. It is clear that it is extremely ambitious to integrate academic and practical skills, and furthermore, to do so would erode the traditional distinction between a liberal arts educational training and a professional training. I will argue that this is a necessary move, but that we need to face our limitations in knowing what count as good decisions and well-developed skills, and we need to proceed carefully. Interdisciplinary courses that focus on difficult decisions in personal and professional lives are important new developments in education, but they are hard to teach well. They challenge our conceptions of what a good course is, and lead us to reevaluate how to include values in our teaching.

The "Standard Approach" in Teaching Ethical End-of-Life Issues

Let us consider how ethical issues at the end of life are standardly set up in textbooks for courses on death and dying. These courses are taught in a variety of departments, or in special interdisciplinary slots. Sometimes they are based in psychology, sometimes sociology, and sometimes philosophy and religion. However, the courses are solidly interdisciplinary. For example, *The Last Dance: Encountering Death and Dying* by Lynne Ann DeSpelder and Albert Lee Strickland, includes the methods of psychology, sociology, anthropology, history, religious studies, medical sociology, political science and policy study, medicine, medical ethics, and law, applied to a variety of topics within death and dying.[1] This is a popular book for use in college courses, and its approach is typical. The emphasis of the book is very much on descriptive social sciences.

The chapter "End-of-Life Issues and Decisions" is very much in the same vein, taking a descriptive approach to the way that the ethical and legal issues are set out. It provides discussion on the principles of medical ethics, the nature of informed consent and the right to refuse treatment, the nature of the caregiver-patient relationship, and the ethics of withholding treatment and helping people die more quickly or more comfortably, as well as a discussion of advance directives, which ends the ethics section.

Books that present medical ethics have a very different focus. One of the major textbooks in this area is *Ethical Issues in Death and Dying*, by Tom L. Beauchamp and Robert M. Veatch.[2] The discussion here is far more in depth, and at a more advanced level. The topics are the definition of death, truth-telling with dying patients, suicide, physician-assisted suicide and euthanasia, forgoing treatment and causing death, decisions for forgoing treatment, and futile treatment and terminal care. The collection of articles focuses on legal cases. This approach is typical for discussions of medical ethics when it comes to end-of-life issues. Other textbooks set out the major theories of ethics, such as Aristotelian virtue theory, Kantian deontology, Mill's Utilitarianism, and feminist ethics of care, and then apply these theories to difficult cases.

I want to raise the question whether these approaches to medical ethics in death and dying courses are the most useful. In order to do this, we need to ask what courses in death and dying aim to achieve.

Aims of Death and Dying Courses

Consider the following learning outcomes given by some instructors for death and dying courses.

GRNT(PSYC) 5266/7266
Course Title: Death, Dying, and Bereavement
University of Georgia
By the end of this course, students should have learned:

1. about classic and current research and theories about death, dying and bereavement;
2. to apply a broad set of approaches to understanding death, dying and bereavement;
3. more about their own feelings, attitudes, and beliefs about death, dying and bereavement, and perhaps to expand or change some of them;
4. about demographic, legal, public policy, and ethical issues that pertain to death, dying and bereavement;

5. how life-span human development and culture interact with death, dying and bereavement experiences.[3]

Sociology of Death and Dying
Bachelor of Science in Life and Health Sciences
SOC 304
Breyer State University
Instructor: Dominick L. Flarey, PhD, DCH, RN, CS, CH-C
Course Objectives: Upon completion of this course, you will be able to:

1. Discuss your own beliefs and attitudes about death and dying.
2. Understand and discuss "death anxiety."
3. Identify competing ideas about death and dying.
4. Discuss biomedical approaches to the definition of death.
5. Identify gender differences related to death anxiety.
6. Identify age differences related to death anxiety.
7. Discuss issues of religious beliefs related to death anxiety.
8. Discuss death as an agent of personal and social change.
9. Identify and understand components and functions of the death system.
10. Identify and discuss the history of death education and counseling.
11. Identify major causes of death past, present and future.
12. Identify and discuss the trajectories of dying from beginning to end.
13. Discuss issues of feelings and counseling related to death and dying.
14. Discuss major issues of communications with dying patients.
15. Identify factors that influence the death experience.
16. Discuss theoretical models of the dying process.
17. Discuss a developmental coping model of the dying process.
18. Discuss the hospice approach to care of the dying.
19. Identify and discuss major "end of life" issues and decision making.
20. Understand how people recover from grief.
21. Discuss issues of bereavement in later life.
22. Identify support systems for the bereaved.
23. Identify and discuss the funeral process and what it means.
24. Identify and discuss ways to improve the funeral process.
25. Discuss the issues and experiences of people related to near death experiences.
26. Define and discuss the roles of death educators/bereavement counselors.
27. Discuss the need for death counselors to be counseled.

28. Understand sociological and individual perspectives of the death experience.
29. Discuss issues related to death by suicide.
30. Define and discuss issues related to beliefs in life after death.
31. Identify issues related to children dying.[4]

Grieving & Loss: Encouraging Students and Ourselves
Lin Reese, MST
The Heritage Institute
As a result of taking this class participants will learn:

1. To identify grief or loss related books to use in the classroom
2. To share grief or loss related articles/books with their students
3. To become a "wounded healer"
4. To see when someone is hurting even though words are never spoken
5. To nurture and encourage students and others in their time of loss
6. To teach students how to be peer mentors and help others in grief/loss situations
7. To help students work through their grief[5]

What is striking about these different course descriptions and learning outcomes is how diverse they are. Most are more about learning knowledge, and some are about learning skills that go beyond being able to communicate knowledge. Some of the skills students learn are especially related to counseling and helping others deal with death. It is particularly striking that none of them mentions the skills of decision making when facing ethically difficult circumstances.

When students take a course in death and dying as an elective rather than as a requirement for a major or minor or a particular training program, then we need to ask what purpose the course can serve for them, and whether existing courses are serving that purpose.

It is clear that people often face ethical problems when they have life-threatening conditions or they know people who are dying, and that the emergence of new medical technology has made such ethical quandaries occur more often.[6] As we gain the ability to extend life for longer, we have to ask whether it is right to do so, and under what conditions it is better to deliberately end life or let people die.

Every student will face the death of a friend or family member, and is likely to eventually face his or her own death. The interdisciplinary nature of the course means that so much is covered that some of it is bound to be relevant to the student in a fairly direct way. Most obviously, understanding the processes through which people face their own possibly terminal illnesses, and cope with the death of loved ones, may help students in understanding their emotions and the emotions of others when they find themselves in such situations. Learning about the legal issues concerning wills and estates could be useful. Understanding the death rituals of different cultures could be helpful to people who have taken a death and dying course and encounter the death of someone from a different culture.

What I want to emphasize here is that people are also likely to experience difficult ethical decisions concerning people who are dying, and a death and dying course should also aim to help people make such decisions well.

Do Standard Approaches in Death and Dying Help People in Ethical Decision Making?

I have identified two main approaches to teaching medical ethics in death and dying courses. The first is largely a social sciences approach, and the other is a review of articles in medical ethics with emphasis on landmark legal cases. Of course, any particular approach will be unique and eclectic, depending on the students in the class, the background of the instructor, the aims of the course, and any number of incidental factors. To make discussion of the standard approaches possible, I will stick with the two approaches I have identified, assuming that points that I make about them will apply to all other approaches to the extent that they include those standard approaches.

The Social Sciences Approach

Consider the sorts of information used in the textbook *The Last Dance*, a text that is used in a great many college courses on death and dying. As we saw previously, it places heavy emphasis on sociology, psychology, history, anthropology, and medicine. My claim here is that these approaches are strongly descriptive, and give students very little help in learning how to make decisions. For some areas, my claim is clearly true. For example, a cross-cultural examination of different views of the nature of death, ways of referring to the dead, and marking the passing of the dead is very descriptive. In order to make the leap from the descriptive to the prescriptive, a person would need to determine to which cultural tradition he or she belongs, and whether he or she wants to follow the traditions of that culture. Gathering information about the cultures is a necessary part of the rational decision-making process, but it is only a part of it. The textbook provides no guidance to its readers on how to decide which culture or culture a person is part of, or would want to be part of.

There are other areas of death and dying where it might seem that this social sciences approach does more to help students make decisions. Let us consider the treatment in *The Last Dance* of living with life-threatening illness. The chapter explains some personal and social meanings of life-threatening illness, emphasizing the stigma that can be associated with the dying, the possible self-blame that people attach to illness, and the help that therapeutic tools can provide. The chapter proceeds with a fairly extended discussion of how people cope with having life-threatening illnesses, referring to the work of Barney Glaser and Anselm Strauss; Elisabeth Kübler-Ross; Charles Corr; Kenneth Doka; and Robert Kastenbaum and Sharon Thuell. The discussion moves on to the particular case of cancer and the types of treatment options that are available. It describes surgery, radiation therapy, chemotherapy, complementary therapies, and unorthodox treatment. It then proceeds with a discussion of pain management. It finishes with sections on the dying trajectory and the social role of the dying patient. All of this could be helpful for a person who wanted to decide now what treatment to choose if he or she needed to make such a decision. The text describes not only the different options available but also some merits and problems associated with each. However, when it comes to deciding, the book takes a distinctly nonprescriptive approach, writing that "although proposals appear from time to time concerning an *ars morendi*, or art of dying, the notion that there is a 'right way to die' that applies to everyone is unlikely to be valid within modern pluralistic societies that place a high value on individualism."[7] The book highlights the fact that there is no one best course of action, so the mere list of pros and cons for each course of action cannot decide which is the right one. The authors provide no guidance about how a person might try to evaluate which decision is best.

So as not to base my whole argument here on a discussion of one book, I can point out that my comments apply equally to one of the other main textbooks used in death and dying courses, Robert Kastenbaum's *Death, Society, and Human Experience*.[8] The book has fifteen chapters, most covering sociological, psychological, and medical aspects of death. There are some places in the book that aim to get the reader to think about his or her own values. In the first chapter, the reader is asked to do an inventory of his or her won attitudes, beliefs, and feelings concerning death, some of which explicitly address values. The second chapter, "What is Death?" includes a section on the meaning of death, and spells out a variety of interpretations. However, it makes almost no effort to evaluate which interpretations are plausible, and it does not discuss how a person should go about selecting an interpretation. It gives the impression that people are passive with respect to which interpretation they adopt, as if it were something that happened to them. The sixth chapter, by far the shortest of the book at twenty pages, is titled "End of Life Issues and Decisions." It surveys living wills, right-to-die decisions, the patient self-determination act, advance directives, cryonics, organ donation, and funeral-related decisions. These short sections spell out some options and some of the legal issues related to those options. There's even some discussion of the pros and cons of cryonics. The chapter ends by saying that society is "actively engaged in rethinking and restructuring the ways in which we treat each other near the end of life," and goes on to explain that people often think about the quality of their lives as well as simply living longer, and also mentions some other factors.[9] Yet nowhere in this chapter on end-of-life decisions is there any guidance on how to make a decision. The final chapter also discusses a shift in the meaning of death, but again, there's very little emphasis on what meaning we should promote or adopt.

Medical Ethics–focused Courses in Death and Dying

While it may not be surprising that courses based in the social sciences take a largely descriptive approach to teaching death and dying, one would expect a medical ethics–centered approach to place much more emphasis on decision making. Consider the section on forgoing treatment and causing death in Beauchamp and Veatch. It has a number of different articles, covering a range of areas, including "Active and Passive Euthanasia"; "Intending and Causing Death"; "Deciding to Forego Life-Sustaining Treatment"; "Intending to Kill and the Principle of Double Effect"; and "Patient Refusal of Hydration and Nutrition: An Alternative to Physician-Assisted Suicide or Voluntary Active Euthanasia." Using these resources, students could carefully study arguments for and against central positions, with detailed attention to the justifications of each position. On deciding which positions are presented most convincingly, students could use this information to form a rational opinion on the ethics of euthanasia, for example. There's no reason in principle why students should not be able to use the text as a way to educate themselves about how to form their values concerning death and dying.

So, my claim here concerning the use of such academic articles has to be a relatively weak claim. My experience in using such an approach is that it tends to be very difficult to get students to use these texts in ways that help them become better decision-makers concerning death and dying. However, simply reporting that I found it difficult is hardly an argument: it may simply reflect my own deficiencies as a teacher. In order to make the argument, I have to show that there is a lack of fit between the content of the papers and the skills that we want to impart to students.

Moral Theory and Particular Cases

There are well-known moral problems, regularly taught in death and dying courses, concerning whether doctors should help dying people take their own lives, and under what circumstances we should disconnect life-sustaining machines from people. When bringing these sorts of issues to students, courses tend to go through a number of familiar steps. They introduce distinctions between killing and letting die, active and passive euthanasia, different criteria of death, and different models of the relationship between physician and patient. They often also bring in a variety of moral theories, such as Kantian deontology, Utilitarianism, virtue-based approaches stemming from Aristotle, and occasionally casuistry and theories of care. Often, medical ethics courses and even courses on death and dying may bring in some moral approaches that have arisen specifically in medical ethics: the best known is Beauchamp and Childress's principalist approach.[10] The course may also address some metaethical questions concerning moral absolutism, moral relativism, moral contextualism, and moral nihilism. In courses that are able to address this sort of issue more fully, there may be some attention paid to the relation between moral belief and religious belief, and the role of religion in moral decision making.

There is a debate in medical ethics and in the rest of ethics about what methods will enable us reach the moral truth and find the best solutions to moral problems. Defenders of different absolutist views disagree as to what the correct moral theory is, and proffer reasons for their views and against competing views. Some have argued that approaches that use rules or principles are not easy to implement when applying them to real life cases.

Pedagogically, the central issue facing a teacher when explaining this complex array of ideas to students is what are the main aims of the course. One can aim to enable students to

1. master the different moral theories and meta-theories, showing an ability to understand the complexities of the theories, compare them, evaluate their strengths and weaknesses, and consider how they apply to particular cases. Call this the *moral theory aim*.

2. become better decision makers when personally facing difficult moral problems concerning death and dying. Call this the *decision-making aim*.

Consider the relation between the moral theory aim and the decision-making aim. Does learning moral theory help in decision making? I argue that, at least often, it does not. Indeed, it can happen that learning moral theory can even worsen decision-making skills. I will sketch my reasons supporting this claim.

There is no neutral way to analyze the relation between the moral theory aim and the decision-making aim because what counts as good decision making will depend partly on what moral theory one supports. However, there has been work on what counts as good decision-making within the field of medical ethics itself, concerning how we can judge when people are competent to make their own decisions. So I propose that we adopt criteria commonly used in that context, and use them to understand what it would be to make students better decision-makers through teaching a course in death and dying.

One useful analysis of informed consent and ethical decision-making in medical decisions is provided by Jessica W. Berg et al. They explain that informed consent is best understood as a process rather than event, and has the following stages:

1. Establishment of a relationship with a physician
2. Definition of the problem
3. Ascertainment of the goals of treatment
4. Selection of a therapeutic plan
5. Follow-up[11]

In cases of people with terminal illnesses, the competence of the dying person may sometimes be compromised, and families or others may need to make surrogate decisions. Even when the dying person is competent, she may want to bring her family or others into deliberations about what to do. These can be very difficult emotional decisions. So the necessary skills in such decision making are not just cognitive and intellectual such as gathering information, understanding it, and assessing it: they also require communication skills, and skills of coping with one's own emotions and those of others while making a decision. Furthermore, when the decision involves a moral dilemma, it will be especially important to find a way to bring one's ethical values to bear on assessing the different options.

Being able to master moral theory involves some related skills. It requires the ability to understand often dense prose, technical language, complex ideas, and sophisticated arguments, and it also requires being able to understand viewpoints that can be quite foreign to one's own. One needs to be able to compare different theories, consider how they relate to thought experiments and real-world situations, and assess their strengths and weaknesses. One can devote a great deal of time to understanding moral theory, up to and beyond writing a PhD dissertation on the topic. Thus, when addressing basic moral theory in a single undergraduate course, one has to be quite selective in how much to cover, and there are limitations on how much one is able to teach.

One way in which the moral theory aim conflicts with the decision-making aim is very simple: there is a limited amount of time to devote to such issues in a course, and so the more one spends on one aim, the less time available to devote to the other. Since teaching moral theory can be time consuming, with the need for close readings of text and careful attention to details of arguments, an instructor designing a syllabus on death and dying covering both moral theory and decision making will have to be careful how much to include.

The second way in which teaching moral theory can conflict with teaching decision-making skills is more subtle and probably more controversial. Put simply, my claim is this: when presented with an array of different theories with sophisticated arguments for each, students often become confused about what values they should hold, and indeed can have their skeptical assumptions confirmed about the usefulness of philosophy. Students quite often draw similar conclusions about philosophy as the Sophists, believing that it is possible to argue for any view, and that justifications of ethical stances often go in circles. Even if they do not go this far, it is generally clear by the end of a survey of ethical theory that no single theory is a plausible candidate for the truth because each theory has implausible aspects. Very few students come away from an ethics course with firmer moral convictions, some students have their personal views unchanged by their exposure to theory, and some have their moral convictions undermined by their exposure to moral philosophy.

One might argue that confusion and skepticism are appropriate responses when one starts to learn about the problems of providing a basis for one's ethical views, and certainly it may be inappropriate to be unquestioningly certain of one's moral convictions. If philosophy injects some epistemological uncertainty about moral truth in students, this may be a good thing. This may indeed improve a person's decision-making skills, if we see unjustified confidence in one's views as a deficit in decision making. Ethics is complicated, and a sophisticated decision maker facing a moral dilemma will do well to be aware of those complexities.

However, when teaching a course on death and dying where one is only able to teach a certain amount of ethical theory, there is a real question about how productive it will be to invest a certain portion of the class on it, and whether students' time might not be better spent on developing their decision-making skills.

The answer to this conundrum depends greatly on empirical questions about the effects of teaching moral theory. I have asserted possible links between the content of a course and effects on students, based on my personal experience, but there has been little systematic empirical study of such a connection. What research there has been is focused on medical school education and the effects of adding medical ethics to the curriculum.[12] The research generally shows that medical ethics education is beneficial to medical students.[13] However, even the literature concerning medical students is full of calls for more research and discussion of the best interpretation of the available data. Thus, it would be a stretch to draw any implications for the teaching of undergraduates in courses on death and dying.

Practical Aims and Teaching Skills

If I am right that there is a tension between the moral theory aim and the decision-making aim, then the question becomes which aim should courses on death and dying focus on when teaching the medical ethics component. Most professors trained in the academy, and especially in social sciences and philosophy, will be more comfortable and ready in teaching theory and facts, since that is what their training generally prepares them for. However, there is a strong case to be made for making such courses more practical in the sense of preparing students for experiences they are likely to encounter later in life. People are likely to experience family and friends dying or they may experience life-threatening illnesses themselves, and they may have to make decisions about what sorts of treatment to recommend or choose. They may also have to decide on whether to continue treatment and when to opt for hospice care. They may have to decide on what sorts of ceremony they want to commemorate the death of a loved one. These are all common experiences in modern life in North America and Western Europe. It is a much rarer event for people to have to go to court, so while the precedent-setting cases often featured in medical ethics sections of death and dying courses may provide some useful background, they do not give information that will be directly useful to most students.

While there may be a strong case for including practical skills in the outcomes of courses on death and dying, there is a concern about how teachers will be prepared to help students learn the necessary skills. As mentioned above, most of those trained in social sciences and even those in philosophy have little training in how to make ethical decisions. So, if there is a need for courses that do emphasize such practical skills, then either graduate programs for people in social sciences and similar areas that train people to teach courses in death and dying should start to offer appropriate training, or else schools should offer professional development opportunities for people who are teaching such courses. As an interdisciplinary course, wherever it is housed, one on death and dying is frequently in a difficult position; since people come from particular disciplines, they rarely have graduate training in multiple disciplines. This means that people who teach these courses will especially benefit from the opportunity to develop their teaching skills to include helping students make difficult decisions.

Conclusion: Life Skills and Liberal Education

In considering whether courses in death and dying should teach some practical life skills in making difficult decisions about the end of life, one may be concerned about how it fits with a liberal education. It clearly makes sense to teach practical ethical skills to those going into medicine because such professional training aims to make students into talented health care professionals. Given the survey of textbooks and courses in death and dying earlier in this paper, it is likely that there is much less focus on such practical aims in most undergraduate courses. However, most understandings of liberal education are clearly compatible with these aims of promoting ethical skills. While there is no generally accepted definition of liberal education, it is clear that in contrast with professional or technical education, it helps to prepare a person for life quite broadly, and conveys knowledge and skills that they can build on through a variety of roles and circumstances.

It is hard to find an articulated reason for why liberal arts approaches to teaching death and dying tend not to delve into personal ethical decisions and the skills that are necessary to make them well. One possible reason is that it is too personal, and just as liberal arts education does not aim to help with one's love life, marriage skills, or child-rearing, is also does not aim to help people with dying. However, considering this sort of case gives us cause to reconsider this attitude. There's little doubt that some preparation for major life events could be extremely helpful to people. Including courses that address such events in a liberal arts education provides a way for students to approach these issues, and especially the difficult parts that require ethical judgment, in a more thoughtful and systematic way. Such preparation could indeed be liberating, and thus would be at the heart of a liberal education.

NOTES

1. Lynne Ann DeSpelder and Albert Lee Strickland, *The Last Dance: Encountering Death and Dying*, 7th ed. (New York: McGraw-Hill, 2005).

2. Tom L. Beauchamp and Robert M. Veatch, *Ethical Issues in Death and Dying*, 2nd ed. (Upper Saddle River, NJ: Prentice Hall, 1996).

3. https://www.capa.uga.edu/cgi/Capa/BrowsePrefix_DisplayCourse .exe?13120I13120 (accessed June 17, 2007).

4. http://www.breyerstate.com/soc304.htm (accessed June 14, 2007).

5. http://www.hol.edu/syllabusuploads/Grieving%20%20&%20Loss.pdf (accessed June 14, 2007).

6. Albert R. Jonsen, "Introduction to the History of Bioethics," in *Bioethics: An Introduction to the History, Methods, and Practice*, ed. Nancy S. Jecker, Albert R. Jonsen, and Robert A. Perlman (Sudbury, MA: Jones & Bartless, 1997), 3–11.

7. DeSpelder and Strickland, *Last Dance*, 212.

8. Robert Kastenbaum, *Death, Society, and Human Experience*, 9th ed. (Boston: Allyn & Bacon, 2007).

9. Ibid., 190.

10. T. L. Beauchamp and J. F. Childress, *Principles of Biomedical Ethics*, 5th ed. (New York: Oxford University Press, 2001).

11. Jessica W. Berg, Paul S. Appelbaum, Charles W. Lidz, and Lisa S. Parker, *Informed Consent: Legal Theory and Clinical Practice*, 2nd ed. (New York: Oxford University Press, 2001), 174.

12. See, for example, D. J. Self, F. D. Wolinsky, and D. C. Baldwin Jr., "The Effect of Teaching Medical Ethics on Medical Students' Moral Reasoning," *Academic Medicine* 64, no. 12 (1989): 755–59; Risa P. Hayes et al., "Changing Attitudes about End-of-Life Decision Making of Medical Students during Third-Year Clinical Clerkships," *Psychosomatics* 40 (June 1999): 205–11; S. Roff and P. Preece, "Helping Medical Students to Find Their Moral Compasses: Ethics Teaching for Second and Third Year Undergraduates," *Journal of Medical Ethics* 30, no. 5 (2004): 487–89; K. Mattick and J. Bligh, "Teaching and Assessing Medical Ethics: Where Are We Now?" *Journal of Medical Ethics* 32, no. 3 (2006): 181–85; R. E. Eckles et al., "Medical Ethics Education: Where Are We? Where Should We Be Going? A Review," *Academic Medicine* 80, no. 12 (2005): 1143–52.

13. Self suggests that medical ethics education may inhibit moral development: D. J. Self et al., "The Moral Development of Medical Students: A Pilot Study of the Possible Influence of Medical Education," *Journal of Medical Education* 27, no. 1 (1993): 26–34.

BIBLIOGRAPHY

Beauchamp, T. L., and J. F. Childress. *Principles of Biomedical Ethics*. 5th ed. New York: Oxford University Press, 2001.

Berg, Jessica W., Paul S. Appelbaum, Charles W. Lidz, and Lisa S. Parker. *Informed Consent: Legal Theory and Clinical Practice*. 2nd ed. New York: Oxford University Press, 2001.

Eckles, R. E., E. M. Meslin, M. Gaffney, and P. R. Helft. "Medical Ethics Education: Where Are We? Where Should We Be Going? A Review." *Academic Medicine* 80, no. 12 (2005): 1143–52.

Hayes, Risa P., Alan S. Stoudemire, Kathy Kinlaw, Mary Lynn Dell, and Amy Loomis. "Changing Attitudes about End-of-Life Decision Making of Medical Students during Third-Year Clinical Clerkships." *Psychosomatics* 40 (June 1999): 205–11.

Kastenbaum, Robert. *Death, Society, and Human Experience.* 9th ed. Boston: Allyn & Bacon, 2007.

Kymlicka, Will. "Moral Philosophy and Public Policy: The Case of New Reproductive Technologies." *Bioethics* 7, no. 1 (1993): 1–26. Reprinted in *Philosophical Perspectives on Bioethics,* ed. L. W. Sumner and Joseph Boyle, 244–70. Toronto: University of Toronto Press, 1996.

Lawlor, R. "Moral Theories in Teaching Applied Ethics." *Journal of Medical Ethics* 33, no. 6 (2007): 370–72.

Mattick, K, and J. Bligh. "Teaching and Assessing Medical Ethics: Where Are We Now?" *Journal of Medical Ethics* 32, no. 3 (2006): 181–85.

Roff, S., and P. Preece. "Helping Medical Students to Find Their Moral Compasses: Ethics Teaching for Second and Third Year Undergraduates." *Journal of Medical Ethics* 30, no. 5 (2004): 487–89.

Self, D. J., F. D. Wolinsky, and D. C. Baldwin Jr. "The Effect of Teaching Medical Ethics on Medical Students' Moral Reasoning." *Academic Medicine* 64, no. 12 (1989): 755–59.

———, D. E. Schrader, D. C. Baldwin Jr., and F. D. Wolinsky. "The Moral Development of Medical Students: A Pilot Study of the Possible Influence of Medical Education." *Journal of Medical Education* 27, no. 1 (1993): 26–34.

4

Teaching Death and Dying in the Context of Religious Studies

Vanessa R. Sasson

A number of years ago when I was first thrust into the teaching arena, I was given the oft-dreaded Introduction to World Religions course to teach. Over the period of one short semester, I was expected to cram all relevant information about five major world religions (these being Judaism, Christianity, Islam, Hinduism, and Buddhism) into my students' heads. I attempted to unravel the many layers that religions embody, such as their history, literature, beliefs, customs, rituals, and festivals, only to find my students drowning in foreign terms, scribbling down notes at a maddening speed, and barely lifting their heads up to ask a question or reflect on the material. Needless to say, it was a dramatic failure in my eyes, and I vowed never to teach such a survey course again.

Unsurprisingly, the next term came around and my department chair asked me, ever so politely, to teach the course again. I could not very well refuse, nor could I go in for a second round of peda-gogical torture, so I opted for a third course of action: I changed the content (I was rather vague about my plans with my chair at the time and we happily laugh about it today, thank goodness!). I remained faithful to the concept of introducing the students to five religions (with repeated urging that my students take awareness of religions that I unfortunately do not have time to cover in one short semester), but I chose to do this through the medium of a theme. The course investigates how each of the five religions deals with death and dying. In this chapter, I would like to present my experiences with this course: how it is set up and how it has worked over the years, what has been successful and where I have struggled.

The Religious Studies Side of Things

Teaching survey courses can be incredibly useful if done properly and taught by the right teacher. One needs to have a solid grasp of a large spectrum of ideas and how they developed over time. My thesis supervisor once told me that the only ones who should teach survey courses are very experienced, older teachers. The more specialized material belongs to the young. Unfortunately, it never works out this way. Young, new teachers are given the survey courses even though they are the least capable of handling the material, which is probably why they are so disastrous so often. The more experience I accumulate, the more I realize how true this is. In another twenty years, I believe I will finally be ready to teach an introductory course.

In the meantime, I have refined the dreaded survey course to be focused around the theme of death and dying. This has proven immensely useful for a number of reasons, many of which I did not initially anticipate. Since I could not yet produce a survey with elegance and accuracy, I focused the lectures on this theme to give me something to hold on to and pivot around. What I discovered, however, was that such a focus made the material easier on the students. Rather than get lost in a sea of information that would surely be forgotten simultaneously to its being learned, I found that the students engaged in and even wrestled with it with an enthusiasm I had not encountered before.

The course is broken down into five sections—one for each of five world religions covered in the course. Each section opens with an introductory subsection that usually involves approximately two lectures (sometimes more) in which the students are introduced to the major features of the religion. Since I am a storyteller by nature, each religion is introduced with a founding story that embodies many of the central doctrines and priorities of that tradition. So, for example, Christianity is introduced with the story of Christ (an obvious choice) and Buddhism begins with the story of the Buddha, and his relationship to previous Buddhas and Buddhas to come. Immediately after 9/11 and for a few years thereafter, the question of Jihad was unavoidable when discussing Islam, but thankfully these questions are quietly subsiding, evidence that Jihad is not at the forefront of students' imaginations anymore. After the introductory session is completed, the discussion surrounding death begins. We explore together how each religion tackles the crucial questions of body disposal, mourning, and concepts of afterlife.

The course material is not restricted to religion, however. What immediately became apparent was the growing and almost desperate need students had to discuss death more broadly. Discussions of aging, beauty myths, gender, suicide, and near death experiences were clearly on their minds and they consistently insisted on bringing these into the classroom. The course therefore expanded outward beyond the religious studies hemisphere and I found myself reserving lecture times for these discussions. Indeed, in the smaller groups (at McGill this class has turned into an auditorium of two hundred students, but Marianopolis continues to provide the opportunity to teach classes of thirty students), the religions have become a jumping-off point for discussing the broader concept of death and dying, and this, it seems, is a discussion the students really want to have.

Indeed, framing an introductory course on world religions around death and dying is immensely rewarding. The students are given a solid structure upon which to ask their questions about death and dying, and they often find, to their own surprise, that the religions they grew up around had similar questions, or at times even provided some rather interesting solutions that they are suddenly more inclined to examine. Consider, for example, the question of mourning. How does one mourn the dead? How does one honor the deceased and yet at the same time prepare oneself to let them go? Is this even a realistic expectation? According to the Jewish tradition, the answer to the last question is yes, and it has put together an intricate system of mourning that is virtually unmatched by any other religious tradition practiced today, with the possible exception of Hinduism.[1] A few of these rituals deserve to be described in some detail below for comparison to be possible.

The Jewish mourning process begins with *shiva* (literally "seven" in Hebrew) and refers to the first seven days of the mourning period. During this time, family and friends congregate at the mourners' home (usually the spouse's home if there is one, or the home of one of the children). The mourners are not permitted to leave the home during this time, nor are they permitted to work, shave, clean the house, or even cook for themselves (among many other prohibitions). They must simply sit on a low stool and mourn their loss. The community is consequently charged with the task of feeding and caring for them. And since they cannot leave the home and thus cannot go to synagogue to perform the prayers required at this time, the synagogue comes to them, and twice a day prayers are conducted in their home. In short, the community takes over and the mourners are granted the privilege of being able to fall completely apart. They do not have to look good or even smell good, and they are even forbidden from hosting their guests. They cannot cook for them or serve them anything, nor indeed, if we are to follow Talmudic requirements to the letter, are they permitted to greet their visitors. They must sit on their stools and be fully in their mourning, leaning on the community completely for survival.

After this seven-day period, however, the tradition requires their mourners to get up from their low chairs. It is time once again to go outside, enjoy the sunlight, and get back to work. They are still called mourners, and they will continue to be identified as such for the first full year after the death of their loved one,[2] but they are slowly and gently encouraged to return to the world. Over the next year, these mourners will slowly re-integrate themselves into society and find their footing on what was, for a time, uncertain ground. The restrictions and prohibitions will gradually be released until the year—and hopefully the mourning—has come to an end.

The one requirement imposed upon mourners during this time (most of the literature is otherwise concerned with restrictions) centers around the recitation of the Kaddish—the prayer recited by mourners.[3] Every day, twice a day, mourners (traditionally only the men) must find their way to a synagogue to recite this old Aramaic prayer with a group of nine other men. No matter where they are in the world or what is going on in their lives, for almost one full year their days are organized around the prayer times of the Kaddish.

Although this may feel like a terrible inconvenience at first, what the students are quickly shown is how profoundly moving and healing the recitation of this prayer can be. In most communities, the only people who attend synagogue daily are mourners. This means that, twice a day, mourners are organically brought together in a small chapel to sing a song of God's praises. Since the mourning period is so long, they are given the opportunity to develop friendships during this time, and in the process, a kind of support group emerges. Those who have been performing the Kaddish for some time welcome in the newest mourners and show them how it is done. Since they themselves have processed the mourning period longer, they often serve as mentors to the newer members, helping them along. By the end of the year, if they have used that year fully and wisely, their own feelings of grief have subsided. They have processed the death and have even been of service to the newer members of the mourning community around them. Indeed, it has always been obvious to me that the easiest way to get over one's own suffering is to help out somebody else with theirs. The mourning period developed by the rabbinic leaders of the Jewish tradition provides such an opportunity. Not only can the mourners help each other, but in some circles it is believed that pronouncing the Kaddish daily actually functions as a kind of intercessionary prayer for the dead. They are therefore able to help the living and the dead in this process, and hopefully, in the midst of it all, themselves.[4]

Consistently over the years, I have watched my students become filled with admiration for the Jewish tradition as they listen to the wisdom of something set up so long ago. They discover a solution to a question they are struggling with and are introduced to a community that has been actively adopting this solution for centuries. They discover ritual, liturgy, history, philosophy, and the literature of the tradition all in the context of this one simple yet particularly poignant example. And, if I have understood correctly what one of the main objectives of a survey course in religious studies implies, students are introduced to the tradition sympathetically and compassionately. In other words, they walk out of the classroom encouraged and wanting to learn more.

They are also given a framework out of which to then compare one religion with the next. It is one thing to tell students that Judaism and Christianity developed to a large degree in opposition to each other. It is another thing entirely to show this to them through the medium of an example and have them come to the conclusion themselves. For example, it is clear from the above discussion that Judaism is largely orthopraxic. When a death occurs, the question Judaism tackles is not so much about what one is to *believe* as it is about what one is to *do*. How does one mourn? Where does one go to mourn? Who even is expected to mourn and for how long? Christianity, on the other hand, rarely institutionalizes answers to these questions. The answers, rather, are often left to local custom to sort out. The more significant issue in Christianity has to do with belief and intention—and this can be traced all the way back to the Gospels and the emphasis placed by the authors on intention over and above action.

Indeed, much of Jesus' critique of the Judaism of his day (I hope, here, that I am not simplifying too much) had to do with the fact that Judaism was too behavior-oriented to the expense of the heart. The Sermon on the Mount (Matt. 5–7) pivots primarily around this very issue, condemning Jews for praying or fasting outwardly without necessarily having to take these experiences inward.[5] Even more directly, when a potential disciple requests some time to bury his father before following him, Jesus replies, "Let the dead bury their own dead" (Matt. 8:22 and Luke 9:60)—a radical statement that acknowledges, among other things, the lengthy and complex ritual requirements that burying the dead in the Jewish context involves.[6] Recognizing that these requirements can unfortunately become behavior models stripped of inner transformative work if one is not careful, Jesus urges his audience to leave such rituals behind.[7] Satisfying ritual requirements means nothing without an emphasis placed on the heart. Obviously, the Jewish ideal would be one in which transformative work is accomplished precisely *through* ritual enactment, but this is not always achieved or highlighted in the literature. Jesus is therefore warning his audience that too much emphasis placed on praxis can easily leave the heart behind.

The above example leads the students to the discovery that the two religions have been talking to each other and reacting against each other for a very long time. They developed in the context of this relationship, criticizing each other but also learning from each other and trying to expand their respective horizons. There is wisdom in performing one's way to healing, just as there is wisdom in letting ritual go.

Another example that I have always found poignant has to do with body washing. In the Jewish tradition, the Hevra Kaddisha—a select group of men and women—is responsible for preparing the dead for burial. The members of the Hevra Kaddisha remain relatively anonymous in the larger community, usually arriving at the funeral home early in the morning to perform the purification of the body, long before the rest of the city or town has woken up. The customs vary from community to community as to how the purification is to be performed, but one prohibition is enforced across the board: a son may never wash the body of his father. It is not clear exactly why this is the case; the most common interpretation is that it would be disrespectful for the son to see his father in such an undignified and fragile state. It has also been suggested that it would not be fair to ask a son to perform what would obviously be an emotionally difficult task. Whatever the reason, it is absolutely clear that, short of a major emergency, sons do not wash their fathers after death.[8]

In Islam, however, the opposite is the case. A body washing is performed by a group of select members of the community in a very similar form to the Jewish version described above with one significant difference: the son *must* wash his father, just as his father did for him when he was young and vulnerable, and incapable of taking care of himself. It is believed to be a privilege and an honor to care for one's father at this time, possibly the most important task one will ever perform. A son washes his father (and conversely a daughter washes her mother) as a sign of respect, love, and commitment. I remember speaking with a Pakistani Muslim woman once about this. She did not participate in her mother's body washing because she felt too distraught to participate at the time. Although her mother died many years ago, this remained her biggest regret. She felt that she had failed her mother because she could not take care of her when she was needed most.[9]

This is a striking comparative example for it informs us that two religious traditions can directly contradict each other and yet both be right. How could one not sympathize with the Jewish decision not to include the son in the process? The decision comes out of respect for both the father and the son. And yet, how could one not admire the Islamic tradition for insisting on the son's presence? Both traditions are right. Moreover, this example is a wonderful reminder of how similar the two religions are. In both religious traditions, and indeed in all religious traditions, the dead are carefully attended to. They are washed by a loving community, wrapped in white shrouds and gently placed into the earth. With or without the son's participation, the differences in this case are few—an important reminder in a time when Judaism and Islam are perceived as being worlds apart.

Although in some respects differences between religions are often minimal, in others the differences can be remarkable. Teaching world religions in the framework of death and dying provides an opportunity to present students with some of these significant differences that do not always come out in a survey course and here the Buddhism section serves as a good example. I have taught many introductions to Buddhism over the years and have found it consistently challenging. Students generally walk into the classroom with so many preconceived notions about it—most of which are naively idealistic and quite far from the truth. For a number of reasons that cannot be addressed here, Buddhism finds itself on a pedestal at the moment and it makes for a rather tricky classroom experience.[10] I do not want to yank Buddhism violently off of its pedestal, and yet I also do not want to leave it up there. How do you teach Buddhism sympathetically and compassionately and yet critically all at once?

One of the best ways I have found of bringing Buddhism into the classroom is, ironically, by teaching about its dealings with death—particularly in the Tibetan tradition. The Tibetan form of Buddhism has produced an impressively extensive literature on death. The now famous *Tibetan Book of the Dead* (*Bardo Thos Grol*) has become staple reading in popular Western Buddhist circles since the publication of Evans-Wentz's translation, but it is by no means the only source on the subject.[11] Hundreds of primary sources flank Tibetan Buddhist libraries, addressing a wide range of issues from clinical descriptions of death to elaborate religious teachings about its significance and role in religious training. I introduce the students briefly to this massive corpus of literature and give them some sense of its complexity and depth, but the moment that seems to impress them the most, for a wide range of reasons, is when the traditional form of body disposal is described.

In precommunist Tibet, the most common form of body disposal involved what modern scholarship today calls the "sky burial." A few days after the death has occurred and at the astrologically appointed time, the body is brought to a sacred area reserved for this very purpose, usually on the edge of a high mountain or rock face. Ritual specialists called *rogyapas* (body cutters) take the body from the family members and proceed to slice it up into sections. The flesh is cut into small handfuls and the bones are crushed and mixed with *tsampa*—a local food mixture consisting of barley flour and yak butter. The skull is cracked open to release whatever consciousness remains and all the pieces are placed in the center of the circle. During this time, one of the *rogyapas* circles the area with a whip to keep the vultures at bay, but when the entire body has been dismembered and prepared, the pieces are placed at the center and the *rogyapa* with the whip steps back. Vultures then pounce on their long awaited feast while the few mourners who chose to attend the event stand by and watch. So a friend of mine tells me who accidentally stumbled upon a sky burial while he was mountain climbing (it was quite a surprise), the entire procedure takes no more than half an hour.[12]

This form of body disposal never ceases to illicit more than a slight gasp from the students. They usually cannot believe that their beloved and idealized Buddhism engages in such a practice. This is the beginning of the end of the pedestal. And yet, what I quickly step in to explain to them is that not only is this practice ecologically sound but it is also a poignant expression of all that Buddhism holds dear. Although the practice surely developed as a response to the physical environment—most of the Tibetan landscape is above tree level, making cremations too expensive an endeavor, and the land itself is frozen most of the year, making burial rather impractical—it also serves to express the long cherished principles of impermanence and generosity (among many others) so central to Buddhist doctrine. As Thubten Jinpa, one of my colleagues, once said to me, form is irrelevant when it comes to Buddhist funerals. It does not matter what form a Buddhist funeral takes so long as the mourners and participants walk away with some notion of impermanence. The sky burial achieves this with great precision. Those left behind watch their loved one come apart and learn quickly and clearly that there is nothing left to hold on to—not even a tombstone to talk to. Nothing is left behind except a lesson taken from the earliest strata of Buddhist literature, namely, that nothing stays the same. Everything changes and everything comes to an end. Moreover, the dying know ahead of time what will happen to their bodies and they accept this form of disposal for themselves. In this way, they willingly offer themselves up to others. They give their bodies as food for the birds, using the very last bit they have left as an opportunity to be of service. In short, the sky burial expresses the most important Buddhist teachings, serving as an excellent introduction to the tradition. At the same time, the students discover that Buddhism is not just a philosophy with happy monks smiling at the camera and robes fluttering romantically in the air. It is a religion with ritual, history, literature, and practices that are often drastically different from what they initially imagined. In this way, Buddhism is gently displaced from its pedestal and brought into a more interesting and productive dialogue with other traditions.

The Death and Dying Side of Things

A religious studies course on death and dying naturally addresses more than the academic material. Broader discussions concerning death and dying are inevitable, particularly when faced with a classroom of eighteen to twenty-one year olds. The examples above have enabled me to introduce the students to various world religions in a context that I feel is conducive to genuine learning and comparative analysis. I am also very grateful that it seems to leave many of the students with a desire to learn and understand more about religion. But this is not the only result. I have also discovered in many students a longing to discuss their mortality in a safe and nonjudgmental context. Sometimes the discussion emerges in the very first lecture, and with other groups it comes later, but always, the discussion happens.

I have learned the hard way that students are not always what they seem. We don't know what goes on in their lives, where they come from, or who they are. All too often, I discover that a student I thought was fine and comfortable is actually struggling terribly behind the scenes. Students carry all kinds of secrets that are often excruciating to them, and a class in which the subject of mortality is addressed seems for many to be a welcome relief. I am clear with the students that my classroom is not about group therapy, nor am I a therapist of any kind prepared to deal with their individual situations. When I come across a serious problem, I use the services provided by the institution and send them there. That being said, however, this material simply evokes personal discussions and the teacher needs to be ready for it. I am not afraid to admit that it is often these very discussions that have become the most meaningful part of the course for me, and I imagine this must be the case for many of the students, too. I will never forget a particular student I had, many years ago, who told me privately one day that she attempted suicide by slicing her wrists a few months earlier. This news obviously concerned me and I asked her a few times if she was sure this course was a good idea for her, but she was adamant. She was ready, in her opinion, to open up a discussion that was haunting her.

She never said anything in class about this, but I kept watch over her and we wound up having a very good semester together. The last day of class, however, when we were wrapping things up before the final test, she raised her hand and asked me if she could address the class. I said yes, and she turned toward her classmates and told them about her attempt. It was very emotional. Tears flooded the room from everyone as we listened to her honest, compassionate and heartbreaking story. The students had so many questions for her and she answered them all carefully and kindly. Some of the questions were difficult, such as the selfishness so often associated with suicide, but she handled herself and the classroom beautifully and gave us all an insight into an experience most of us will likely never have to face.

I realized that day how important the subject of suicide is for young people. For many of them, death is associated with old age and is thus often very far from their reality. But suicide—and by extension self-mutilation, anorexia, and all other forms of destructive behavior—they understand and relate to all too well. At times, the discussions are harder for me to bear than for them. These lectures/discussions don't have much to do with religion; indeed, most religions simply prohibit suicide and little more needs to be said. But it seems to be a required discussion for the students, and thus it belongs in the classroom. Since this conversation has the potential for becoming incredibly personal, I often invite a therapist who specializes in suicide for this talk, and it usually leaves everyone in the room feeling safe enough to be honest.

Another topic that has found its way unexpectedly into the classroom has to do with Elizabeth Kübler-Ross's five stages of dying.[13] Students invariably relate stories about how they have struggled with the death of someone close to them. They talk about the anger they felt or the sense of betrayal, or they wonder openly if acceptance is ever possible in reality. I obviously don't have the answers to these questions; these are questions we all have to settle for ourselves. But Kübler-Ross's work seems to be helpful in this regard; we thus explore the famous five stages of dying that she outlined and I incorporate a few personal anecdotes along the way from my time as a volunteer in a palliative care unit. I tell them about the various patients I have been with, the ones who were angry and fighting until their very last breath to remain alive, and others who were so drugged one would think they didn't even notice when death happened. But there were also gentle and even loving deaths, and this has made a tremendous impact on me.

One of the stories I often tell them has to do with a French-Canadian woman I spent some time with. She had been dying for what seemed to her to have been many long, interminable months. When I met her, she was exasperated with her situation. She was a devout Catholic and could not understand why God was making her suffer for so long. Most of our interactions involved my listening quietly to various expressions of her fury. She ranted and raved against the God she loved and complained about her misery. But near the end, in the last few weeks of her life, her heart seemed to soften. Rather than require an audience for her complaints, she asked me to read her Psalms from the Bible. She was slowly moving away from anger and into a state of serenity that was inspiring to behold.

One day, I was sitting with her silently when her husband came into the room. She was near the end and could barely speak at all anymore. She was only skin and bones, barely making a dent on her mattress or under her sheets. Her husband sat himself down in the back of the room, hiding himself in the shadows, apparently unable to approach her in her final hours. I knew that she was very worried about him and feared leaving him behind, and her fears were obviously well founded to some degree. I left her bedside and joined him in the darkness. At first, he didn't say very much, or he muttered only sadness and despair, but all of a sudden he lightened up and whispered to me with such love and mischief in his eyes, "You know, she is not the easiest person in the world to live with. She can be quite difficult at times!" He then began to tell me all kinds of beautiful things about his wife and talked about her with such intimate knowledge, love, and humor. He cried and laughed and just reveled in the beauty that is the woman he married and I just sat back and listened to him. And then, we both looked over at her bed and somehow we knew that she had passed. She died while listening to her husband speak of his love for her, and I am sure that this is what allowed her to let go. I believe that for her, at that very moment, the acceptance Kübler-Ross described in her work was finally achieved.

Teaching this course over the past few years has taught me many things. I have learned so much about the religions I teach and about the connections between them. I have learned about similarities and differences and have developed a sense of comfort amidst both. But I have also learned from my students and about them. I have learned that they are often not what they seem, that many have touched a depth of existence they yearn to speak of, and that if you listen, they will in fact speak. Teaching material relative to death and dying in a religious studies context has been immensely rewarding and I only hope that others might do the same.

NOTES

1. The minor Talmudic tractate *Semachot* is one of the earliest sources focusing on this subject. For a modern outline of the laws and rituals surrounding mourning, see C. B. Goldberg, *Mourning in Halachah: The Laws and Customs of the Year of Mourning* (New York: Mesorah, 1991). This book is not an academic discussion of the subject, but rather a step-by-step manual for mourners and is often distributed by funeral homes to mourners to help them decipher the technicalities of their obligations.

2. The mourning period lasts a year more or less, depending on the rabbinic injunction one follows.

3. This requirement does not appear in the Talmud. It is a prayer and a tradition that developed over time and only seems to have become associated with mourning in the middle ages. See T. Rabinowicz, *A Guide to Life: Jewish Laws and Customs of Mourning* (New Jersey: Jason Aronson, 1989), 70. For a discussion of the Kaddish more specifically, see L. Wieseltier, *Kaddish* (New York: Alfred A. Knopf, 1998).

4. For further reading on the subject, see in particular S. C. Heilman, *When a Jew Dies: The Ethnography of a Bereaved Son* (Berkeley: University of California Press, 2001); also helpful is E. Levine, "Jewish Views and Customs on Death," in *Death and Bereavement across Cultures*, ed. C. Murray Parkes, P. Laungani, and B. Young (London: Routledge, 1997), 98–130.

5. All biblical quotations are drawn from the King James Version.

6. For a discussion of this controversial verse, see B. R. McCane, "Let the Dead Bury Their Own Dead: Secondary Burial and Matt. 8:21–22," *Harvard Theological Review* 83: 1 (1990): 31–43; B. R. McCane, *Roll Back the Stone: Death and Burial in the World of Jesus* (Harrisburg, PA: Trinity, 2003), 73–77; M. Bockmuehl, "'Let the Dead Bury Their Dead' (Matt. 8:22 / Luke 9:60): Jesus and Halakhah," *Journal of Theological Studies* 49: 2 (1998): 553–81.

7. The role of ritual in the Gospels is not a simple one. Numerous passages in the New Testament have been used to either uphold the place of ritual or to denounce it. For the purposes of this argument, however, and for the purposes of a survey course more broadly, such generalizations are necessary.

8. For an excellent discussion and description of this purification process, see S. C. Heilman, *When a Jew Dies*, 31–71.

9. For a discussion of Muslim preparation and funeral customs, see A. S. Tritton, "Muslim Funeral Customs," *Bulletin of the School of Oriental and African Studies* 9: 3 (1938): 653–61.

10. For an excellent discussion of this idealization, see D. S. Lopez, *Prisoners of Shangri-La: Tibetan Buddhism and the West* (Chicago: University of Chicago Press, 1998).

11. *The Tibetan Book of the Dead*, trans. W. Y. Evans-Wentz, 3rd ed. (London: Oxford University Press, 1960). For alternative English translations, see *The Tibetan Book of the Dead: The Great Liberation through Hearing in the Bardo*, trans. F. Fremantle and C. Trungpa, Shambhala Dragon Editions (Boston: Shambhala, 1987); and *The Tibetan Book of the Dead: Liberation through Understanding in the Between*, trans. R. A. F. Thurman (New York: Bantam, 1994).

12. For a description of the sky burial, see J. Powers, *An Introduction to Tibetan Buddhism* (Ithaca, NY: Snow Lion, 1995), 307–9. For further discussion, see (among many others) F. Fremantle, *Luminous Emptiness: Understanding the "Tibetan Book of the Dead"* (Boston: Shambhala, 2003); Dalai Lama, *Advice on Dying: And Living a Better Life*, trans. J. Hopkins (New York: Atria, 2002); G. H. Mullin, *Living in the Face of Death: The Tibetan Tradition* (Ithaca, NY: Snow Lion, 1998); and G. Orofino, *Sacred Tibetan Teachings: On Death and Liberation* (Bridgeport, CN: Prism, 1999).

13. E. Kübler-Ross, *On Death and Dying: What the Dying Have to Teach Doctors, Nurses, Clergy and Their Own Families* (New York: Simon & Schuster, 1997).

BIBLIOGRAPHY

The Tibetan Book of the Dead. Translated by W. Y. Evans-Wentz. 3rd ed. London: Oxford University Press, 1960.

The Tibetan Book of the Dead: The Great Liberation through Hearing in the Bardo. Translated by F. Fremantle and C. Trungpa. Shambhala Dragon Editions. Boston: Shambhala, 1987.

The Tibetan Book of the Dead: Liberation through Understanding in the Between. Translated by R. A. F. Thurman. New York: Bantam, 1994.

Bockmuehl, M. " 'Let the Dead Bury Their Dead' (Matt. 8:22 / Luke 9:60): Jesus and Halakhah." *Journal of Theological Studies* 49: 2 (1998): 553–81.

Dalai Lama. *Advice on Dying: And Living a Better Life.* Translated by J. Hopkins. New York: Atria, 2002.

Fremantle, F. *Luminous Emptiness: Understanding the "Tibetan Book of the Dead."* Boston: Shambhala, 2003.

Goldberg, C. B. *Mourning in Halachah: The Laws and Customs of the Year of Mourning.* New York: Mesorah, 1991.

Heilman, S. C. *When a Jew Dies: The Ethnography of a Bereaved Son.* Berkeley: University of California Press, 2001.

Kübler-Ross, E. *On Death and Dying: What the Dying have to Teach Doctors, Nurses, Clergy and Their Own Families.* New York: Simon & Schuster, 1997.

Lopez, D. S. *Prisoners of Shangri-La: Tibetan Buddhism and the West.* Chicago: University of Chicago Press, 1998.

McCane, B. R. "Let the Dead Bury Their Own Dead: Secondary Burial and Matt. 8: 21–22." *Harvard Theological Review* 83: 1 (1990): 31–43.

McCane, B. R. *Roll Back the Stone: Death and Burial in the World of Jesus.* Harrisburg, PA: Trinity, 2003.

Mullin, G. H. *Living in the Face of Death: The Tibetan Tradition.* Ithaca, NY: Snow Lion, 1998.

Orofino, G. *Sacred Tibetan Teachings: On Death and Liberation.* Bridgeport, CT: Prism, 1999.

Parkes, C. Murray, P. Laungani, and B. Young, eds. *Death and Bereavement across Cultures.* London: Routledge, 1997.

Powers, J. *An Introduction to Tibetan Buddhism.* Ithaca, NY: Snow Lion, 1995.

Rabinowicz, T. *A Guide to Life: Jewish Laws and Customs of Mourning.* New Jersey: Jason Aronson, 1989.

Tritton, A. S. "Muslim Funeral Customs." *Bulletin of the School of Oriental and African Studies* 9: 3 (1938): 653–61.

Wieseltier, L. *Kaddish.* New York: Alfred A. Knopf, 1998.

Practical Applications of a Course on Death

5

Teaching Death and Dying: A Pastoral Theological Approach

G. Lee Ramsey Jr.

"Caius really was mortal, and it was right for him to die; but for me, little Vanya, Ivan Iliych, with all my thoughts and emotions, it's altogether a different matter. It cannot be that I ought to die. That would be too terrible . . . It's impossible! But here it is. How is this? How is one to understand it?[1]

Interpretations and responses to death and dying—emotional, physical, cognitive, and spiritual—are conditioned by the deepest religious convictions of the one who is dying and the ones who are grieving the coming or recent loss of another to death. While death is a universal human experience, one's own religious beliefs and practices—whether Jewish, Christian, Muslim, or Hindu—shape the experience of death for both the dying and the bereaved. Within schools of Christian theological education, such as the one where I teach, students not only need to learn psychosocial frameworks for understanding loss, death, and grief as a human phenomenon, but they need to examine their religious tradition's distinctive interpretations of death within the larger divine story of creation, redemption, and resurrection. If seminary students, many of whom will become or already are pastoral leaders within Christian congregations, are sufficiently grounded in the religious tradition's understandings of death and dying, then they will be more adequately prepared to render the authentic spiritual care that is needed as individuals and families undergo the transition from life to death and whatever awaits beyond.

This educational context calls for an approach to teaching death and dying that is theologically based and practically oriented. To these ends, I seek to challenge students to plumb the depths of their own informal theologies of death and dying, which is in part based upon their own personal experiences of loss, and to critically examine it in the light of scripture, Christian belief, and church tradition. These religious understandings must be correlated with psychosocial views of death and dying to provide a comprehensive theoretical knowledge of how individuals and communities respond to death. At the same time, I attempt to equip the student with the practical skills that, when informed by sound theological understandings, can lead to effective pastoral care in the varieties of situations of loss that are encountered in ministry.

Within the seminary setting, I organize the teaching of death and dying in four distinctive yet interlocking sections, each of which will be explained in detail below: (1) exploration of the students' own experiences of loss and grief and examination of their own responses to death; (2) review of distinctive biblical and theological understandings of death that help students locate themselves within the Christian religious tradition; (3) examination of psychosocial theories of death and dying and correlation of these approaches with theology; and (4) presentation of pastoral and congregational resources for assisting individuals, families, and congregations as they grieve the death of loved ones and prepare for their own eventual deaths.

Context and Pedagogy for Theological Education

Before we look at the content of these four areas, a few comments about context and basic pedagogical assumptions are necessary. I teach in a Christian seminary whose student body is made up of adult learners with an average age of forty. They are first-, second-, and third-career students, mostly from a wide spectrum of evangelical Protestant traditions in the mid–southern section of the United States, with a smattering of Episcopalians and Roman Catholics, and the occasional Jewish student. The student body of approximately 325 is roughly 45 percent African-American, 50 percent Caucasian, and 5 percent International. Women comprise about 40 percent of our student body and men, 60 percent. Most, though not all, of our students have significant leadership experience in Christian congregations or other ministry settings.

Because of the high degree of diversity among our students and faculty, the way that context shapes belief is always a factor in the classroom. Denominational diversity means that interdenominational dialogue is a subtext for every class. For example, Pentecostals neither understand nor ritualize death and dying in the same manner as mainstream United Methodists. Similarly, the black-white racial diversity within the school means that religion and race is an equally important subtext. African-American Baptists approach death and dying and its attendant grief rituals in a manner distinct from Caucasian Presbyterians. Similar comparisons can be drawn between the ways that men and women seem to deal with death and dying and how they provide pastoral leadership during times of grief and loss.

The diversity creates a rich learning environment for theology students and teachers. Diversity in the classroom invites an "open" learning environment where teacher and students value shared learning. Adult learners from diverse contexts bring a wealth of knowledge and skills into the seminary classroom before they ever open a book about death and dying. Life experiences, previous reading, professional work in related fields, and the theoretical knowledge gained from other seminary courses all come into play in the classroom as we grapple together with the topic of death and dying. My role as teacher is to provide a conducive and trustworthy learning environment, a basic set of resources and foundational understandings, particularly from the Christian tradition, and a variety of ways to help students remain accountable to individual and classroom learning.

I strive to be an expert in the classroom, but not about death and dying. I, too, am a learner with other adult learners. Together, we go through a semester-long journey of exploration of the many faces of death and response within the Christian community. My aspiring expertise, if it can be called that, aims towards pedagogy. The questions that I ask myself and the answers that hopefully benefit my students are these: What are the best conditions that make for optimal learning about this topic and in this context? What do I need to do to help bring about those conditions? What and who are the best available resources—books, films, videos, guest presenters—that I can bring to the table? What other resources do I need to continue to seek? Given this particular group of students (and each class is different), who needs to be encouraged to speak more and who needs to be encouraged to listen more? Once underway, do we need to alter the course map (syllabus) to allow for the unforeseen? Why? These sound like the questions of any teacher in higher education who might be interested in shared learning in the classroom.

But a distinct set of questions guides pedagogy in the seminary classroom. At least, I assume that these questions are different from those openly pursued by many college and university instructors. How is this course on a very difficult and existentially relevant topic—death and dying—shaping the faith of the student? Who is struggling spiritually because of the course or because of the intersection between the course and life? Can or should the class address the spiritual, theological, and emotional responses of its own members? In other words, should and in what ways do the students and the teacher care for each other as we move into the mystery of death together? Where is the boundary between classroom and church when the student minister becomes the one who needs a minister? These are some of the distinctive issues that animate the seminary classroom. They are particularly acute in a seminar on death and dying among adult learners. I strive to understand how best to teach when such faith questions and matters of student diversity are always on the front burner.

Beginning with Experience

I start a seminary course on death and dying with the assumption that experience precedes theory. Each student and the instructor bring various experiences of loss into the classroom. Many have been visited by death within their own families and congregations; they know grief. Indeed, some students show up at theological seminaries attempting to make spiritual and emotional sense of recent or traumatic loss. Crisis often propels persons into the religious arena to seek solace, guidance, and understanding of the powerful emotions and spiritual questions that they are undergoing. Confronted at the border between life and death, knowing the void that follows the loss of a loved one, the seminary is a good place to find honest companions and to ask the questions that are naturally within the purview of religious studies: Where is God at times of loss or disaster? What is the purpose of life? Does life go on after death? Does it matter? They bring all of these existential questions into the classroom, and I invite them to offer these concerns at the very beginning of the course.

Another reason for beginning with experience is that theological education is not simply to inform students about biblical interpretation or church history or denominational polity. Nor is it simply about transmitting professional skills such as preaching, teaching, caregiving, or church administration. Theological education seeks to *form* students as certain kinds of persons, for example pastoral leaders who minister (serve) not only by what they know but by *who* they are.[2] Seminary education strives to help the student integrate head, heart, and body as a complete person; a person who lives by certain habits and practices that are distinctively Christian, what theologian Ed Farley calls "habitus."[3] When such a person leads a congregation as its pastor or priest, others can sense this deep formation and are more likely to respond to the leadership being offered.[4]

Thus, the student who participates in a class on death and dying is invited to grapple with his or her own feelings, mental associations, and beliefs with respect to the topic. Only the minister who knows how to recognize his or her own grief, and attend to it appropriately, will be able to help others as they confront death and dying. The minister who is terrified of death will avoid persons who are terminally ill or bereaved. He or she will withdraw from others at the very point that a ministry of care is most needed. Unfortunately, this happens too often in Christian ministry. So, one of the primary aims of the course on death and dying is to help students begin, if they have not already, to come to "terms" with death. Jesus of Nazareth's recalling of the proverb, "Doctor, cure yourself," is always appropriate when dealing with ministers and other caregivers.[5]

A caution, however, is important. The classroom should not become an extended therapy session for the student who might be wrestling with grief as the class occurs. Some students are living so close to the experience of death and dying that everything said or read in the class seems personally directed at them. When this occurs, I offer some time within the class to respond to the personal concerns of the student. It is an occasion for me and the students to provide basic pastoral care through listening and supporting. But if necessary, because the student's needs for support are so great that they begin to dominate class time, I will speak to the student and invite him to talk with me outside of class where we can more adequately deal with his personal concerns. Usually, other students will follow up outside of class as well. Such therapeutic "turns" in the class need to be monitored closely so they do not overtake the larger educational goals of the course. Nevertheless, it is unavoidable, if teacher and students are honest with one another, that a certain amount of therapeutic material will arise in a class on death and dying. This is helpful. Since the course begins experientially, the challenge for the instructor is to guide the sharing and response to those experiences toward maximum learning for everyone.

I begin the first session by inviting students to reflect upon personal experiences of death and dying, grief and loss. But I lead them into the water slowly, first by introducing them to a song, a poem, or a movie clip that deals with grief or death and dying. Kate Campbell's song "Tupelo's Too Far" or Ann Peebles's classic "I Can't Stand the Rain" are good choices for my students. Short clips from movies like *In the Bedroom* or *Steel Magnolias* work well.[6] From these artistic sights and sounds of death, loss, and grief, it is only one small step to our own subjective responses to death and dying. When the class seems ready, I will invite each student (class size is always limited to twelve to fifteen students) to share a personal experience of having lost someone to death. I give students the option to "pass" with or without explanation. This signals to the students that I want the classroom to be a safe place to explore this emotionally and spiritually relevant topic. I guide students to simply listen to what is being offered by their classmates.

What students begin to hear in their own stories and those of their classmates is both the commonality of human loss and the uniqueness of grief. Right away, they begin to make emotional and mental connections with each other because of the universal experience of loss that leads to grief. At the same time, the stories are usually so different—sometimes a tragic death by car accident, sometimes a mysterious death, other times a death at the end of a long and fruitful life, sometimes a murder—that they cannot rush to generalize feelings or understandings within the class. We all grieve differently. When one student tries to "help" another student by either sympathizing or rationalizing their experience (clergy types are particularly prone to both), I will gently remind them that the first class session is for story-telling and story-listening rather than interpretation or active response. By the end of the first session, if I have done a good enough job of creating a conducive environment for shared learning, the students are in touch with some of their own emotions and beliefs with respect to death and dying and are eager to begin working towards greater understanding of themselves and of the resources of the Christian tradition.

Death and Dying: Biblical and Theological Understandings

After one or two sessions that help students explore their own experiences of loss and their own responses to the deaths of others, they are ready to more formally engage theological and biblical understandings of death and dying. I begin these sessions with an artistic response to death, such as Ralph Stanley's haunting song "O Death" or a clip from the movie *Iris*, which is based on the life and death of the British writer Iris Murdoch.[7] These artistic pieces provide springboards into discussions about theological and biblical views of death. I encourage students to "tease out" the theology of death that seems to govern the song or film. I ask them if they agree or disagree with this theology and why? And then I ask them if the assigned reading material for the class session would support or contradict the theology of the songwriter or film director.

Primary texts for this section of the course might be Kenneth Mitchell and Herbert Anderson's *All Our Losses, All Our Griefs*, Lucy Bregman's *Beyond Silence and Denial: Death and Dying Reconsidered*, Kathleen Billman and Daniel Migliore's *Rachel's Cry*, or assigned readings from Rodney Hunter et. al.,

Dictionary of Pastoral Care and Counseling.[8] The main concern is to push the students toward a deeper understanding of the various ways that the Christian tradition understands death and dying and to motivate them to begin to articulate their own theology of death and dying.

This is both a theological and pastoral matter. Without any clear notion of what we believe about the relationship between ourselves, God, life, and death, ministers can easily slip into an approach to pastoral care that either is sentimental, is marked by false assurances, avoids the reality of death, or is so bland that it fails to connect believers to the sources of the Christian faith. Only if the pastor understands that her task is both theological and pastoral, can she lead persons to the engagement with God, Jesus Christ, the Holy Spirit, and Christian faith that believers want and expect as they pass through the crisis of death. As Charles Gerkin said many years ago, ministers cannot go into the grave with their parishioners, but they can go up to the edge and peer over into the darkness with them.[9]

At a minimum, an adequate discussion of death and dying from a Christian theological perspective will address the issue of body and spirit, the Judeo-Christian understandings of both, and the strange split that has occurred between the two in the Western Christian tradition. This necessitates a review of Greek beliefs in the immortality of the soul in contrast to the Christian belief in the resurrection of the body. The differences are crucial, but many Westerners have become so captive to a Greek-influenced dualism that it takes careful (and often lengthy) discussion to even begin to dislodge the notions. The preponderance of Christian scripture, the Nicene Creed and its attendant controversies, and the weight of 2,000 years of Christian tradition lead us toward an affirmation of body and spirit together that is not negated but fulfilled and completed in death.

This assumes that the doctrine of the resurrection is the keystone doctrine when it comes to a theology of death and dying. But many seminary students have not fully plumbed the depths of this doctrine. Christian believers, even in the face of wasted bodies and horrific human pain, will affirm the goodness of creation and the promise of redemption of the whole person—body, mind, and spirit. David Buttrick argues correctly that "the risen Christ is the crucified Christ."[10] This foundational mystery is something that seminary students must approach if they are to minister with theological integrity and hope among the sick and dying. The power of the resurrection is precisely its power over death, both the death of Jesus Christ and the death of all his followers.

In Christian belief, the resurrection of Jesus Christ is God's act of new creation. God calls back to life not just Jesus' soul but his entire self—body and soul. Through the resurrected Christ, God is at work to vanquish death and bring forth a whole new life for those who are "in Christ" and, indeed, for all creation. As the apostle Paul said to the church at Corinth, "If anyone is in Christ, there is a new creation: everything old has passed away; see, everything has become new."[11] Such a claim, as unreasonable as it may seem to the skeptic or the nonbeliever, is the hinge upon which a Christian theology of death swings. Paradoxically, death for the Christian opens a door to new life where the believer receives his full humanity, a humanity bestowed by God and redeemed by Jesus Christ. Since Jesus mediates such salvation, he must really fall to the sword of death. That is the only way to overcome it. These are general, and many would say, controversial claims, but they are the theological claims that orient seminary students and Christian ministers who grapple with death and dying on a regular basis.

With respect to biblical interpretation, students need to see the range of positions within scripture. Hebrew and Christian scripture do not present a unified understanding of death and dying. Rather, there are multiple views within scripture. The student should recognize them all as she develops her own biblically informed theology of death and dying. These include the following main positions, though others can be found as well:

1. Death is a natural part of human creation that causes grief for those who survive the loss of a loved one, for example Abraham's death in Genesis 25 and Moses' death in Deuteronomy 34.

2. Death is a constant threat to the fulfillment of human life and we should strive to drive it away, for example the death of Absalom in 2 Samuel 18 and the death of Jairus's daughter in Mark 5.

3. Death is the result of human sin. Suffering is divine punishment for violation of God's laws and covenant, for example Genesis 2–3 and Romans 6:23: "For the wages of sin is death."

4. Death and loss are God's enemies, and they will be defeated at the end of human history, for example I Corinthians 15:26: "The last enemy to be destroyed is death."

5. Death, loss, and suffering are redemptive insofar as God through Christ suffers with us and, thereby, yields hope in the resurrection. Death isn't desirable but is unavoidable, leading the Christian to the fullness of new life. See, for example, Philippians 3:10–11.[12]

Students may find their own beliefs about death and dying among any or all of these positions. To push them toward a hard-won integration of a pastoral and theological view of death and dying, I assign readings from Nicholas Wolterstorff's *Lament for a Son*, so that they can see how a theologian personally wrestles with the tragic death of a son.[13] We note the range of biblical interpretations of death to encourage the seminary student to think the whole matter through and to be aware that in ministry she will encounter most if not all of these views among the congregation. Sometimes the minister may want to gently offer a more helpful understanding for the bereaved congregation or family member. And other times, she may simply reaffirm the theology that is being expressed by adding one's own exclamation point.

Psychosocial Theories of Death and Dying

After establishing the theological and biblical framework for understanding death and dying, we are ready to turn to the psychological and sociological resources that will aid the Christian minister as he cares for the dying and bereaved. Many of these resources are discussed in other articles in this volume, so I will only touch here on the way that I include them in the seminary classroom.

Seminary students should be familiar with some of the classic twentieth-century texts that elucidate death and grief from psychological and sociological perspectives. In this section of the course, they might read from Erich Lindemann's "Symptomatology and Management of Acute Grief," in *Beyond Grief: Studies in Crisis Intervention*; Elisabeth Kübler-Ross's *On Death and Dying*; Ernest Becker's *The Denial of Death*; and Karla Holloway's more recent *Passed On: African American Mourning Stories*. An additional resource for this section of the course is Therese A. Rando's encyclopedic *Grief, Dying, and Death: Clinical Interventions for Caregivers*.[14] Each of these texts help students understand the vocabulary and theories of death, loss, and grief that continue to shape cultural attitudes and responses to death and dying. In some cases, the primary texts will deepen or correct understanding, as with the work of Kübler-Ross. In other cases, the ideas will challenge students to stretch and grow conceptually, Becker's work on the denial of death being one example.

With each of these resources, I ask students how the ideas and clinical applications relate to their own theological and biblical understandings of death and dying. In other words, how do they correlate psychosocial theories of death and dying with theological understandings? What do the theories assume about the nature of humanity, the origins and ends of creation, and the purpose of human life that is either compatible or incompatible with their own evolving Christian views? What difference does this make when it comes to the practice of Christian ministry?[15]

The purpose of this section in the course is twofold. First, Christian ministers need the wisdom of the social science disciplines to adequately provide pastoral care among the dying and bereaved. Anyone without a working knowledge of the psychological, social, and physiological manifestations of grief should not be attempting pastoral care in the twenty-first century. Secondly, students need to determine *for themselves* which psychosocial understandings of death and grief are most compatible with their own religious views. Some psychologies are less open to religious correlation than others. Christian ministers can ill afford to unknowingly embrace a set of theories and applications that explicitly or implicitly undermine the beliefs and values that they are attempting to sustain. On the other hand, the gains afforded by many psychosocial understandings of death and dying are so great that the clergy who dismiss them do a disservice to their parishioners.

Pastoral and Congregational Resources

The final goal of the course is to provide pastoral and congregational resources to assist the minister and the congregation in their ministry to the dying. This is the practical turn in the course that most likely motivates the student to enroll in the first place. It isn't that practical concerns have been absent throughout the course, but the final section devotes full attention to them. By design, the course is circling back around to the experiential and the practical as students seek tangible resources for ministry within their own situations and contexts.

Here, we cover a wide range of material. This includes attention to life-cycle theory and ministry, with special focus upon death, dying, and ministry among children and adolescents. A chaplain from our local children's hospital visits with the class to discuss her work among families with children who are terminally ill. We review ministry with the dying patient and discuss hospice care with a local hospice chaplain. We explore the differences between normal and pathological manifestations of grief and the best ways to respond to both. We discuss ethical dilemmas surrounding death and dying—for example, assisted suicide. Resources here include Sally Geis and Donald Messer, *How Shall We Die: Helping Christians Debate Assisted Suicide*; David Barnard, Anna Towers, Patricia Boston, and Yanna Lambrinidou, *Crossing Over*; and a viewing of the movie, *Wit*. Each of these resources usually triggers discussions among the students about situations in ministry where they are grappling with how to best provide pastoral care.[16]

We give careful attention in the final weeks of the course to funerals and other rituals for persons who are dying and bereaved. Students learn of the distinctive funeral traditions that are represented among the class members who come from different denominations and cultural backgrounds. We read portions of Mitchell and Anderson's *All Our Losses, All Our Griefs*, Holloway's *Passed On*, and Edward Wimberly's *African American Pastoral Care*.[17] If not already familiar with their denominational prayer books and resources, students review the relevant rituals and assess them for strengths and weaknesses. We meet with a local funeral home director and learn of the funeral home's understanding of their work both as a business and as a service to the community.

Finally, we discuss the minister's own grief, the grief that Wayne Oates characterizes as "the tragic sense of life" in *Grief, Transition, and Loss*.[18] Clergy discuss the importance of self-care as they minister within a congregation or other setting where death is always present or just around the next corner. This is critically important for ministers who wish to remain vital in ministry. Providing ongoing care for the dying and bereaved takes an emotional and spiritual toll on the minister. The minister, just as the social worker, the nurse, the community worker, and the counselor, must find ways to nurture her own spiritual, psychological, and physical health if she intends to carry on a ministry of pastoral care that aids the sick, the dying, and the bereaved.[19]

Assignments in this section push the student to integrate the theoretical with the practical, the pastoral with the theological. In the final assignment, the student develops a project on one of the course topics in which he demonstrates integration of the various resources of the course. For example, he may choose to design a funeral ritual for the family of a child who dies during birth. The ritual must be fully explained theologically, psychologically, and practically. In assessing the work, I want to see how well the student is able to synthesize and expand upon the material covered throughout the course. Does the ritual make sense in light of the student's own expressed beliefs and what she understands about the beliefs of the grieving family? Is it emotionally therapeutic for the bereaved parents and congregation? Why or why not? Does the ritual progress both logically and symbolically in a way that affords honesty, support, hope, faith, and community care for those who are grieving? If so, why? If not, what is missing or needs to be changed? How does the ritual communicate to the believer the nearness or absence of God? What else needs to happen in the days following the funeral to continue to care for the grieving family? These are the practical and theological questions that conclude the course and point the student away from the classroom and toward the congregation and community where Christian ministry occurs.

Conclusion

Because of the theological context for education, this approach to the teaching of death and dying is distinct from that of many approaches in college and university settings. A seminary context requires an integration of religious *and* psychosocial understandings that will assist the inquiring student as she prepares herself for Christian ministry. Because of the personal nature of the material, many seminary students must first grapple with their own fears and doubts concerning death and dying before their examined experience can be turned towards life-giving ministry. But when, among a group of trusted peers, the seminary student begins to face his own mortality and the accompanying emotions and beliefs surrounding his own finiteness, he can then begin to learn from the rich resources available about how to best extend care to others as they seek to live faithfully in the face of death and dying.

NOTES

1. Leo Tolstoy, *The Death of Ivan Iliych and Other Stories*, afterword by Hugh McLean (New York: New American Library, 2003), 129.

2. On the formation of students in theological education, and the accompanying pedagogies that aim at such formation, see Charles R. Foster, Lisa Dahill, Larry Goleman, and Barbara Wang Tolentino, *Educating Clergy: Teaching Practices and Pastoral Imagination*, J. B. Carnegie Foundation for the Advancement of Teaching (San Francisco: Jossey Bass, 2006); and C. R. Dykstra, "The Pastoral Imagination," *Initiatives in Religion* 9 (2001): 2–3, 15.

3. Edward Farley, *Theologia: The Fragmentation and Unity of Theological Education* (Philadelphia: Fortress, 1983).

4. I am not suggesting that all seminaries do such formation very well, but formation of the whole person is usually a primary goal within formal theological education.

5. Luke 4:23, New Revised Standard Version of the Bible. All biblical quotes from NRSV.

6. Kate Campbell, "Tupelo's Too Far," on *Moonpie Dreams* (Compass Records, 1997); Ann Peebles, "I Can't Stand the Rain," on *I Can't Stand the Rain* (Hi Records, 1974); *In the Bedroom* (Miramax, 2002); *Steel Magnolias* (Rastar Films, 1989).

7. Ralph Stanley, "O Death," on *Oh Brother, Where Art Thou?* soundtrack (Lost Highway, 2000); *Iris* (British Broadcasting Corporation, 2001).

8. Kenneth R. Mitchell and Herbert Anderson, *All Our Losses, All Our Griefs: Resources for Pastoral Care* (Louisville: Westminster John Knox, 1983); Lucy Bregman, *Beyond Silence and Denial: Death and Dying Reconsidered* (Louisville: Westminster John Knox, 1999); Kathleen D. Billman and Daniel L. Migliore, *Rachel's Cry* (Cleveland:

United Church Press, 1999); Rodney L. Hunter and Nancy J. Ramsay, eds., *Dictionary of Pastoral Care and Counseling* (Nashville: Abingdon, 2005).

9. Charles V. Gerkin, *Crisis Experience in Modern Life: Theory and Theology for Pastoral Care* (Nashville: Abingdon, 1979).

10. David Buttrick, *The Mystery and the Passion: A Homiletic Reading of the Gospel Traditions* (Minneapolis: Fortress, 1992), 29.

11. 2 Corinthians 5:17.

12. Most of these positions are delineated in Mitchell and Anderson, *All Our Losses, All Our Griefs.*

13. Nicholas Wolterstorff, *Lament for a Son* (Grand Rapids, MI: Eerdman's, 1987).

14. Erich Lindemann, "Symptomatology and Management of Acute Grief," in *Beyond Grief: Studies in Crisis Intervention*, ed. Erich Lindemann and Elizabeth Lindemann, p. 59–77 (New York: Jason Aronson, 1985); Elisabeth Kübler-Ross, *On Death and Dying* (New York: Macmillan, 1969); Ernest Becker, *The Denial of Death* (New York: Free Press, 1973); Karla F. C. Holloway, *Passed On: African American Mourning Stories* (Durham: Duke University Press, 2002); Therese Rando, *Grief, Dying, and Death: Clinical Interventions for Caregivers* (Champagne, IL: Research Press, 1984).

15. To help them through this tough work of correlation, I assign readings from Hunter et al., *Dictionary of Pastoral Care and Counseling*, such as James Loder's "Theology and Psychology," J. D. Carter's "Integration of Psychology and Theology," Kenneth Mitchell's "Theology and Psychotherapy," and Walt Lowe's "Christology and Pastoral Care."

16. Sally B. Geis and Donald E. Messer, eds., *How Shall We Die? Helping Christians Debate Assisted Suicide* (Nashville: Abingdon, 1997); David Barnard, Anna Towers, Patricia Boston, and Yanna Lambrinidou, eds., *Crossing Over: Narratives of Palliative Care* (Oxford: Oxford University Press, 2000); *Wit* (Avenue Pictures Productions, 2001).

17. Edward P. Wimberly, *African American Pastoral Care and Counseling: The Politics of Oppression and Empowerment* (Cleveland: Pilgrim Press, 2006).

18. Wayne Oates, *Grief, Transition, and Loss: A Pastor's Practical Guide* (Minneapolis: Fortresss, 1997).

19. Of the many good resources for pastors regarding clergy self-care, see Roy M. Oswald, *Clergy Self-Care: Finding a Balance for Effective Ministry* (Washington, DC: Alban Institute, 1991), and for a theological understanding of sustaining excellence in ministry, see Greg Jones and Kevin Armstrong, *Resurrecting Excellence: Shaping Faithful Christian Ministry* (Grand Rapids, MI: Eerdman's, 2006).

BIBLIOGRAPHY

Barnard, David, Anna Towers, Patricia Boston, and Yanna Lambrinidou. *Crossing Over: Narratives of Palliative Care.* Oxford: Oxford University Press, 2000.

Becker, Ernest. *The Denial of Death.* New York: Free Press, 1973.

Billman, Kathleen D., and Daniel L. Migliore. *Rachel's Cry.* Cleveland: United Church Press, 1999.

Bregman, Lucy. *Beyond Silence and Denial: Death and Dying Reconsidered.* Louisville: Westminster John Knox, 1999.

Buttrick, David. *The Mystery and the Passion: A Homiletic Reading of the Gospel Traditions.* Minneapolis: Fortress, 1992.

Dykstra, C. R. "The Pastoral Imagination." *Initiatives in Religion* 9 (2001): 2–3, 15.

Farley, Edward. *Theologia: The Fragmentation and Unity of Theological Education.* Philadelphia: Fortress Press, 1983.

Foster, Charles R., Lisa Dahill, Larry Goleman, and Barbara Wang Tolentino. *Educating Clergy: Teaching Practices and Pastoral Imagination.* J. B. Carnegie Foundation for the Advancement of Teaching. San Francisco: Jossey Bass, 2006.

Geis, Sally B., and Donald E. Messer, eds. *How Shall We Die? Helping Christians Debate Assisted Suicide.* Nashville: Abingdon, 1997.

Gerkin, Charles V. *Crisis Experience in Modern Life: Theory and Theology for Pastoral Care.* Nashville: Abingdon, 1979.

Holloway, Karla F. C. *Passed On: African American Mourning Stories.* Durham: Duke University Press, 2002.

Hunter, Rodney L., and Nancy J. Ramsay, eds. *Dictionary of Pastoral Care and Counseling.* Nashville: Abingdon, 2005.

Jones, Greg, and Kevin Armstrong. *Resurrecting Excellence: Shaping Faithful Christian Ministry.* Grand Rapids, MI: Eerdman's, 2006.

Kübler-Ross, Elisabeth. *On Death and Dying.* New York: Macmillan, 1969.

Erich Lindemann. "Symptomatology and Management of Acute Grief." In *Beyond Grief: Studies in Crisis Intervention,* edited by Erich Lindemann and Elizabeth Lindemann, p. 59–77. New York: Jason Aronson, 1985.

Lindemann, Erich, and Elizabeth Lindemann. *Beyond Grief: Studies in Crisis Intervention.* New York: Jason Aronson, 1985.

Mitchell, Kenneth R., and Herbert Anderson. *All Our Losses, All Our Griefs: Resources for Pastoral Care.* Louisville: Westminster John Knox, 1983.

Oates, Wayne. *Grief, Transition, and Loss: A Pastor's Practical Guide.* Minneapolis: Fortress, 1997.

Oswald, Roy M. *Clergy Self-Care: Finding a Balance for Effective Ministry.* Washington, DC: Alban Institute, 1991.

Rando, Therese. *Grief, Dying, and Death: Clinical Interventions for Caregivers.* Champagne, IL: Research Press, 1984.

Tolstoy, Leo. *The Death of Ivan Iliych and Other Stories.* Afterword by Hugh McLean. New York: New American Library, 2003.

Wimberly, Edward P. *African American Pastoral Care and Counseling: The Politics of Oppression and Empowerment.* Cleveland: Pilgrim Press, 2006.

Wolterstorff, Nicholas. *Lament for a Son.* Grand Rapids, MI: Eerdman's, 1987.

6

Death, Loss, and Bereavement: The Role of Social Work

Estelle Hopmeyer

Fifteen years ago, I helped a mother start a group for the survivors of suicide: Family Survivors of Suicide (FSOS). Although I had practiced and taught at McGill University for over twenty-five years, this was my first introduction to sudden death, bereavement, and the impact of a death on a family. As I learned about these areas, I realized that graduate social work students needed to have the practice skills that I was acquiring and relevant knowledge about loss and bereavement to inform this practice. Two colleagues who worked at the Montreal Children's Hospital joined me several years later to teach the first class on bereavement and loss to four students. The first year we provided considerable theoretical material about life threatening illness and bereavement and shared our practice with the students. We learned halfway through the term that the four students would go for coffee after the class to debrief, as the course material was having a profound personal impact on them. As one student reported, "At work I have professional boundaries but this class is making me look at my personal losses and my own mortality." We learned from this feedback, and as a result, I have made significant changes in course content, format, and assignments.

This book chapter will present current course goals, content, and format. It will also address strategies utilized to assist students in processing and integrating this powerful practice material. Unlike other chapters in the book, it will present many examples of clinical practice related to death and dying and nonbereavement loss.

Course Goals, Content, and Format

The seminar entitled Life Threatening Illness and Bereavement: Non Bereavement Loss taught at McGill is at the graduate level and is part of the master of social work program. It is a three-credit, or one-half-year, course that is open to all the master's-level social work and other health care provider students. Its primary focus is on the psychosocial concerns of individuals living with life-threatening illnesses and/or experiencing the death of a family member. It also addresses nonbereavement loss issues.

The course is designed for students who are interested in the field of loss and bereavement and who want to achieve the following goals:

1. To gain theoretical knowledge and the application of this knowledge in social work practice and research
2. To gain an appreciation of the impact of culture on the illness and bereavement process
3. To develop a loss perspective in nonbereavement loss areas of social work practice
4. To explore the personal and professional impact of course content related to loss and bereavement in small group discussions and written assignments

The course begins with four classes related to life threatening illness. The specific areas covered are prediagnosis and diagnosis, the chronic phase, the terminal phase, and finally, anticipatory grief and bereavement. This section of the course is followed by classes that deal with psychosocial loss (severe mental illness, child welfare, relocation due to immigration or refugee status) and disenfranchised grief (AIDS, perinatal loss), interspersed with a series of classes that deal specifically with issues related to end of life or bereavement: sudden-death, suicide, ethical issues, and cross-cultural practice relating to life-threatening illness and bereavement; intergenerational loss issues; and spirituality.

Throughout the course, there is an integration of theory, practice, and the impact of this work on the professional. The course format provides for didactic teaching, films,[1] case material, class discussion, and small group discussions in fixed groups to permit the students to safely discuss personal reactions should they choose to do so. Students are expected to cover three areas in these small groups. The first is to discuss major points of interest that had been presented in the more formal teaching part of the class. The second requires students to consider the role(s) of the social work professional related to the theme of the class. The third, and perhaps the most important part, asks students to reflect on the "personal" impact of the material presented in class. At the end of the thirty-to-forty-five-minute discussion, students rotate to present a summary of their small group discussion to the entire class (while protecting the confidentiality of group members). The last few minutes of the class is spent in summarizing the content of the day.

Assignments require students to write practice papers related to class content and to write a journal after each class. The journal is focused on personal reflections related to the impact of course content and discussion. Two weeks following each topic, the theoretical assignments are handed in: two deal with a phase of life threatening illness, one with bereavement loss, one with nonbereavement loss, one with cultural or ethical issues, and the final one with the impact on the social worker. The goal of these assignments is to integrate theory and practice through an analysis of selected theoretical material (a minimum of three readings per assignment) and the linkage of central themes to case examples. Students are expected to include a discussion of the role(s) for a social worker. The final assignment is a poster presentation on a topic of each student's choice. This is presented in the last class and is an opportunity for each student to share in a creative and scholarly manner. Students are encouraged to submit posters to conferences related to their topic.

The above discussion has briefly presented course content and format. It does not, however, do justice to the richness of the presentations, class participation, and the written assignments of the students. Further, it does not address the formidable task faced by the students as they confront the very powerful material presented in this class. Students must challenge themselves both as emerging professionals wanting to become skillful in working with individuals and their families and personally as they are forced to face issues relating to their own loss history and mortality. These challenges will be addressed in the following section where certain of the classes will be described in greater detail to highlight the integration of theory with practice and emerging skill-building and self-awareness on the part of the students.

As stated earlier, theoretical material related to prediagnosis and diagnosis is presented in the first class, once the housekeeping business of a new class has been addressed. My colleague, who is a pediatric oncology social worker, and I presently team-teach the course. She brings her current practice with children and their families into the classroom to illustrate the linkage of theory to practice. This year she used the case of a five-year-old child recently diagnosed with acute leukemia. She described her work with the family, newly arrived immigrants, who were totally overwhelmed by the devastating news, and their entry into a complex and seemingly unresponsive medical system. The students asked my colleague how she intervenes (her role[s] and practice skills) and how she deals with the overwhelming sadness of the parents. Students, even those who have previous work experience, can be immobilized by feelings of impotence, and wonder if they will be able to help families facing a life crisis that has little or no chance of a positive health outcome. The fact that the patient is a young child presents even more difficulties for beginning practitioners. This is highlighted in a subsequent class on the terminal phase. Here, we present a film entitled *Letting Go: The Hospice Journey*. It follows three people through the final stages of illness to their deaths. One of the patients is a young boy in a coma. We share intimate moments with his father, young sister, and the health-care team. The mother is estranged from the family and only sees her son just prior to his death. This film and the one we show in class on bereavement, *Surviving Death: Stories of Grief*, also provide insightful material on a child's experience of having a parent or sibling die. In the latter film, the boy's aunt, and the subsequent legal guardian, was advised by a psychiatrist not to tell the young boy (approximately nine years of age) that his mother, a single mom, was dying from AIDS. In the film, it became clear that the young boy would have preferred to be told about the impending death of his mother and not have been protected from this truth. Class discussion was lively on this topic with little support for the position taken by the health-care professional. This then led to a serious discussion on what children understand about death and age-appropriate interventions with this young population.

The journal written after each class, as stated earlier, provides the opportunity for the students to explore personal reactions to class material. The first class this year generated several personal accounts related to the diagnosis phase of an illness. This is not surprising, as we all have our own loss history and emotions that can be triggered, often unexpectedly, when a subject comes close to our own experiences. One student wrote that her mother, who lives in another city, had recently discovered a lump on her breast and was going for a biopsy the following week. Her worries were not only for her mother but also for herself and the rest of the family if their worst fears were to be realized. Another student described her own agonizing wait for her diagnosis and the surprising sense of relief when her worst fears were confirmed. She now had a diagnosis and some possibility of regaining control. She talked about her need to have a social worker to give her and her family support during this highly stressful time. It is evident even in the journals that students are linking theoretical material presented in class, including potential role(s) for social workers.

An example from another class highlights the cross-cultural emphasis in the course. The McGill Master of Social Work program attracts international students from many different countries. In 2004, the loss and bereavement class had students from across Canada, the United States, Indonesia, Israel, Jordan, Palestine, Africa, and the Caribbean. Classroom teachers were very aware that most of the films and case material were presented from a "Western" perspective. In the ethics class, for example, one of the films used was entitled *Intensive Care: Who Decides?* This *Dateline NBC* documentary presented three case studies from a large Chicago hospital. The ethics team faced decisions related to providing or not providing life-sustaining treatment. It was important for us to explore non-Western perspectives as well as to discuss the ethical dilemmas presented in the film. For some students this was not a decision for a physician or family to make. Learning from this class discussion is then transferred to the work with individuals and families from many cultural and religious groups.[2] Students are encouraged to learn from their clients so that they can work from the clients' worldviews in a nonjudgmental and supportive manner. This work can require social workers to intervene as advocates on behalf of their clients with other care providers. For example, in some cultures, all communication with the family is to go through the male, even in the case of perinatal death. The wife/mother may not be asked to participate in the grief work as would be expected in other cultural groups.[3] Another cultural practice issue relates to "truth telling" in the case of a terminal illness. In Western countries, we generally work to include the patient in decision making related to his or her health and treatment. It is important to give the patient as much control as possible. Other cultures do not want the patient to know his or her health status in the case of a terminal illness, as it is believed that this may lead to an accelerated death with the patient's lack of hope. In relation to truth telling, several years ago we had a student in a class who was from a culture that did not believe in truth telling at the end of life. She was doing her field placement in a local hospital and was asked to see a very ill sixteen-year-old adolescent of her same culture. She described her "bicultural" dilemma. Having spent several years in Canada and having been increasingly educated in the Western frame at the end of life, she was conflicted about whether she should discuss this issue with the young man to help him find meaning in his premature death. We advised her to let the young man take the lead. She did, and he never asked her if he was dying. At the very end, she held his hand and said it was okay. He died very soon after, and she worried that she had betrayed her culture by giving him permission to die. We all learned from this student's efforts to reconcile her emerging professional and personal beliefs which were complicated by her bicultural location.

Selected themes related to bereavement will now be discussed. Areas to be covered include suicide—a sudden, stigmatized death—disenfranchised grief, and psychosocial loss.

The first section of the course deals with illness and the possible, probable, or inevitable outcome of the disease through classes on the progressive stages of an illness from diagnosis to death.[4] It addresses both concrete tasks and roles for the individual, the family, and the health-care team, and also the belief systems ascribed to this illness for all concerned.[5] The class on sudden death provides a new framework for analysis. There is no timeline or phases of illness; rather, there is a sudden and often unexpected death. Further, in the case of suicide, this is very likely to be a stigmatized death.[6] One of the reasons that Family Survivors of Suicide (FSOS) was established is that when Esther, the founding member of the group, and I went to a Compassionate Friends meeting (a self-help group for parents whose child had died), Esther did not feel that she could tell them that her daughter had killed herself. All of the other parents had children who died from an illness, which seemed more acceptable than the manner of her daughter's death.

My ongoing work as consultant to FSOS has provided me with considerable expert knowledge and interventive skill in practice related to the aftermath of suicide. I bring case examples from this practice into the classroom as a way of illustrating the devastating impact of suicide on those who have been left behind.

The class on suicide begins with a presentation on the factors related to a sudden death and its aftermath. The bereavement path can follow the avoidance-confrontation-reconciliation trajectory presented by Theresa Rando,[7] but also has elements that differ in intensity for the griever. This can lead to a complicated mourning, which is briefly presented theoretically.[8] In a sudden death, there is no opportunity to say goodbye, to deal with unfinished business, to say "I love you" or "I forgive you," or ask "Can you forgive me?" or "Did I not love you enough?" The "why" haunts those left behind from a suicide death, as it is impossible to imagine the hopelessness, helplessness, or despair felt by another. In describing the psychic pain experienced by those who kill themselves, one of the FSOS group members shared her brother's suicide note, which told his family that he had "cancer of the soul."

In working with FSOS, it became clear that one of the strongest emotions felt by suicide survivors is guilt. The what-ifs and if-onlys are played and replayed in the survivors' minds. One group member took months of meetings to begin to forgive herself for her husband's death. They had separated and she felt that this had been the precipitating factor for his suicide. She described the decision to separate as the drop of water that made the bucket overflow. The process of self-forgiveness began when she acknowledged that she did not kill him, for if she had she would be in jail. She shared that she was beginning to be more accepting intellectually that it had been his choice and that she would have prevented it if she could have. However, there was a long distance between her head and her heart.

The issue of a timeframe for grieving after the death of a loved one can be usefully discussed in this class. There is an expectation, in our quick-fix society, that people will get on with their lives after a death in a relatively short period of time. Grievers and others do not expect that for those left behind, the second year after the death may be more difficult than the first year. This can be explained through understanding that the avoidance phase may take a considerable length of time and that a second birthday or holiday event without the person confirms that they are permanently gone. We must also recognize that a suicide death is very traumatic for the survivors, and there is no timeframe for refocusing back on the person's life rather than staying fixed on the manner of the death. One FSOS group member told us that it took two years for her to say her son's name and much longer to talk about his life.

This same group member attended her first meeting eighteen years after the death of her son. She explained that she had returned to work and participated actively in hobbies, including music. However, attending the Group permitted her to do important work with her aged parents and her other children. The latter felt that the family had never done the essential grief work required after the death of their brother.

An important expressed outcome for suicide survivors is to make meaning from the suicide death of a loved one. Group members have helped others through continuing leadership in FSOS, through advocacy (e.g., against gambling addiction/VLTs [video lottery terminals]), through public education (radio and television presentations) and open meetings, and through being available to meet individually with families needing support. Breaking the silence is very important in a stigmatized death and in our contemporary society where suicide is still taboo in some religious groups, which can affect funeral rites and burial.

The class on suicide also features a film entitled *The Choice of a Lifetime: Returning from the Brink of Suicide*. A woman named Nila Bogue, who had made an unsuccessful suicide attempt, produced this film. She felt challenged to hear and record the stories of others who were on the brink of suicide but were drawn back by a lifeline. This film very powerfully portrays the stories of three men and three women and provides insight into the acute pain experienced by them. One of the strengths of the film is the diversity of the participants who represent different ages, genders, sexual orientations, socioeconomic status, and ethnic and cultural backgrounds. This provides an understanding of the complexity of suicide risk and generates an excellent class discussion.

Suicide is the ultimate tragic outcome of a film entitled *Richard Cardinal: Cry from a Diary of a Métis Child*, shown in the class on loss and child welfare. Richard was the victim of multiple foster homes, most of which did not provide, to put it mildly, the nurturing and care he required. The story uses his diary to effectively provide some of the narrative for portraying his short life. Fortunately, this event had a positive outcome for others in the child welfare system. In the Province of Alberta, in Canada, where Richard lived and died, new policies were introduced to better protect the rights of children. Nevertheless, this is a very difficult film to watch, particularly for those students who have worked or continue to work in the area of child protection or with an Aboriginal clientele. It does, however, help them to understand the need to provide a loss framework for much of their work.

Disenfranchised grief is a new area of learning for the majority of students. Disenfranchised grief is defined by Kenneth Doka as follows: "There are circumstances, in which a person experiences a sense of loss but does not have a socially recognized right, role or capacity to grieve. In these cases the grief is disenfranchised. The person suffering the loss has little or no opportunity to mourn publicly."[9] Doka goes on to distinguish three categories of disenfranchised grievers. In the first instance, the relationship is not recognized, in the second case, the loss is not recognized, and in the third category, the griever is not recognized (e.g., the very old, the very young, the severely intellectually disabled). While many categories of mourners fit into these categories, we have chosen to use perinatal loss (including infertility, abortion, miscarriage, and very-early infant death), foster parents, and nontraditional relationships as clinical examples to discuss this aspect of grief. We have encouraged students to, in their class discussions and journals, extend their analysis to other categories of relationships, including ex-wives or ex-husbands, ex-daughters-in-law or ex-sons-in-law, mistresses, coworkers, roommates, friends, classmates, and even health-care providers, to name a few examples.

Perinatal loss is a good example of Doka's second category. In this instance, the loss is not recognized. The literature on miscarriage addresses how the mothers form a very early attachment with their child and the devastating sense of loss when the pregnancy is prematurely terminated.[10] Very often, only the couple and very close family members know about the pregnancy. Others, then, are unlikely to be aware of the miscarriage. Well-meaning practitioners may tell the couple that they are young and can still have children. This in no way addresses the enormous sense of loss faced by the parents and other close family members, such as grandparents, and tends to trivialize the loss. The secrecy about the pregnancy and miscarriage may not enable the couple to have the social support of others at this difficult time.

In addition to FSOS, the school of social work, under my direction, offers or has offered other bereavement groups that meet regularly at the school as a public service at no cost to the members. The groups are facilitated by professional social workers, graduates of the school, with expertise attained in our class in the area of bereavement. I act as a consultant to the groups and/or the facilitators, which enables me to bring current practice to the classroom. One of the groups was for parents who had experienced a perinatal loss. The group was facilitated by a social worker who herself had experienced a similar loss. During the first two years, the group membership was homogenous in that all of the families had experienced a death at childbirth or shortly afterward. At the beginning of the third year, I was called for a consultation, as the facilitator did not believe that the group could work together due to the very heterogeneous membership. The group was to be composed of one couple who had experienced a death of their child at birth, a woman who had multiple miscarriages, another woman who had a therapeutic abortion, and finally a woman who had an abortion. I understood her concerns, but suggested that she emphasize the commonality of the loss of a baby rather than the differences among the group members. This was a very difficult practice experience and ultimately she worked with only two women—the one with multiple miscarriages and the woman who had the abortion. The latter disclosed that she had been pressured by a family member to have the abortion and was grieving the loss of her child the same way as the other woman was grieving her inability to complete a pregnancy. The two women became very supportive of one another and continued to meet for coffee after the group ended.

The child welfare system provides multiple examples of loss, some of which can be considered disenfranchised grief. Foster parents and siblings provide a good example of Doka's second category where the loss is not recognized. The loss experienced by natural parents whose children are placed in foster care and the multiple losses faced by the children themselves are identified and worked with by competent social workers. However, even though the foster parents can become very attached to those in their care, children can come and go in foster homes with very little input from their temporary caregivers into the decision making of the placement of the children. We teach the students that attention needs to be paid by professionals to the need for grief work in these areas. Several years ago, we had a student in the class, who was the only natural child of a family that cared for foster children from the local child and family agency. She shared, in her journal, the devastating loss she experienced each time a child was taken out of her home. She lost siblings and no one in the system ever discussed with her how she felt about these significant ongoing losses. The class became the catalyst for action and she wrote a proposal to the agency where she now works to start a group for foster family siblings.

There are many instances where the relationship is not recognized or publicly sanctioned (Doka's first category). Homosexual relationships, for example, can have limited legal standing, which can create complications in cases of serious illness and/or death. The partner may not have the authority to make decisions or, at times, be present in the hospital room as death nears.

One student poignantly presented several years ago in class the experience of being an ex-daughter-in-law. Her former mother-in-law, with whom she had been very close, died in another city, and her grandson (the son of the student) was invited to attend the funeral. No invitation was extended to the boy's mother, though the boy was too young to travel on his own. She questioned whether she was a "legitimate" mourner because of her status, particularly since she had happily remarried. With support, she determined that she was in fact a legitimate mourner and went to the funeral with her son.

A final brief example will conclude the discussion related to disenfranchised grief. I was invited by a local agency serving the intellectually disabled to develop a bereavement program for all of their professional and residential staff. They wanted to be able to work with the residents, many of whom were nonverbal. The staff were aware that their clientele were aging and soon would be facing the death of their (non custodial) parents. The need for the program became more urgent as the agency was facing the death of one of their clients who had been in long-term residential care. The resident had become very ill, was hospitalized, and her agency caregivers wanted her to return "home" to spend the end of her life with her reconstructed family. They did not want these clients to be disenfranchised and not recognized.

Many practice examples from this training experience were brought into the classroom as my team and I were called in to debrief the staff after this expected death and a sudden death of another client by choking during a meal. To elaborate, in the home where the caretakers wanted their terminal resident to die at "home," she did die shortly thereafter. At the debriefing, an issue arose between the night staff and day staff. One of the night staff closed the door to the now empty room while one of the day caregivers opened the door as soon as she came on duty. We opened communication and addressed different grieving patterns. They were then able to respect each other's preferred way of mourning the death of someone whom they had both loved very much. In the case of the sudden death, there were two main challenges: first, to deal with the staff over the traumatic death, and second, to explain the death to the nonverbal residents. In the first instance, we did a form of posttraumatic stress debriefing. For the residents, a picture of the deceased was put in front of his place at the supper table. His favorite music played in the background as the staff told them in simple language what had happened. After dinner they visited his room as a group to see the empty room and bed. Once again, a simple explanation was given about the finality of death. This ritual was repeated many times.

As indicated in my discussion of the course content and the illustrations provided in this chapter, we spend some class time on nonbereavement loss, as we believe that grief work is a component of much of the work we do as social workers. A discussion of psychosocial loss will further elaborate this point.

Psychosocial loss, or ambiguous loss, relates to nondeath loss, and is the recognition that the person is no longer the same: that he or she may still be alive but that an illness (e.g., severe brain injury, severe mental illness, dementia) has changed the person into someone else.[11] The person may look the same but his or her personality may be very different, and with this comes changed social relationships. In the classroom, we have used the example of severe mental illness (SMI) to illustrate this concept of "social death." I and a former student, whose father had a severe mental illness, wrote a scenario from a child's perspective to highlight the overwhelming number of nondeath losses that are experienced by the family. Brief excerpts will be presented to illustrate firstly the impact on the individual and family and then the similarities and differences with a death loss.

For the child, the parent with SMI has changed in ways that are not understood. It is very hard for a child to understand that Mommy or Daddy looks the same but is so different in response. The ability to count on the parent for love, stability, and support may no longer be possible. The child may feel responsible for the problem, and when the parent acts like his or her old self the child feels that everything is okay and that he or she is good. When the response changes, the child experiences the loss all over again. Because of the cyclical nature of SMI, an improvement in the condition raises hope, but each new episode leads to a severe loss (regrieving). When the illness persists, there may be chronic grief, which is a deep and continuing sorrow. For the person with the mental illness, there is also much loss, as he knows who he was before. Often he may look in the mirror and wonder at the reflection looking back. Who am I? may be a question asked as the loss of who he "was" is hopelessly mourned. There is the loss of the past, of the the present, as he knew it, and of the dreams and goals for the future. Mona Wasow speaks to the constant loneliness of the mentally ill person, experiencing the loss of relationships and caring from others.[12] She writes about how she asked her son, who is a schizophrenic, if he had a good day, and he replied that it was great; someone had asked him for a match and it felt like he was a "regular" person. There is the distinct recognition that the person who now exists is so unlike the person who existed before. It is difficult to reconcile oneself to these changes.

Unlike the physical death of a person, psychosocial death does not create space for social detachment; rather, demands on time and energy may increase. An emancipation from ties—see, for example, Worden's four tasks, the last of which is to withdraw emotional energy from the deceased and invest in others—which is essential for grief work, is precluded.[13] There is a need to recognize multiple losses being experienced while still providing care. Mona Wasow, a social worker, suggests that you need to believe that you did the best you could in a situation where there are few frames of reference to acknowledge all of your losses. Unfortunately, these losses and the need to grieve them go largely unnoticed or unsanctioned by society, making it difficult to achieve resolution. Unlike a death loss, there is no tangible evidence here that would allow for actual mourning, ritual (e.g., funeral), or social support. One student wrote the following in her journal after a class on nonbereavement loss:

> There is great difficulty in obtaining genuine closure where there is a loss of a parent to mental illness, until there is the actual death. It was only when my father died, almost two years ago, that I could attempt to finalize this chapter in my life. The sorrow will never be completely gone and yet, somehow, I have managed to make meaning from it. I learned the prayers for the dead and prayed that my father and I would find peace . . . for me there was great comfort in participating in a ritual that had been around for[ever]. I found meaning and finally roots.

We have learned the importance of ritual in nonbereavement loss from the individuals and families with whom we do grief work. We bring these insights into the classroom, which enriches the students' learning experience.

The Personal and the Profession

The final section of this chapter will provide a discussion on the means we have developed to assist the students to process and integrate powerful class material both personally and professionally. As I write these "final" words, I reflect on the reasons why this is the last section, as in many books on the subject of death and dying.[14] Surely we can only be effective as health-care professionals if we are self-aware, as we use ourselves as the primary tool in our work.

Perhaps this is where we should begin, and we do so in our first class. We alert students that the loss and bereavement course will address material that will affect them personally. We talk about the Western discomfort in discussing death and dying and the need to be open to struggling with difficult feelings, such as fear, uncertainty, powerlessness, and guilt in not being helpful enough, in order to acquire the skills to work effectively with individuals and families facing life-threatening illness and bereavement, and to recognize nonbereavement and how it is dealt with by different groups. We tell students that in this course, we provide structures to assist in this work, namely, the small groups and the journals. We assure them of the confidentially of their work so that they can safely disclose personal stories should they choose to do so (only the classroom instructors will read and have access to the students' journals). We also assure them that throughout the course we will be addressing the impact on the professional and have provided specific readings on this subject (see reference list). Finally, one class (regrettably, usually one of the last classes) will focus on care for the caregiver.

Central to the discussion of the personal impact of work with illness and loss is a heightened awareness of our own mortality. Alicia Cook and Daniel Dworkin state, "As a therapist in this field you will come face to face with your own mortality and your fear of dying and losing loved ones."[15] John Rolland elaborates that a "we-they attitude towards the families we encounter is impossible. We are helping families with issues that are inevitable in our own lives and families."[16] These authors and others insist upon the need for the professional to explore their own losses, both past and present, in order to be effective helpers.[17]

Some of the specific themes we address related to this area are the following: boundaries and self-disclosure, showing emotion, participating in rituals, knowing our limitations, and self-care. These topics will be briefly described below. Boundary setting and self-disclosure to clients are not particular to working with loss and bereavement but nevertheless need to be addressed in this course.[18] Guest lecturers have provided insightful suggestions for the students in the area of personal boundaries with clients. The first guest, Dr. Barbara Sourkes, reminded students that clients are not family members and that our relationships have to be considered within this frame. We, as professionals, cannot become overinvolved with those we are helping. Cook and Dworkin cite Alan Wolfelt, who suggests that therapists working with grief and loss can become "co-dependant bereavement caregivers and can confuse care giving with care taking."[19] The second guest, a psychiatrist, told the class that fences make good neighbors and, continuing with the analogy, elaborated that the fence could have spaces between the slats and a door that therapists could open if they choose to do so. This analogy can usefully be applied to guidelines for self-disclosure. We teach that the most important considerations for self-disclosure are for what purpose and whose benefit the self-disclosure is intended. In broad terms, the purpose for therapist self-disclosure is for building a therapeutic alliance for normalizing, for modeling, and/or for demonstrating empathy. The self-disclosure must be for the benefit of the client(s) and not an opportunity for the therapist to work on his own issues, either past or present.

Students share concerns about showing emotion, like crying, when working with a family after the death of a patient with whom they have grown close to during their illness. Due to "professional" behavior, they may hesitate to cry in front of a family, but as a person, they may need to express their sadness. I believe that it is normal and helpful to shed a tear but remind the class that our patients are not family and we must be respectful of that difference. I provide the same answers when students question whether they "should" attend funerals and other rituals like memorial services. There is value in attending funerals for the purpose of closure and coping with the profound losses experienced with the death of patients. However, equally important is the need to set limits.

The discussion on limit setting and self-care has many dimensions. Briefly, in class we address issues such as vicarious traumatization or compassion fatigue.[20] Here the helper can be overcome with the pain and trauma clients and families are facing. This year, for example, the students, working with refugees (many from countries with genocide) formed their own peer support group to help deal with their reactions to the horrendous stories of rape, torture, and death of family members that they were hearing from their clients. Professional reactions, if not addressed, can lead to distancing or psychic numbing and ultimately to burn out. Strategies of coping and self-care become an important part of these discussions. Students are encouraged to explore solutions like the one cited above.

Setting limits can also be reframed to helping students accept the limits of their ability to change the inevitable: for example, off-time deaths (as was addressed in the section on diagnosis) and the increasing losses associated with many chronic illnesses. This may be difficult in a cure-oriented setting like a hospital, where one has to accept personal and professional limits and not see them as failures. Michael Sternoff, in his article, "The Last Journey: Embracing our Mortality," says it very well:

> When the client is close to the end, I have to tolerate my discomfort
> that nothing I will do will change the outcome and appreciate the

power of being present with those clients, being genuinely curious about their dreams and aspirations even as they are ending life. . . . Being present with the dying can be frightening. Like most people, I spend a lot of time with the panicky thought. "This could be me."[21]

This is the essence of the "we-they" that Rolland described and the interface between the personal and professional that we address in the classroom.

NOTES

1. Films that I have used with success, and that will be mentioned in this chapter, include *The Man Who Learned to Fall*, dir. Garry Beitel (Beitel/Lazar Productions, 2004); *Tuesdays with Morrie*, dir. Mick Jackson (Harpo Productions, 1999); *When Strangers Reunite*, dir. Florchita Bautista and Marie Boti (National Film Board of Canada, 1999); *Surviving Death: Stories of Grief*, dir. Elizabeth Murray (National Film Board of Canada, 1998); *Letting Go: A Hospice Journey*, dir. Debora Dickson, Susan Frömke, and Albert Maysles (Films for the Sciences and Humanities, 1996); *Richard Cardinal: Cry from a Diary of a Métis Child*, dir. Alanis Obomsawin (National Film Board of Canada, 1986); *Living with Dying* VHS, dir. L. Jaffe, A. Jaffe, and R. Love (Alfred University School of Health Related Professions, 1976); *Fight to Die* (CNN Special Presentation, 1995); *Intensive Care: Who Decides* (*Dateline NBC*, date unknown).

2. E. Shapiro, *Grief as a Family Process: A Developmental Approach to Clinical Practice* (New York: Guilford Press, 1994).

3. M. P. Hebert, "Perinatal Bereavement in Its Cultural Context," *Death Studies* 22: 1 (1998): 61–78.

4. J. Rolland, *Families, Illness, and Disability: An Integrative Treatment Model* (New York: Basic Books, 1994).

5. F. Walsh and M. McGoldrick, eds., *Living Beyond Loss; Death in the Family* (New York: W. W. Norton, 1991).

6. G. Sprang and J. McNeil, *The Nature and Treatment of Natural, Traumatic, and Stigmatized Death* (New York: Bruner & Mazel, 1995).

7. T. A. Rando, *Grief, Dying, and Death: Clinical Interventions for Caregivers* (Champaign, IL: Research Press, 1984).

8. T. A. Rando, *Treatment of Complicated Mourning* (Champaign, IL: Research Press, 1993).

9. K. Doka, Living with Life-Threatening Illness: A Guide for Patients, Their Families, and Caregivers (New York: Lexington Books, 1993), 3.

10. K. Kluger-Bell, *Unspeakable Losses: Understanding the Experience of Pregnancy Loss, Miscarriage, and Abortion* (New York: W. W. Norton, 1998).

11. See K. Doka, *Disenfranchised Grief: Recognizing Hidden Sorrow* (New York: Lexington Books, 1989); and F. Walsh and M. McGoldrick, "A Family Systems Perspective on Loss, Recovery and Resilience," in *Working with the Dying and Bereaved*, ed. P. Sutcliffe, G. Tufnell, and U. Cornish, p. 1-26 (New York: Routledge, 1998).

12. Mona Wasow, *The Skipping Stone*, 2nd ed. (Palo Alto, CA: Science & Behavior Books, 2000).

13. W. Worden, *Grief Counseling and Grief Therapy: A Handbook for the Mental Heath Practitioner*, 3rd ed. (New York: Springer, 2002), p. 27–36.

14. See, for example, A. Cook and D. Dworkin, *Helping the Bereaved: Therapeutic Interventions for Children, Adolescents, and Adults* (New York: Lexington Books, 1992); Doka, *Living with Life-Threatening Illness*; Rolland, *Families, Illness, and Disability*; and Worden, *Grief Counseling.*

15. Cook and Dworkin, *Helping the Bereaved*, 168.

16. Rolland, *Families, Illness, and Disability*, 270.

17. See also M. Sternoff, "The Last Journey: Embracing Our Mortality," *Networker* (January–February 1996): 35–41; and Worden, *Grief Counseling.*

18. Estelle Hopmeyer, "Worker Self-Disclosure in Group Work," in *Social Work with Groups: Social Justice through Personal, Community and Societal Change*, ed. Nancy E. Sullivan et al. (New York: Haworth Press, 2003), 147–58.

19. Cook and Dworkin, *Helping the Bereaved*, 171.

20. See Ibid.; C. R. Figley, ed., *Compassion Fatigue: Coping with Secondary Traumatic Stress Disorder* (New York: Brunner & Mazel, 1995).

21. Sternoff, "Last Journey," 41.

BIBLIOGRAPHY

Cook, A., and D. Dworkin. *Helping the Bereaved: Therapeutic Interventions for Children, Adolescents and Adults.* New York: Lexington Books, 1992.

Doka, K. *Disenfranchised Grief: Recognizing Hidden Sorrow.* New York: Lexington Books, 1989.

——. *Living with Life-Threatening Illness: A Guide for Patients, Their Families, and Caregivers.* New York: Lexington Books, 1993.

Figley, C. R., ed. *Compassion Fatigue: Coping with Secondary Traumatic Stress Disorder.* New York: Brunner & Mazel, 1995.

Hebert, M. P. "Perinatal Bereavement in Its Cultural Context." *Death Studies* 22: 1 (1998): 61–78.

Hopmeyer, E. "Worker Self-Disclosure in Group Work." In *Social Work with Groups: Social Justice through Personal, Community, and Societal Change*, edited by Nancy E. Sullivan, Sue Ellen Mesbur, Norma C. Lang, Deborah Goodman, and Lynne Mitchell, 147–58. New York: Haworth Press, 2003.

Kluger-Bell, K. *Unspeakable Losses: Understanding the Experience of Pregnancy Loss, Miscarriage, and Abortion.* New York: W. W. Norton, 1998.

Rando, T. A. *Grief, Dying, and Death: Clinical Interventions for Caregivers.* Champaign, IL: Research Press, 1984.

——. *Treatment of Complicated Mourning.* Champaign, IL: Research Press, 1993.

Rolland, J. *Families, Illness, and Disability: An Integrative Treatment Model.* New York: Basic Books, 1994.

Shapiro, E. *Grief as a Family Process: A Developmental Approach to Clinical Practice.* New York: Guilford Press, 1994.

Sprang, G., and J. McNeil. *The Nature and Treatment of Natural, Traumatic, and Stigmatized Death*. New York: Bruner & Mazel, 1995.

Sternoff, M. "The Last Journey: Embracing Our Mortality." *Networker* (January–February1996): 35–41.

Walsh, F., and M. McGoldrick, eds. *Living beyond Loss: Death in the Family*. New York: W. W. Norton, 1991.

———. "A Family Systems Perspective on Loss, Recovery and Resilience." In *Working with the Dying and Bereaved*, edited by P. Sutcliffe, G. Tufnell, and U. Cornish, p. 1-26. New York: Routledge, 1998.

Wasow, Mona. *The Skipping Stone*. 2nd ed. Palo Alto, CA: Science & Behavior Books, 2000.

Worden, W. *Grief Counseling and Grief Therapy: A Handbook for the Mental Heath Practitioner*. 3rd ed. New York: Springer, 2002.

7

Psychology, Grief, and the Student

David E. Balk

Contemporary approaches to college teaching accept as a given the importance of promoting student learning, not merely teaching students.[1] I wholeheartedly endorse this pedagogical position and believe it has important implications as the overall template for considering any curriculum aimed to reach college students. Discussing "psychology, grief, and the student" seems to me best approached from this commitment to engaging students as learners. Engaging students in learning provides the background for examining the topics of this chapter; and I have reflected on what essential aspects comprise the foreground of the overall gestalt of college students, psychology, and grief.

Three important considerations involving psychology strike me as important for teaching college students about bereavement, grief, and mourning.

A considerable portion of scholarship about grief primarily, if not solely, emphasizes psychological processes. A faculty member may examine these processes within a course and bring into view alternative points of view to the solely psychological.

Because a significant proportion of college students are dealing with loss,[2] they will have strong personal interests in the subject matter of a thanatology course.

College teaching ought to promote active student learning. Engaging students in active learning profoundly exemplifies psychology in action, and within a thanatology course engaging students can make use of the first two points listed above. Furthermore such learning occurs when students are challenged to think critically, to connect disparate ideas, and to examine subject matter within the contexts of their own experiences.

Psychology as a Framework to Understand Grief

Psychology provides the primary, if not the sole framework, whereby many persons understand grief, and psychology's emphasis on the individual has dominated thanatological views. This emphasis is illustrated in religious and in secular approaches: to wit, the medieval Catholic Church's emphasis that a dying person be made aware of his or her condition, repent of sins, and meet God in a state of grace;[3] and the various models, often stage or phase theories, to describe what responding to bereavement entails.[4]

Emphasis on the individual made a profound impact on thanatological thinking in the twentieth century. Freud's famous paper on grief and depression laid out for readers his analysis of what the bereaved individual faced when dealing with the death of someone loved: a long, grueling process whereby the griever faced reminders of the dead person, neutralized the effect of these reminders, and withdrew emotional ties to the dead person.[5] After some reconsideration about personality development, Freud said healthy mourning also led the bereaved individual to incorporate a mental representation of the dead person.[6]

Erich Lindemann, John Bowlby, and Elisabeth Kübler-Ross, three major figures in thanatology, clearly accepted Freud's emphasis on the bereaved individual as the proper focus for attention and the obvious starting point when considering responses to loss. Lindemann operationalized Freud's psychoanalytic explanation of bereavement and said clearly that the 101 bereaved persons seen by his psychiatric team began to recover in a very short time when they (1) allowed themselves to feel the distress their bereavement caused and (2) openly expressed their feelings.[7] Lindemann identified the bereaved individual's recovery from such symptoms as depression, anxiety, hostility, and difficulty concentrating as evidence of recovery from bereavement. Recent evidence has differentiated time-limited psychological symptoms such as depression and anxiety from longer-lasting indicators of grief such as an enduring emptiness and an ongoing sadness;[8] these research results have led to questions about whether six decades of research into coping with normal grief overlooked the fundamental aspects of bereavement and examined related but less central psychological symptoms.

Bowlby's ethological emphasis on attachment as the foundation for individual survival and development became the cornerstone for his explaining an individual's response to a death. He postulated four phases leading the individual to recover from typical grief: shock and numbness, yearning and searching, disorganization and despair, and reorganization. C. Murray Parkes contributed to completing Bowlby's schema of four phases to mourning.[9] While Bowlby's ideas acknowledge the importance of an interpersonal reality at the heart of recovering from bereavement, the emphasis in Bowlby is upon the individual's phased psychological response to the lost attachment, moving beyond the loss, and reinvesting in the world of people.[10]

Kübler-Ross had a profound influence on raising consciousness about the psychological responses of the terminally ill to their dying. She proposed that individuals who are aware they are dying proceed through five stages: denial, anger, bargaining, depression, and acceptance. She noted that not everyone completed the sequence and also that persons might repeat specific stages. Empirical studies have failed to find evidence to support her stages of dying framework,[11] and "many clinicians who work with the dying have found this model to be inadequate, superficial, and misleading."[12]

Kübler-Ross's five stages of dying have been adopted by writers to explain a variety of responses to loss, for instance, corporate CEO failure, divorce, congregational responses to sexual abuse by ministers, leaving previously desired but currently unrewarding careers, and responses to brain injury.[13] Throughout Kübler-Ross's description there is no doubt that the sole focus is on how the individual responds. By applying these ideas to a congregation's response to a minister's sexual abuse, D.J. Andrews obviously has transferred the stage-theory from the individual to a larger system.[14]

Corrections to the "psychologizing" of thanatology have been present for many years, as evidenced in the sociological approach in Robert Fulton's work and in the more recent sociological analysis in Tony Walter's study of bereavement.[15] Walter, for instance, positions grief in society and looks at the rituals whereby societies facilitate or obstruct connections between the living and the dead. Various writers have argued for the value of seeing grief within the interactive processes of family systems and, both by implicit and explicit remarks, maintain (1) that grief fundamentally involves relationships and (2) that resolving bereavement requires adjustments in the roles, responsibilities, and rules that comprise family processes.[16] Dennis Klass has examined the role culture, including religion, plays in dealing with death and bereavement, and has noted that in many cultures the focus is on rituals connecting individuals to the larger society.[17] A massive two-volume work, *Handbook of Death and Dying*, applies sociology to examining such thanatology topics as mourning, terrorism, and AIDS.[18] Robert Kastenbaum has introduced a new concept, *macrothanatology*, to examine such massive incidents of death as the nuclear explosions over Nagasaki and Hiroshima, the Japanese crimes in occupied China, the Nazi extermination of six million Jews, and the Hutu genocide of Tutsis in Rwanda.[19] For Kastenbaum, two elements comprise macrothanatology: deaths on a large scale and challenges to simple cause-and-effect frameworks. A needed complement would be human complicity, unless we are to include natural catastrophes, such as the disasters caused by the massive tsunami of late December 2004 that struck such countries as Sri Lanka and Indonesia.

College Students' Experience with Bereavement

I have reviewed the first of the three considerations and now will move on to the second, college students' experiences with bereavement. College students are more experienced with bereavement than many persons realize. When Louis E. LaGrand conducted a survey of college students in the state of New York, he identified a variety of losses in many of their lives, among them the deaths of family members and friends.[20] Surveys using convenience samples on several campuses consistently have indicated 22–30% of college students are in the first year of grieving the death of a family member or friend, and 35–48% within 13–24 months of such a loss.[21]

In the late 1980s Hannelore Wass, F. M. Berardo, and Robert A. Neimeyer estimated conservatively there were over 3,000 undergraduate courses on death and dying.[22] One can infer from the popularity of such courses that many college students clearly are interested in issues of thanatology and that a significant proportion of students are struggling with issues of death and grief. A colleague who taught an introductory survey course on human development at Kansas State University said at least 10% of her students indicated they were particularly anxious about death.[23]

This definite substrate of bereavement, grief, and death anxiety in the college student population highlights that for a significant portion of the student body, courses on death and dying hold more than academic interest. Something else indicated is that the students' experience holds material readily available for private comparison and contrast with information offered in a thanatology course.

Engaging Students in a Course on Death and Dying

The third consideration for teaching thanatology courses in college deals with the responsibility to engage students in learning. Distinct aspects from educational psychology provide a conceptual framework for engaging students in a course on death and dying.

Teaching that promotes learning engages the student. This important point applies across all subject matter, from anthropology to zoology, and obviously includes thanatology. How do effective teachers promote student learning? They do so, at least in part, by adept use of strategies that foster students to think critically about course content. Students think critically when they become actively involved in the subject matter, connect ideas from various sources, and gain insight by comparing and contrasting their own experiences with the course material. The challenge for faculty is to identify how they will engage students in active involvement, connecting ideas, and making use of experiential contexts.

Let's take as a given the following assertion: our responsibility as teachers is to promote student learning. If we are going to debate that assertion, then we are into a different venue about the role and function of college faculty. I have assumed that readers of this book agree that teaching differs from learning,[24] that good teaching promotes learning, and that the primary responsibility of a college teacher is to promote student learning.

Bloom's taxonomy of cognitive domain educational objectives has influenced me greatly in my work.[25] While I have some familiarity with the affective domain objectives in the taxonomy,[26] I have thought much more about the cognitive domain objectives, and I use them as means to design and deliver courses and to evaluate student learning. Let's review briefly this cognitive domain of objectives.

Bloom's Cognitive Domain of Educational Objectives

There are six categories of cognitive objectives, and mastery of material occurs along a hierarchy of increasing complexity and cognitive challenge. The six cognitive objectives are knowledge of facts, comprehension of information, application of information, analysis of information, synthesis of information, and evaluation of information. You will find examples of these objectives in table 7.1.

While many if not all college faculty endorse the higher cognitive abilities represented by application through evaluation and, from my observations, indicate they aim to attain those sorts of objectives in their teaching, it also seems the case that testing what students know moves very quickly to assessing knowledge and comprehension objectives. Such exams are easier to write and to grade. Perhaps lack of faculty expertise in writing exams that assess the more complex cognitive objectives leads to the widespread reliance on

TABLE 7.1. Cognitive Educational Objectives with Examples

Knowledge of facts, implying "recall or recognition of specific elements in a subject area" (213)

Examples: Who was the sixteenth President of the United States? What is the abbreviation for chlorine? Name the known planets in our solar system. Who wrote the book On Death and Dying?

Comprehension of information, "the first level beyond the category of knowledge" (221) whereby persons state in their own words what they know.

Examples: Tell briefly what Lincoln primarily wanted to accomplish in the War between the States. Tell in your own words what Kübler-Ross meant by bargaining.

Application of information, emphasizing applying "principles and generalizations" (232) to new problems and situations, a cognitive ability making use of knowledge and comprehension.

Examples: How do Lincoln's ideas about a house divided apply to understanding the battle over civil rights in the United States in the 1960s? Use Bowlby's notion of phases of mourning to explain children's reactions to the divorce of their parents.

Analysis of information, breaking down information into constituent parts and making explicit the relationships between various ideas, a "complex ability which makes use of knowledge, comprehension, and application" (249).

Examples: Examine Lincoln's first inaugural address and see if it forecasts his determination to keep the Union together and to end slavery. Interpret the following case study of a terminally ill woman in terms of Kübler-Ross's stages of dying.

Synthesis of information, putting together disparate pieces and combining them in such a way "as to constitute a pattern or structure not clearly there before" (265), a form of convergent thinking making use of knowledge, comprehension, application, and analysis.

Examples: Write a biography of Lincoln. Devise a model for grieving by examining information from major writers in the field of thanatology.

Evaluation of information, assessing the merit or worth "of ideas, works, solutions, methods, material, etc" (276), a form of critical thinking "among the most complex cognitive behaviors" (276) requiring use of the other five types of cognitive behaviors.

Examples: Assess the impact of the Emancipation Proclamation as a factor in ending the War between the States. Judge the value of Kübler-Ross's stages of dying as a therapeutic tool for counselors working with the bereaved.

All quotations are from B. S. Bloom, G. F. Madaus, and J. T. Hastings, *Evaluation to Improve Learning* (New York: McGraw-Hill, 1981).

examination methods that test for recall and paraphrasing. I contend that courses that aim at application, analysis, synthesis, and evaluation objectives need to assess student learning of those objectives. And here is my link to critical thinking, what I believe college teaching is supposed to reach: critical thinking occurs when students achieve these more complex cognitive objectives.

Promoting Active Learning, Connecting Ideas, and Incorporating Experiential Context

Based on some valuable committee work in which I was fortunate to participate in the 1990s with colleagues at Kansas State University (KSU) when devising a university-wide change in general education, I learned general education works best when there is an active learning environment, an opportunity to connect ideas, and an experiential context for the matter being studied. In our document on general education, we wrote that college graduates "should exercise educated habits, which include, at least: critical and analytical thinking, careful and thoughtful reading, writing and speech, an inclination to wonder, a penchant for questioning, and a desire to solve puzzles and problems."[27]

It is one thing for a faculty member to say attaining certain critical thinking objectives are part of the curriculum he or she has devised but then quite another to devise means to achieve those objectives. My KSU colleagues persuaded me of the wisdom of requiring faculty to spell out specifically and clearly in their syllabi at least one example of how they will promote active learning, provide an opportunity to connect ideas, and make use of experiential context when they assert it is their intent to accomplish such noble objectives.

A Set of Curriculum Ideas to Promote Active Learning in a Thanatology Course

A way I have endeavored to promote critical thinking is through students' intensive reading, writing, and discussion of student papers—with timely, concise written feedback from the instructor on each paper. This approach to teaching came about from reflections on my own experiences as a student. We wrote a lot at the University of Illinois. I vividly recall what one professor said: "Writing is an extension of thinking."

In every course I teach, graduate or undergraduate, students read material (usually the same material, but not always), they write review papers about what they have read, and they discuss these papers in small groups. I get a copy of each student's paper. Each person in the small group gets a copy of each group member's paper. Group meetings take place during assigned class sessions. All papers are to be e-mailed as attachments at least one day before the class meeting. Everyone is responsible for making a copy of each paper and bringing the copies to the class meeting.

Four to five students comprise a group. I assign the group members by means of a quasi-random selection process. For instance, if there are forty persons in the course and I want groups of five members each, I will have the students count off from one to eight until each person has a number, and then form groups with persons who have the same numbers. Groups smaller than three or larger than five present logistical problems, such as insufficient time in a fifty- to seventy-five-minute class period to include the work of each group member when group size exceeds five.

Each person reads aloud his or her paper while the other group members follow along with their own copies. The students' review papers are four to six pages long (typed, double-spaced, twelve-point font, one-inch margins). The student is to provide a one-hundred-fifty- to two-hundred-word summary of the material that has been read. For example, in my undergraduate course on death, dying, and bereavement, I assign personal accounts of such things as a medical doctor's reflections on misgivings about keeping infirm, debilitated, aged persons alive at all costs. Students are to answer some questions about the personal account: for example, "Discuss the doctor's personal account in light of the biomedical model that dominates medical care in the United States." Students are asked to provide one or more alternate questions in addition to the questions that are assigned.

Once the students have read their papers, the groups do three things:

1. Discuss the summaries and identify what could be done to strengthen each summary as a clear and reliable presentation of the personal account.
2. Discuss the questions and the various answers given.
3. Complete in writing a discussion worksheet that includes six points:- What are the strengths in each person's review and what are some ways each student can improve his or her review to provide a clear and reliable presentation of the personal account? What were the various points discussed about the personal account? What personal experiences and observations of group members were mentioned as experiences and observations that confirm or call into question the personal account? What are areas on which people reach consensus? What are areas on which people disagree? How could the personal account be strengthened as an introduction to one or more topics about this course? Discussion worksheets are graded and each person in the group gets the group's grade for the worksheet.

Experience has taught me that students dislike group work if one (or more) person in a group does not pull his own weight and does not contribute to the group: if, in short, someone basically takes advantage of everyone else by having them do the work but all get equal credit.

I have come up with a group assessment form each student completes after every group meeting. The group assessment form covers seven topics and is worth a total of forty-six points. Students hand in to me their completed group assessment forms, and I calculate for each student the average score for all the assessments he or she received. I use that average score as part of the points that go into calculating the student's final grade. Copies of the group assessment form and of the discussion worksheet are included in tables 7.2 and 7.3.

Another aspect to consider is how well templates with questions to answer work for student discussions when groups are left to meet on their own. Here are the comments of one student who has participated in several group discussions in which I was present and others from which I was absent:

> As a student myself, I can tell you, Dr. Balk—after 20+ years of traditional, standards-based education, it can be difficult for under-graduates (and even graduate students) to train themselves to think in an entirely different way. I know that often, when my fellow students and I are left to discuss material on our own, our conversations would seem to benefit from a mediator of sorts, to pose guided questions, raise issues, stimulate debate, and generally help navigate the material.[28]

An Exercise to Promote Active Learning and Experiential Context

For many students a course on death, dying, and bereavement involves personal issues such as the death of a friend or family member, a terminal illness in the family, recovery from a serious illness, anxiety about death, and suicidal thoughts. Topics touched on rub some students' camouflaged pain and suffering.

While I think it unethical to cast a thanatology course as a means to help students deal with loss or life crises, it is important to get out in the open experiences that students are willing to share. An exercise that I use now to open all my thanatology courses includes a set of questions that each student answers individually; then I divide the students into small groups of three to four persons to discuss their papers. I have used a variation of this exercise in courses that deal with topics other than thanatology (for example, a course on adolescent development and a course on research methods).[29] One of the important things accomplished is to get students to know some others and to set a precedent for open, respected discussion. Some of the questions asked in the thanatology course are What degree are you pursuing? What do you hope to do when you finish your program of studies? and Have you experienced the death of a family member?

After students have written out answers to their copy of the exercise, I divide them into small groups to discuss their responses and have each person

TABLE 7.2. Form for Students to Assess Group Participation

Group Assessment Form for Discussion of Personal Accounts
Name _____
Meeting Date: _____
Personal account # _____
Group Members: Give **both the first and last name** of each group member
(make copies of this form for use later in the course)

Names of Group Members

Don't evaluate your own participation

1. Was the person present? (Yes/No) Yes = 2, No = 0

2. Did the person arrive on time? (Yes/No) Yes = 2, No = 0

3. Did the person stay the whole meeting? (Yes/No) Yes = 2, No = 0

4. Rate their participation in the discussion. (0–10)
   0 = poor 5 = fair 8 = good 10 = excellent

5. Did the person come prepared? (0–10)
   0 = poor 5 = fair 8 = good 10 = excellent

6. Rate the person's knowledge of the material. (0–10)
   0 = poor 5 = fair 8 = good 10 = excellent

7. Rate the person's contribution to the work of the group. (0–10)
   0 = poor 5 = fair 8 = good 10 = excellent

TABLE 7.3. Worksheet for Use in Discussion of Personal Accounts

For each personal account that is discussed, review these questions and provide written responses documenting your group's discussion: (make copies for use later in the course)
1. What are the strengths in each person's review and what are some ways each student can improve his or her review to provide a clear and reliable presentation of the personal account?
2. What were the various points discussed about the personal account?
3. What personal experiences and observations of group members were mentioned as experiences and observations that confirm or call into question material in the personal account?
4. What are some alternate questions that people think deserve consideration when thinking about this personal account?
4. What are areas on which people reach consensus?
5. What are areas on which people disagree?
6. How could the personal account be strengthened as an introduction to one or more topics about this course?

Synthesize the group's answers to the six items and turn in the worksheet with accompanying pages with summaries of the discussion. The summary is due at the end of the class in which the personal account is being discussed.

Rotate scribe responsibilities for writing summaries to each item. Be sure to give examples that illustrate what was discussed. Don't, for instance, simply say, "We agreed about everything." Give examples that verify or illustrate this agreement.

Title of personal account _____
Date of meeting: _____
Signatures of group members present:

introduce someone from their group to the rest of the students in the course. This last function is skipped if the class is so large that the introductions would take an inordinate amount of time. An important rule given is to only mention things you don't mind others knowing about, and another rule is to learn if what the person told you can be repeated outside your small group. All the questions and the protocol for the exercise can be found in table 7.4.

Psychological Issues that Prompt Ethical Concerns

On occasion, classroom material can produce harrowing moments for students (and the professor) when topics elicit painful emotions openly exhibited. It is clear that people's experiences with death and bereavement make a thanatology course more than academic, and painful reactions to some topic may emerge: tears, sobbing, and even perhaps keening. It is difficult to predict what topic will elicit such reactions. Once at the end of a class lecture on issues

TABLE 7.4. Exercise to Begin Course

Instructor name and course title

Students write out answers to these questions and then discuss with three to four other students:
What degree are you pursuing?
What do you hope to do when you finish your program of studies?
Why are you enrolled in this course?
What will indicate to you that the course is worthwhile?
What will let you know you are learning?
What will make this course a success?
Have you experienced the death of a family member?
If yes, who died, when did the person die, and what was the cause of death?
Have you experienced the death of a friend?
If yes, who died, when did the person die, and what was the cause of death?
Has the death of a pet been difficult?
If yes, what pet died, when did the animal die, and what was the cause of death?

Arrange students in groups of three or four persons per group. Students discuss their answers with other persons in the group.

Get students into circle facing one another. (If class enrollment takes up the whole room, then just have students remain in their small groups.)
Introduce person from your group.

of suicide (what is suicide, who commits suicide, myths about suicide, and what to do with someone who is suicidal), a student visibly upset told the rest of the class in between deep sobs how she could not understand how persons could take their lives when other persons (her sister in particular) who die from terminal illnesses want to live.

Rescuing someone from painful feelings at such times is a severe psychological betrayal. I don't see a thanatology course as a support group for the bereaved or a place for administering naïve therapy, nor is the course a venue to do whatever will get students to express their grief. I am very hesitant as well to turn someone's public pain into a "teachable moment" for the rest of the class. My response has been to listen attentively and continue the discussion, not call a halt to the day's lesson.

These classroom confrontations with pain, almost guaranteed to occur given the subject matter of a thanatology course and the experiences students bring to such a course, need further discussion among thanatologists. The pedagogy evokes psychological processes for everyone in the class: for some persons, the processes involve public expression, perhaps unwilling expression, of grief; for others, the processes involve witnessing someone else in pain and the subsequent reactions that such vicarious experiences evoke.

These classroom experiences present some fundamental matters of ethics to be examined regarding teacher obligations and classroom protocol. Is more than attentive listening required? Should the syllabus contain "informed consent" in which the potential for painful feelings to be elicited gets mentioned and cautions are raised that the course is not the place for someone wanting to resolve bereavement? Does the very subject matter of thanatology courses make self-evident that painful emotions may be elicited and thus persons enter with this awareness? Here are the comments to earlier drafts of the present chapter from some persons who have extensive experience teaching college students about death and dying.

> In terms of the section on classroom ethics, I have pondered this
> through the years. What has worked best for me is to make it
> very clear on the first day of class that this course most likely will not
> fit a paradigm of other college courses they have taken or will take.
> I let them know that we will be discussing material that may be
> quite emotional for some, as well as reading material and watching
> videos that can be quite moving. I also tell my students that if
> they have recently experienced a significant loss they need to be sure
> this is the right time to take this class—this leads into my discussion
> that very clearly states that this course is NOT therapeutic

in nature. I give them direct information about the counseling service on campus. All of this information is delivered in a very compassionate manner but it is made very clear. In my 13 years teaching the course I have had a wonderful, open interchange with the students, but rarely do I have a student whose wounds are too fresh to be in class. I do, however, show some great tear jerking films that we debrief afterwards. I feel no need for any type of informed consent—any psychology course can bring up issues for any student. I am always an advocate for counseling and find a way in all my classes to get that message in.[30]

We did offer a modest warning in the syllabus for our class, noting that students should do whatever they might need if the class became difficult for them and adding our willingness to be helpful in such circumstances. In early years, we sometimes did have a student get up and leave the class in emotional distress (often related to the screening of a video). Since we almost always team taught, one of us could usually follow such a student and offer assistance without abandoning the ongoing needs of the remainder of the students in the class. I don't think the possibility of such confrontations (either privately or publicly) with one's personal experiences is improper for participants who are self-selected members of a class whose title clearly indicates its subjects. However, I would not introduce each new subject or each new video by warning about its potential horrors. That just artificially winds up potential responses.[31]

The initial course exercise (see table 7.4) that I ask students to complete and share with a few peers in the classroom caught the attention of a colleague with considerable experience in teaching thanatology to college students. In short, she expressed clear concerns that the exercise is improper:

I want to comment on the section entitled "An Exercise to Promote Active Learning and Experiential Content." I think your exercise forces students into an unethical situation. If they know they will have to share deeply personal information in a small group and with the entire class in some instances, they may choose not to reveal this information in response to your questions (and you do give them permission to do this). However, this means they have to lie, hold back, not disclose (select the term you prefer) and immediately at the beginning of the class their personal experiences are disconnected from the classroom experience (not something that I think you want to do). I do like your "rules" but I feel like the exercise is "too much too soon" and is forced disclosure. Some students would be uncomfortable with this approach altogether. Remember that Colorado State University's death and dying class usually has a minimum of 65 students and oftentimes up to 90. As an instructor, I have always asked students to complete a confidential survey that only I read to get a sense of the issues/experiences in the class. Then as the semester progresses and students feel more comfortable with their classmates, they sometimes choose to share information about their own losses, and sometimes not; it is not a requirement of the course.[32]

The Importance of Personal Attitudes as Course Focus

One of the goals of death education is to help persons explore their attitudes toward issues of death, dying, and bereavement.[33] To bring such a goal specifically into the heart of the classroom, I have borrowed some material from Kastenbaum and some from the National Issues Forum "At Death's Door: What Are the Choices?"[34] Using the Kastenbaum material, I distribute a survey that asks questions for which there is factual knowledge (for instance, "What are the odds that a death certificate will state the specific cause of death?") and questions that ask about attitudes (for instance, "I believe in some form of afterlife"). Using the National Issues Forum material, I show the students a thirteen-minute video tape on choices facing society in care for terminally ill people who are in pain, then distribute a worksheet each student is to complete, and then break the students into groups of five to discuss their answers. The worksheet asks students to identify each choice presented in the video tape, to indicate two reasons people support the choice, two reasons people oppose the choice, and their personal position on the choice. We spend the following class examining what the students know about the choices and what their personal views are.

Concluding Remarks

In this chapter I have presented my inferences about three considerations salient to teaching college level thanatology courses: the emphasis upon psychological processes within scholarship about grief; the personal experiences of many students with loss; and the salience of promoting active learning in college courses, including courses on thanatology. There seems no reason to doubt that the same considerations apply to undergraduate and graduate students. What is needed is extended and open discussion among college faculty about their experiences at promoting student learning. We need to invoke our collegiality and engage in a discussion of how we teach. With that hope of a discussion in mind, I have written this chapter. My hopes are for an ongoing dialogue to ensue.

NOTES

Thanks to Mary Ann Balk, Janet R. Balk, Alicia S. Cook, Charles A. Corr, Robin Paletti, and Tamina Toray for comments and suggestions to earlier versions of the manuscript.

1. L. D. Spence, "The Case Against Teaching," *Change* 33, no. 6 (2001): 10–19; M. Weimer, "Focus on Learning, Transform Teaching," *Change* 35, no. 5 (2003): 48–54.

2. D. E. Balk, "Death, Bereavement, and College Students: A Descriptive Analysis," *Mortality* 2: 3 (1997): 207–20; H. G. Hardison, R. A. Neimeyer, and K. L. Lichstein, "Insomnia and Complicated Grief Symptoms in Bereaved College Students," *Behavioral Sleep Medicine* 3: 2 (2005): 99–111; L. E. LaGrand, *Coping with Separation and Loss as a Young Adult: Theoretical and Practical Realities* (Springfield, IL: Charles C. Thomas, 1986); R. Wrenn, "College Management of Student Death: A Survey," *Death Studies* 15: 4 (1991): 395–402.

3. See the discussion of "death of the self" in P. Aries, *Images of Man and Death*, trans. J. Lloyd (Cambridge, MA: Harvard University Press, 1985).

4. J. Bowlby, "Processes of Mourning," *International Journal of Psychoanalysis* 42 (1961): 317–40; J. Bowlby, *Attachment and Loss*, 3 vols. (New York: Basic Books, 1969–1980); E. Kübler-Ross, *On Death and Dying* (New York: Macmillan, 1969); J. W. Worden, *Grief Counseling and Grief Therapy: A Handbook for the Mental Health Professional*, 3rd ed. (New York: Springer, 2002).

5. S. Freud, "Mourning and Melancholia," in *Standard Edition of the Complete Psychological Works of Sigmund Freud*, ed. and trans. J. Strachey, 24 vols. (1917; London: Hogarth Press, 1957), 14:243–58.

6. S. Freud, "The Ego and the Id," in *Standard Edition of the Complete Psychological Works of Sigmund Freud*, ed. and trans. J. Strachey, 24 vols. (1923; London: Hogarth Press, 1961), 19:12–66.

7. E. Lindemann, "Symptomatology and Management of Acute Grief," *American Journal of Psychiatry* 101: 6 Suppl. (1944): 141–48.

8. G. Byrne and B. Raphael, "The Psychological Symptoms of Conjugal Bereavement in Elderly Men over the First Thirteen Months," *International Journal of Geriatric Psychiatry* 12: 2 (1997): 241–51; N. A. Neimeyer and N. S. Hogan, "Quantitative or Qualitative? Measurement Issues in the Study of Grief," in *Handbook of Bereavement Research: Consequences, Coping, and Care*, ed. M. S. Stroebe et al.

(Washington, DC: American Psychological Association, 2001), 89–118; H. G. Prigerson et al., "Traumatic Grief as a Risk Factor for Mental and Physical Morbidity," *American Journal of Psychiatry* 154: 5 (1997): 616–623.

9. C. M. Parkes, *Bereavement: Studies of Grief in Adult Life* (New York: International Universities Press, 1972).

10. Bowlby, *Attachment and Loss*.

11. R. Kastenbaum, *Death, Society, and Human Experience,* 7th ed. (Boston: Allyn & Bacon, 2001).

12. C. A. Corr, C. M. Nabe, and D. M. Corr, *Death and Dying, Life and Living,* 4th ed. (Pacific Grove, CA: Brooks/Cole, 2003), 139.

13. J. J. Slocum, C. Ragan, and A. Casey, "On Death and Dying: The Corporate Leadership Capacity of CEOs," *Organizational Dynamics* 30: 3 (2002): 269–81; J. F. Crosby, B. A. Gage, and M. C. Raymond, "The Grief Resolution Process in Divorce," *Journal of Divorce* 7: 1 (1983): 3–18; D. J. Andrews, *Healing in Congregations in the Aftermath of Sexual Abuse by a Pastor* (PhD diss., Hartford Seminary, Hartford, CT, 1999); S. Burnett-Beaulieu, "Occupational Therapy Profession Dropouts: Escape from the Grief Process," *Occupational Therapy in Mental Health* 2: 2 (1982): 45–55; and K. Meredith and G. M. Rassa, "Aligning the Levels of Awareness with the Stages of Grieving," *Journal of Cognitive Rehabilitation* 17: 1 (1999): 10–12.

14. Andrews, *Healing in Congregations*.

15. R. Fulton, *Death and Identity* (New York: Wiley, 1965); T. Walter, *On Bereavement: The Culture of Grief* (Buckingham, UK: Open University Press, 1999).

16. N. L. Moos, "An Integrative Model of Grief," *Death Studies* 19: 4 (1995): 337–64; J. W. Nadeau, *Families Making Sense of Death* (Thousand Oaks, CA: Sage, 1997).

17. R. E. Goss and D. Klass, *Dead but Not Lost: Grief Narratives in Religious Traditions* (Walnut Creek, CA: AltaMira Press, 2005); D. Klass, "Developing a Cross-Cultural Model of Grief: The State of the Field," *Omega: Journal of Death and Dying* 39: 3 (1999): 153–78.

18. C. D. Bryant, ed., *Handbook of Death and Dying*, 2 vols. (Thousand Oaks, CA: Sage, 2003). In vol. 1, *The Presence of Death*, see especially L. G. Vigilant and J. B. Williamson, "On the Role and Meaning of Death in Terrorism," 236–45; and R. D. Moremen, "Dying of AIDS and Social Stigmatization," 397–404. In vol. 2, *The Response to Death*, see especially D. E. Balk, "The Evolution of Mourning in the United States from the Early Nineteenth to the Early Twenty-first Century: Middle and Upper Class European Americans," 829–37.

19. R. Kastenbaum, "Death Writ Large," *Death Studies* 28: 4 (2004): 375–92.

20. LaGrand, *Coping with Separation*.

21. Balk, "Death, Bereavement, and College Students"; D. E. Balk and L. C. Vesta, "Psychological Development during Four Years of Bereavement: A Longitudinal Case Study," *Death Studies* 22: 1(1998): 23–41; Hardison, Neimeyer, and Lichstein, "Insomnia and Complicated Grief Symptoms."

22. H. Wass, F. M. Berardo, and R. A. Neimeyer, "Dying: Integrating the Facts," in *Dying: Facing the Facts*, ed. H. Wass, F. M. Berardo, and R. A. Neimeyer (Washington, DC: Taylor & Francis, 1988), 395–405.

23. Joan N. McNeil, personal communication. However, not all students take courses on death, dying, and bereavement because of losses in their lives. In my courses, as in the courses of my colleagues, there are elementary and secondary school teachers, premed students, and preveterinary students who anticipate dealing directly with grieving persons and families.

24. G. S. Krahenbuhl, "Faculty Work: Integrating Responsibilities and Institutional Needs," *Change* 30, no. 6 (1998): 18–25; Weimer, "Focus on Learning."

25. B. S. Bloom, ed., *Cognitive Domain*, handbook 1 of *Taxonomy of Educational Objectives: The Classification of Educational Goals* (New York: McKay, 1956); B. S. Bloom, J. T. Hastings, and G. F. Madaus, eds., *Handbook of Formative and Summative Evaluation of Student Learning* (New York: McGraw-Hill, 1971); B. S. Bloom, G. F. Madaus, and J. T. Hastings, *Evaluation to Improve Learning* (New York: McGraw-Hill, 1981).

26. D. R. Krathwohl, B. S. Bloom, and B. B. Masia, *Affective Domain*, handbook 2 of *Taxonomy of Educational Objectives: The Classification of Educational Goals* (New York: McKay, 1964).

27. See http://www.k-state.edu/uge/aboutuge/goals.htm

28. Robin Paletti, personal communication.

29. See, for instance, D. E. Balk, "Scholarship, Students, and Practitioners: Bringing Scholarship into the Expectations of Practitioners," *Death Studies* 29: 2 (2005): 123–44.

30. Tamina Toray, personal communication.

31. Charles A. Corr, personal communication.

32. Alicia S. Cook, personal communication.

33. Corr, Nabe, and Corr, *Death and Dying*; H. Wass, "A Perspective on the Current State of DeathEducation," *Death Studies* 28: 4 (2004): 289–308.

34. Kastenbaum, *Death, Society*; M. D. Hinds, *At Death's Door: What Are the Choices?* (Dubuque, IA: Kendall Hunt, 1997).

BIBLIOGRAPHY

Aries, P. *Images of Man and Death*. Trans. J. Lloyd. Cambridge, MA: Harvard University Press, 1985.

Andrews, D. J. *Healing in Congregations in the Aftermath of Sexual Abuse by a Pastor*. PhD diss., Hartford Seminary, Hartford, CT, 1999.

Balk, D. E. "Death, Bereavement, and College Students: A Descriptive Analysis." *Mortality* 2: 3 (1997): 207–20.

———. "Scholarship, Students, and Practitioners: Bringing Scholarship into the Expectations of Practitioners." *Death Studies* 29: 2 (2005): 123–44.

———, and L. C. Vesta. "Psychological Development during Four Years of Bereavement: A Longitudinal Case Study." *Death Studies* 22: 1(1998): 23–41.

Bloom, B. S., ed. *Cognitive Domain*. Handbook 1 of *Taxonomy of Educational Objectives: The Classification of Educational Goals*. New York: McKay, 1956.

————, J. T. Hastings, and G. F. Madaus, eds. *Handbook of Formative and Summative Evaluation of Student Learning*. New York: McGraw-Hill, 1971.

————, G. F. Madaus, and J. T. Hastings. *Evaluation to Improve Learning*. New York: McGraw-Hill, 1981.

Bowlby, J. "Processes of Mourning." *International Journal of Psychoanalysis* 42 (1961): 317–40.

————. *Attachment and Loss*. 3 vols. New York: Basic Books, 1969–1980.

Bryant, C. D., ed. *Handbook of Death and Dying*. 2 vols. Thousand Oaks, CA: Sage, 2003.

Burnett-Beaulieu, S. "Occupational Therapy Profession Dropouts: Escape from the Grief Process." *Occupational Therapy in Mental Health* 2: 2 (1982): 45–55.

Byrne, G., and B. Raphael. "The Psychological Symptoms of Conjugal Bereavement in Elderly Men over the First Thirteen Months." *International Journal of Geriatric Psychiatry* 12: 2 (1997): 241–51.

Corr, C. A., C. M. Nabe, and D. M. Corr. *Death and Dying, Life and Living*. 4th ed. Pacific Grove, CA: Brooks/Cole, 2003.

Crosby, J. F., B. A. Gage, and M. C. Raymond. "The Grief Resolution Process in Divorce." *Journal of Divorce* 7: 1 (1983): 3–18.

Freud, S. "Mourning and Melancholia." 1917. In *Standard Edition of the Complete Psychological Works of Sigmund Freud*, edited and translated by J. Strachey, 14:243–58. London: Hogarth Press, 1957.

————. "The Ego and the Id." 1923. In *Standard Edition of the Complete Psychological Works of Sigmund Freud*, edited and translated by J. Strachey, 19:12–66. London: Hogarth Press, 1961.

Fulton, R. *Death and Identity*. New York: Wiley, 1965.

Goss, R. E., and D. Klass. *Dead but Not Lost: Grief Narratives in Religious Traditions*. Walnut Creek, CA: AltaMira Press, 2005.

Hardison, H. G., R. A. Neimeyer, and K. L. Lichstein. "Insomnia and Complicated Grief Symptoms in Bereaved College Students." *Behavioral Sleep Medicine* 3: 2 (2005): 99–111.

Hinds, M. D. *At Death's Door: What Are the Choices?* Dubuque, IA: Kendall Hunt, 1997.

Kastenbaum, R. *Death, Society, and Human Experience*. 7th ed. Boston: Allyn & Bacon, 2001.

————. "Death Writ Large." *Death Studies* 28: 4 (2004): 375–92.

Klass, D. "Developing a Cross-Cultural Model of Grief: The State of the Field." *Omega: Journal of Death and Dying* 39: 3 (1999): 153–78.

Krahenbuhl, G. S. "Faculty Work: Integrating Responsibilities and Institutional Needs." *Change* 30, no. 6 (1998): 18–25.

Krathwohl, D. R., B. S. Bloom, and B. B. Masia. *Affective Domain*. Handbook 2 of *Taxonomy of Educational Objectives: The Classification of Educational Goals*. New York: McKay, 1964.

Kübler-Ross, E. *On Death and Dying*. New York: Macmillan, 1969.

LaGrand. L. E. *Coping with Separation and Loss as a Young Adult: Theoretical and Practical Realities*. Springfield, IL: Charles C. Thomas, 1986.

Lindemann, E. "Symptomatology and Management of Acute Grief." *American Journal of Psychiatry* 101: 6 Suppl. (1944): 141–48.

Meredith, K., and G. M. Rassa. "Aligning the Levels of Awareness with the Stages of Grieving." *Journal of Cognitive Rehabilitation* 17: 1 (1999): 10–12.

Moos, N. L. "An Integrative Model of Grief." *Death Studies* 19: 4 (1995): 337–64.

Nadeau, J. W. *Families Making Sense of Death*. Thousand Oaks, CA: Sage, 1997.

Neimeyer, R. A., and N. S. Hogan. "Quantitative or Qualitative? Measurement Issues in the Study of Grief." In *Handbook of Bereavement Research: Consequences, Coping, and Care*, edited by M. S. Stroebe, R. O. Hansson, W. Stroebe, and H. Schut, 89–118. Washington, DC: American Psychological Association, 2001.

Parkes, C. M. *Bereavement: Studies of Grief in Adult Life*. New York: International Universities Press, 1972.

Prigerson, H. G., E. Frank, S. V. Kasl, C. F. Reynolds, M. K. Shear, N. Day, L. C. Berry, J. T. Newson, and S. Jacobs. "Traumatic Grief as a Risk Factor for Mental and Physical Morbidity." *American Journal of Psychiatry* 154: 5 (1997): 616–623.

Slocum, J. J., C. Ragan, and A. Casey. "On Death and Dying: The Corporate Leadership Capacity of CEOs." *Organizational Dynamics* 30: 3 (2002): 269–81.

Spence, L. D. "The Case Against Teaching." *Change* 33, no. 6 (2001): 10–19.

Walter, T. *On Bereavement: The Culture of Grief*. Buckingham, UK: Open University Press, 1999.

Wass, H. "A Perspective on the Current State of DeathEducation." *Death Studies* 28: 4 (2004): 289–308.

———, F. M. Berardo, and R. A. Neimeyer. "Dying: Integrating the Facts." In *Dying: Facing the Facts*, edited by H. Wass, F. M. Berardo, and R. A. Neimeyer, 395–405. Washington, DC: Taylor & Francis, 1988.

Weimer, M. "Focus on Learning, Transform Teaching." *Change* 35, no. 5 (2003): 48–54.

Worden, J. W. *Grief Counseling and Grief Therapy: A Handbook for the Mental Health Professional*. 3rd ed. New York: Springer, 2002.

Wrenn R. "College Management of Student Death: A Survey." *Death Studies* 15: 4 (1991): 395–402.

PART III

Media as Teacher and Aid to Teaching

8

The Virtual Resurrection: Technology, Violence, and Interpretations of Death in a Southern University Classroom

Diana Walsh Pasulka

Justin, a student in my introductory religion course, approached me one day after class. "Please don't get me wrong," he said. "I don't want you to take this the wrong way." I smiled in expectation, although inside I was a little nervous. We had been discussing Christianity, and the historical-critical method I use to dissect the scriptures sometimes creates a tense environment that I am usually able to ease through an easy-going teaching style. However, occasionally a student confronts me directly with the equivalent of a modern day accusation of heresy. Facing Justin, I was bracing for this. "It's not that I disagree with what you are saying, but I think that your emphasis is wrong. The message is about resurrection. Death is not the end. This is why I converted to Christianity." He smiled and then walked away. That was not so bad, I thought to myself as I headed back to my office. However, his simple statement resonated with me for days. It provided an answer to a puzzle that had presented itself to me in the preceding few years that I had been teaching university students. The puzzle involves the connections between violence and technology, death and notions of immortality.

The Interpretation of Death when Violence Is the Background

As a university instructor at a major regional university in the South, I teach introductory religious studies courses as well as those that focus on my own area of expertise, which involves analyzing ideas of transcendence in U.S. religions and popular culture. What appears as an occasional glimpse into the general paradigm of youth culture regarding death and conceptions of immortality is clarified in my upper-level courses as students speak more directly to the subject of death and its manifestations in religion and culture. In my first few years of teaching, what struck me most was what appeared to me to be a blindness or insensitivity on the part of students to representations of violence. It seemed to me that violence was so ubiquitous as to become the background within which they lived their lives. In the most real and ordinary sense, it had become banal. This was most evident to me when we discussed specific examples from course texts that involved issues of death and immortality, like Plato's *Apology*, which deals with the death of Plato's teacher, Socrates. In order to make sense of Socrates' willing acceptance of what appeared to be an unjust death sentence by the Athenian lawmakers, students used an interpretive framework that involved popular culture. Examples used most often came from the television series *Buffy the Vampire Slayer* and more recently the movie adaptation of the graphic novel featuring the Greek-Persian Battle of Thermopylae, *300*.[1] The *Apology* is a moving account of the death of the beloved wise teacher, Socrates, written by his student Plato. It is Socrates' defense of his life of teaching, for which he is being tried by the Athenian government who accuse him of atheism and corrupting the youth of the state. After he is sentenced to death, Socrates' friends arrange to help him escape. Socrates refuses the escape, saying that he has lived a good life within the Athenian legal system, and he will now die by the system that had granted him such a life. Additionally, he has not been given a "sign" from his inner oracle, or daimon, to escape, and therefore he must do what is presented to him as his destiny. He then goes on to discuss different ideas of immortality, something of which he has great hope but no sure knowledge. As he states to his friends just prior to his death, "I regard this as a proof that what has happened to me is a good, and that those of us who think that death is an evil are in error." Specifically regarding immortality, he says, "There is great reason to hope that death is a good, for one of two things: either death is a state of nothingness and utter unconsciousness, or, as men say, there is a change and migration of the soul from this world to another." Although he hopes that in postdeath he might live on to converse with the great philosophers of history, Socrates maintains that what has made his life important is the goodness that he engaged in day to day, "a man who is good for anything ought not to calculate the chance of living or dying; he ought only to consider whether in doing anything he is doing right or wrong—acting the part of a good man or of a bad." In this way, Socrates breaks the connection between goodness as instrumentally connected to achieving immortality. Goodness is intrinsically good—an end in itself. Good men and women are good because it is the best way to be or it is its own reward. One is not to be good to gain a place in a heaven.[2]

The popular culture references that my students used to interpret Socrates' message about life, death, and goodness reveal an unmistakable pattern. For the most part, students feel that they understand Socrates to be affirming a notion of immortality that has nothing to do with literalism or metaphor. Whether a personal soul or part of the personality progressed onward to a post-death life matters not . . . or I should say this is not how they articulate the problem of immortality. To students, Socrates is interpreted as stating that there is indeed an immortal world, and this is a continuation of one's present action and life. I was able to understand this form of immortality through the examples they used to explain Socrates' decision.

The example used most often as analogous to Socrates' plight was from the controversial movie and graphic novel 300. At its release, 300 was routinely panned by movie critics as being racist and saturated with violence. Critics such as Roger Moore and Dana Stevens noted that the portrayal of the Persians as effeminate, especially in comparison to the movie's masculine representations of the Greeks, was race baiting at its worst. By and large, the message my students seemed to draw from the movie was that in the face of sure death, immortality was assured through heroic action and spectacular death. Perhaps this is what explains the popularity of this movie despite widespread condemnation by those in the university and the educated media. The violence of the movie, as well as its use of racial stereotypes, was secondary or nonexistent to what the students perceived as its most important point—the heroic sacrifice of one's life for a noble reason. The violence that accompanied the death of the heroes—the 300 Greeks who, as the movie constructed it, wished and chose to die in battle—made the meaning of the deaths that much more spectacular. A death accompanied by raging special effects was the proper way for one to depart this life and create everlasting meaning. To my students, the 300 Greeks were the modern-day popular-culture equivalents of Socrates.

This was also the pattern evident in another example routinely used by my students: episodes of the television series *Buffy the Vampire Slayer*. This successful television series ran from 1997 to 2003, and virtually all of my students are familiar with its characters and the story line that features a high school girl (Sarah Michelle Geller) whose job is to slay demons and vampires. The main action of the show occurs at high school, and although it is steeped in violence and the weekly vicious deaths of high school children, the show's self-conscious trivializing of life and death attempts to blunt the edge of these weighty matters. To my students, the grisly deaths of friends of the main characters, which in many cases are graphically portrayed as the bloody murders of children who are then much grieved for, is secondary or nonexistent to the main point of the show—that immortality is achieved by being willing to die for a noble cause. The meaning is maximized if this death is particularly gruesome and spectacular.

Metaphors abound in the series. The high school where the action takes place is atop a "Hellmouth," a place where hell literally threatens to erupt on earth. The protagonist Buffy must sacrifice herself in the first season to save the world from destruction, and thankfully she is resurrected to live on in the episodes of subsequent seasons. When these features of the show are pointed to specifically, however, my students do not accept metaphor as an interpretive framework. To them, high school *is literally* a hell on earth, and many of them say they would choose to sacrifice themselves to make the world a better place. Just as Socrates chooses the hemlock and not the escape, Buffy chooses to die. She has lived a heroic life—the life of a warrior, in the modern day war zone that these students identify as high school. These popular cultural references, shockingly violent perhaps to me, are for my students real references, not metaphors. They are linked to the conception of immortality that hearkens back to the ancient Greek notion of immortality conferred through heroic action, most often granted to warriors in battle.

Another interesting aspect of my students' understanding of immortality is that they do not make a distinction between popular culture and real life. If I insisted on reading the Buffy references as metaphors, they would correct me with examples from everyday life, most commonly the Columbine High School shootings. To them, the victims and the perpetrators of this tragedy are now immortal due to the spectacular nature of their deaths, and the occurrence of the massacre revealed the correlation of modern high school with a zone of violence. Disturbingly, my students read the motives of the perpetrators as being a choice made in some way under duress—the marginal status of the high schoolers and the alienation and ostracizing by fellow classmates made their actions somewhat comprehensible to my students. The deaths had meaning, and they pointed out to me that all of the victims of Columbine, like Buffy, will not soon be forgotten. Both live on in popular and mainstream culture.

Could it be that the ubiquitous presence of violence in the lives of university students, either real or as fictionalized representation, formed this unique construction of immortality? And, perhaps as portrayed in the fictional series *Buffy the Vampire Slayer*, death by horrific and violent means seems possible if not probable, so perhaps an idea of immortality that is assured somehow blunts the intensity of this realization. How did the fictional and factual become so blurred in the minds of my students, such that questions of the meaning of life and death were inextricable from references to popular culture? These questions were almost constantly abuzz in my mind as I taught and learned from my students.

A Homogeneity beyond Religious Affiliation

Beyond the realization that students were equating spectacular violent death with immortality and rejecting the issue of immortality as a problem of literalism or metaphor, it was evident that most of the students, beyond specific religious affiliation, adhered in degrees to a set of beliefs. First, death was meaningful if one had died a public, violent death, preferably for a noble cause. Second, as far as immortality is concerned, one is immortal if the first condition is met, as immortality is not to be conceived within a framework of literalism or metaphor. The evidence my students used to provide for this second contention was that "weren't we discussing it?" thus equating the life of public discourse and popular culture with postdeath survival. Another fascinating feature of this phenomenon was that, with few exceptions, most of the students felt this way. If pushed on their personal religious beliefs, which as their instructor I felt duty bound to do, they found no contradiction in holding a traditional, literal belief in immortality with this new type of virtual immortality, simultaneously. To my students, both conceptions of immortality were compatible, and neither took precedence.

Although this set of beliefs was articulated mostly in my upper-level courses that dealt specifically with issues of immortality, I witnessed it in my basic introductory courses as well. One class exercise I use to great effect in every introductory course involves examining the definition of religion. Religion, as everyone who has studied it as a category knows, is not such an easy thing to identify. In order to come to a better understanding of what types of beliefs and practices make up a religion, I confuse the issue by taking a few controversial cases from popular culture in order to bring the students to a recognition of what constitutes religion. One example I use is the "religion" based on the fictional Star Wars books and films. A Web-based religion, the religious practitioners of Jediism, describe themselves as believing "in the Force as our religion and the Jedi path as our philosophy and way of life."[3] While I do not disregard the religious claims of Jedi practitioners, I do compare some traditional religions such as Judaism with Jediism, in an effort to bring students to a better understanding of the definition of religion. For example, I push students to ascertain what truth claims Judaism makes with regard to the transcendent, and to compare these with the claims of Jediism. For the most part, students do come to see that Judaism makes truth claims about the objectivity of the transcendent, while Jediism's ideas of transcendence are more subjective. In other words, for most practicing Jews, G-d exists no matter whether you believe or not, whereas practitioners of Jediism are more relaxed about the beliefs of its members. They can believe in God or not, it doesn't really matter as long as they *feel* they are Jedi Knights.

My aim in assigning this work is to hopefully reveal to students that most religions have strong truth claims that are usually viewed by practitioners as objective. Although students do see my point, for the most part they reject it. Therefore, according to their beliefs, the Jedi practitioners have it right. If I ask them whether it should matter or not whether Jesus was actually the Son of God, for example, they respond that it doesn't matter to Christians, that they will still live and act like Christians regardless. Or, if the Buddha had not actually achieved nirvana, would Buddhists still be justified in believing in the Four Noble Truths? What matters is not the objectivity of the claims being made, but the everyday actions of practitioners. It is the ongoing lived tradition that seemed to define objective reality to the students. At first I thought this was just an example of not thinking through the issues at stake and identifying conclusions, but over time I recognized the persistence of the belief as another version of the idea that public discourse (and practice, it seems) equals reality, or, that public presence confers reality.

Another striking example of the students' linkage between violence, death, and perceived virtual immortality occurred one day when I was teaching a class on Buddhism and popular culture. In this class, I routinely mention the plight of Vietnamese Buddhist Thich Quang Duc, the monk who famously immolated himself as a protest of the South Vietnamese regime in 1963 Vietnam. The American press used the provocative image as a means to promote their agenda during the U.S.-Vietnam conflict, and later appropriations include his image on a CD cover for the once-popular band Rage Against the Machine. My point is to reveal the ways in which images of Buddhism and Buddhist monks are employed gratuitously by the media of mass culture, a phenomena known as "Orientalism" and coined by Edward Said.[4] After my lecture, a student, a self-proclaimed Christian, revealed a tattoo on his back of the monk engulfed in flames. Surprised, I asked the student how he came to have the monk on his back, where did he learn of his story? He replied that he didn't know who the monk was, just that he had seen him on the cover of the Rage Against the Machine CD, thought it was an image that cohered with the meaning of the crucified Christ, which was the other image visible on his arm. I was too surprised to ask if the student thought that Thich Quang Duc was resurrected in the same manner as Christ, as no doubt the Christian belief of the student dictated a belief in resurrection. In time, I have come to believe that this is precisely what motivated the student to tattoo the monk's image in the first place. He must understand Thich Quang Duc as *virtually* resurrected due to his violent death for a noble cause, and most important, through his ongoing incarnations in popular culture. Although the student never stated this directly, his actions, especially his correlation of the monk with the image of the resurrected Jesus, suggests it.

The Place of Media in the Formation of Beliefs Regarding Immortality

As instructors of religious studies, we must take the media, technology, and popular culture seriously as formative in the construction of beliefs about immortality and the supernatural. Lynn Schofield Clark makes the point that "research into young people and their beliefs has often assumed that they have learned of and formed their beliefs about angels, God or Allah, and the devil—the more traditionally 'religious' supernatural beings, in the context of the church, synagogue or mosque."[5] In actuality, youth of today are involved in an extended religious culture that informs them as much as, if not more than, the traditional cultures of their parents and grandparents. If my experiences and Schofield Clark's analysis are any indication, distinct patterns emerge that indicate that young people are making similar types of judgments regarding these matters. Seemingly regardless of religious affiliation, students adopt a framework of *virtual reality* to confer meaning on events, and lives.

One of the more compelling reasons that Schofield Clark cites in her analysis accounting for the fascination of today's youth with religious elements and the supernatural in popular culture is their need to feel powerful and competent when faced with forces beyond their control. Confronted with the daily display of war and violence in the news and fictionalized on television, teens and young people identify with an imaginary realm where evil is overcome, demons are vanquished and the good are immortalized. This would certainly cohere with my own experiences of witnessing how students betray an apparently resigned acceptance of violence with a parallel belief in immortality. Beyond this, however, is the issue of the conflation of reality with fantasy. Just as metaphor and literalism are insignificant frameworks in their assessment of religious claims, students have adopted an alternative framework that blurs the boundaries between reality and the imaginary, or what they view on television or in virtual space. It is this aspect that I find most interesting, and disturbing, about the belief system I have encountered.

Strategies and Practices

In the first few years teaching, I mostly viewed these interpretations of death and immortality as anomalous and not worth much attention. I soon became aware of the persistence and prevalence of the interpretations. Additionally, my work on the place of popular culture in the formation of nineteenth-century theology focused my attention on the function of popular culture in the formation of religious beliefs. I now feel I am witnessing firsthand how mass culture is impacting the beliefs of a particular demographic—my students. Are my students representative of a larger population? Most probably, although they do not represent all of the young people in the United States. Still, the likelihood that other instructors at other institutions are witnessing the same phenomenon is great, as we are all in some degree affected by mass culture.

With this realization came a pedagogical problem. Although I felt that the beliefs held by my students were for the most part not thought through and often incompatible, I did not necessarily feel that their religious ideas were something I needed to correct. We are not theologians, but academics whose approach to teaching is a nonconfessional and mostly historical method to be safeguarded carefully. If my students chose to blur the boundaries between what they saw on television with what they learned in the classroom, or for that matter what they learned in the mosque or church, who was I to stop them? The more I saw how the violence of the media and popular culture seemed to be impacting their ideas of reality, the more I felt a sense of obligation. In my upper-level courses, I emphasized the methods I used in my research on nineteenth-century popular culture in which the connections between popular media and a community's beliefs are directly correlated. I hoped students would make the connections with their own lives. The point at which I decided to make the issue more explicit came one day when several of my honors students requested that I show episodes from the History Channel to teach about Islam and early Christianity. "Its history and it is entertaining," one young man opined. At this point, I felt something had to be done.

During this time, I had been reading Angela Davis's work on the connections between the prison, labor, and the media. In her essay "The Prison Industrial Complex," she details the significant place that the media has in perpetuating the widespread notion that crime is out of control and that the need for prisons is great. She states that "during the same period when crime rates were declining, the prison populations soared" and quotes Vincent Beiser's statements about representations of crime versus its actuality:

> The media, especially television . . . have a vested interest in perpetuating the notion that crime is out of control. With new competition from cable networks and 24-hour news channels, TV news and programs about crime . . . have proliferated madly. According to the Center for Media and Public Affairs, crime coverage was the number-one topic on the nightly news over the past decade.
> From 1990 to 1998, homicide rates dropped by half nationwide, but homicide stories on the three major networks rose almost fourfold.[6]

I used essays, statistics, and facts to show my students how the world they witnessed on television did not correlate directly with their own lives, and that the representation of violence was not unbiased or reflective of reality. Although this would seem like common sense, based on the testimonies and beliefs of my students, it was not common sense to them. I was witnessing firsthand the "the matrix effect," the idea documented in the popular movie *The Matrix*.[7] The directors of *The Matrix* were inspired by the works of philosopher Jean Baudrillard, who coined the term "hyperreality"—the theory that people in the United States were so affected by media and television that they often blurred the boundaries between reality and fiction.[8] The hyperrealism of the media determined in large part what my students believed. The media was not innocent in its portrayals of violence, as the news was often constructed so as to get the best ratings. However, to most students, the raw edge of representation has a visceral effect and analysis seems no match for emotive, graphic content.

Jean Baudrillard is not the first to elaborate on how media affects beliefs and practices. Before him, Marshall McLuhan became famous for his work on the impact of the media on society. His famous statement "The medium is the message" is a summary of his belief that the act of engaging with modern media actually structures cognition. He was a strong advocate for media awareness, as he thought that without the ability to know how the media affects one's reality, one's place within society was bound to be determined by forces of advertising and corporate manipulation. He even went so far as to suggest that an uninformed population was vulnerable to forces of terror and totalitarianism.[9] With this in mind, I devised several ways to educate my students.

It is important that students see for themselves how the media is not an unbiased source of information. While using statistics and sharing important studies is one significant way to address this issue (and one I use often in my courses), students need to see firsthand how the media treat information. One way I get them to do this is to have them choose a contemporary newsworthy event and to keep a log of that event over two weeks. They are to document how various news media treat this event. I generally urge them to follow the major national networks such as CBS, NBC, ABC, and CNN, as well as international networks like the BBC, in addition to national radio networks. After two weeks, they are to do a comparison of these and determine the major differences. I then have the students seek out even-more-alternative news media to get other views of the same event. The students are always surprised by the various ways in which one event is interpreted. The students follow up the assignment by paying attention to the advertising on each network when the event is covered, and I have them ask questions such as "What type of audience does this advertisement assume?" and "What are the connections between the portrayal of the event and the companies who advertise on the network?" This assignment is effective in revealing how the media is not an objective recorder of reality but has vested interests in a particular portrayal.

Another teaching exercise I use involves having students compare a religious text with a text from popular culture. An example of this involves Plato's texts about the death of Socrates. I require students to examine the theme of death and immortality in the text of Plato and compare this with the exact same themes in an example from popular culture, such as *Buffy the Vampire Slayer*. Students draft a graph comparing and contrasting the two texts, which allows them to visualize the differences and similarities. They are then able to interpret these differences within frameworks suggested by me—sociologically, historically, and philosophically. Questions I pose, such as "What accounts for the differences in the way in which death is portrayed in each text?" lead students to identify cultural influences on belief. In this way, they start to identify their own beliefs as being shaped by cultural, historical influences. These exercises engage students in an active process of analysis, the goal of which is to reveal to them how their religious ideas of death and immortality have been shaped by the media.

Conclusion: A New God

Friedrich Nietzsche said, "Two thousand years have come and gone—and not a single new god!" proclaiming that the time was ripe for the arrival of a new way of conceiving of the transcendent.[10] Martin Heidegger, influenced by Nietzsche, thought he found this new ethos when he proclaimed, "Technology is Truth."[11] The truth of technology for Heidegger was that it dominated and determined modern man and woman's very being in the world. Certainly, these two philosophers would not be surprised if they were to catch a glimpse of the theological developments shaped by the contemporary world. Although I am not ready to proclaim the arrival of a new religion, I think it is safe to say that the transcendent has not escaped the marks of the media and technology, and as my students age and become the next generation of citizens, religion will no doubt bear these marks. Religious studies and education will change accordingly, taking more of an interest in the present instead of the past and in the ways in which media and technology shape and form beliefs, and people.

NOTES

1. *Buffy the Vampire Slayer*, dir. Joss Wedon (WB network, 1997–2003); *300*, dir. Zack Snyder (Warner Bros. Pictures, 2007).

2. Benjamin Jowett, trans., *Plato's Euthyphro, Apology, Crito, Phaedo (Great Books in Philosophy)* (Buffalo, NY: Prometheus Books: 1988), 51.

3. The Jediism Way, at http://www.thejediismway.org (accessed on September 15, 2007).

4. Edward Said, *Orientalism* (New York: Vintage, 1979).

5. Lynn Schofield Clark, *From Angels to Aliens: Teenagers, the Media, and the Supernatural* (New York: Oxford University Press, 2003), 4.

6. Angela Davis, "The Prison Industrial Complex," in *The Feminist Philosophy Reader*, ed. Alison Bailey and Chris Cuomo (New York: McGraw-Hill Higher Education: 2008), p. 415. Quote from Vince Beiser, "How We Got to Two Million: How Did the Land of the Free Become the World's Leading Jailer?" *Debt to Society*, MotherJones.com Special Report, July 10, 2001, http://www.motherjones.com/news/special_reports/prisons/overview.html.

7. *The Matrix*, dir. Andy Wachowski and Larry Wachowski (Warner Bros. Pictures, 1999).

8. Jean Baudrillard, *Simulacra and Simulation*, trans. Sheila Faria Glaser (Ann Arbor: University of Michigan Press, 1995); see also Mark Poste, ed., *Jean Baudrillard: Selected Writings* (Stanford: Stanford University Press, 1988).

9. Marshall McLuhan, *Understanding Media: The Extensions of Man* (1964; Cambridge, MA: MIT Press, 1994).

10. Freidrich Nietzsche, *The Anti-Christ*, trans. H. L. Mencken (Tucson, AZ: See Sharp Press, 1999), 19.

11. Martin Heidegger, "The Question Concerning Technology," *Basic Writings: From Being and Time to the Task of Thinking*, ed. David Farrell Krell p. 307–42 (New York: Harper Collins, 1993), 334.

BIBLIOGRAPHY

Baudrillard, Jean. *Simulacra and Simulation*. Translated by Sheila Faria Glaser. Ann Arbor: University of Michigan Press, 1995.

Beiser, Vince. "How We Got to Two Million: How Did the Land of the Free Become the World's Leading Jailer?" *Debt to Society*. MotherJones.com Special Report, July 10, 2001. Available at http://www.motherjones.com/news/special_reports/prisons/overview.html.

Davis, Angela. "The Prison Industrial Complex." In *The Feminist Philosophy Reader*, edited by Alison Bailey and Chris Cuomo, 412–21. New York: McGraw-Hill Higher Education, 2008.

Heidegger, Martin. "The Question Concerning Technology." In *Basic Writings: From Being and Time to the Task of Thinking*, edited by David Farrell Krell, 307–42. New York: Harper Collins: 1993.

Jowett, Benjamin, trans. *Plato's Euthyphro, Apology, Crito, Phaedo (Great Books in Philosophy)*. Buffalo, NY: Prometheus Books: 1988.

McLuhan, Marshall. *Understanding Media: The Extensions of Man*. Cambridge, MA: MIT Press, 1964/1994.

Nietzsche, Freidrich. *The Antichrist*. Translated by H. L. Mencken. Tucson, AZ: See Sharp Press, 1999.

Poste, Mark, ed. *Jean Baudrillard: Selected Writings*. Stanford: Stanford University Press, 1988.

Said, Edward. *Orientalism*. New York: Vintage, 1979.

Schofield Clark, Lynn. *From Angels to Aliens: Teenagers, the Media, and the Supernatural*. New York: Oxford University Press: 2003.

9

What Would Spielberg Do? Using Mainstream Films to Teach Visions of the Afterlife

Michael McKenzie

"I really wouldn't like to be reincarnated in a place similar to where I grew up. Out of all the films we watched, I liked What Dreams May Come *the best, and how it portrayed the afterlife as beautiful and somewhat exotic, a place you created yourself. I'm from Buffalo and really don't want to go back there."*

—Alicia, Keuka College freshman[1]

In teaching introductory courses in comparative religions, I sometimes feel like an academic version of Art Linkletter: college students sometimes *do* "say the darnedest things." As many surveys and studies on the spirituality and religiosity of the modern college student have noted, and as I have also noticed, there is a genuine openness on the part of students to talk about religion and spirituality.[2] But we shouldn't be surprised at this phenomenon, and Dean Kelley is no doubt right when he says simply, "Humans are incorribly religious creatures."[3]

I am frankly pleased with this student openness to discussing religion and spirituality;[4] in fact this vigorous give-and-take is a large part of what keeps my classes alive and vibrant. Unlike some of my colleagues I run into at conferences, I actually enjoy teaching introductory religion courses to undergraduates—since students bring little in the way of bromides or pat answers. This unbridled honesty is of course mixed with ignorance, but frankly, I don't mind the trade-off, and I find their input mostly refreshing and academically stimulating.

To reach these students I have developed a pedagogy that seems to be working quite well, despite combining what some may worry are the oil and water of teaching religions: primary religious texts and mainstream Hollywood films. From class evaluations by students and peers, enrollment numbers, and my own sense of the learning that goes on in the course, it seems clear that both these elements are indeed creating a nice synergy. Despite a grading rubric that is more challenging than my other courses, the class is quite popular and I am consistently forced to turn students away each semester.

What follows is the story of how I came to employ mainstream films in teaching an introductory religion course, focusing on how I employ such films to teach on the various visions of death and the afterlife, a topic that is a significant component of the course. To support my contention that films can work to enhance teaching a religion course that discusses death and dying, I have included representative student comments from discussion groups that relate the class films to the assigned readings. These comments suggest that students have demonstrated a significant and appropriate level of learning, especially for an introductory course. Hollywood films have served to prompt students to reflect both on their own mortality and how various religions cope with death.[5] Finally, I conclude in a somewhat speculative manner, suggesting that this sort of film viewing can add a sense of community to the learning environment.

The Strange *Via Media* of the "Church-Related" College

Before describing this integration of films into my teaching on death and dying, it is necessary to touch on the specific college environment in which I now teach. As one who has taught in widely divergent campus environments, I understand that my approach may be considered somewhat heterodoxical at institutions with more creedal stances regarding religiosity and faith. As part of my normal teaching load each semester I teach Religion 103, Introduction to Religion, at Keuka College, a liberal arts–based college in the Finger Lakes region of western New York. The college itself was founded in 1890 by George Harvey Ball under the auspices of the Freewill Baptists, and is currently what is known as a "church-related" college, affiliated with a mainline denomination, the American Baptist Churches of America.[6] Out of the sixteen colleges and universities affiliated with this particular denomination, Keuka ranks toward the "less confessional" end of the scale, and for some time the campus community has been in the midst of a vigorous discussion on the proper role and scope for religion at the college.

On the one hand, it is obvious that the overt presence of religion at Keuka has declined over the past twenty-five years or so. For example, the college has done away with the various religion majors as well as the religious studies department, there are no daily chapel services (mandatory or optional), and out of the thousand or so students on campus, in annual surveys given by the college only 4 percent identify themselves as Baptists.[7] In discussions with older alumnae (until the mid-1980s Keuka was a women's college), I have noted a fair number who majored in religious education and who are somewhat dismayed at the loss of that major and at the decline of campus religiosity in general.

It would be a serious mistake, however, to infer from the above observations that many of today's Keuka students neither care about religion's voice nor see themselves as spiritual. Whether I'm teaching religion, ethics, or philosophy, students are not shy in talking about religion or spirituality—either in the abstract or in more personal terms. And, in conversations with colleagues in other disciplines, many of them report the same phenomenon: if students sense they are in a safe environment, they don't seem overly reticent in talking about spirituality any more than, say, the issues surrounding student parking or the quality of food in the cafeteria.

According to the 2004 National Survey of Student Engagement, 61 percent of Keuka College freshmen (the largest target group for this introductory religion course) report participating in formal religious activities "sometimes," "often," or "very often," compared to 67 percent of freshmen nationwide. However, this same category drops to 40 percent for Keuka seniors, contrasting sharply to 67 percent for seniors nationwide. Whatever the reasons for this decline in the reported spiritual activities of Keuka seniors, it is nonetheless clear that a substantial portion of Keuka students—especially first-year students—identify themselves as participating in religious activities.[8]

And this same openness to the spiritual might be said of the Keuka faculty, albeit accompanied by more nuanced reflection and caution regarding the role(s) that campus religiosity ought to play. Under the auspices of a grant from the Lilly Foundation, obtained through the Rhodes Foundation, for a study on the future of church-related colleges, I facilitated a series of faculty discussions during the 2000–2001 school year on the place of spirituality on the Keuka College campus. Faculty participants were asked to read and reflect on Parker Palmer's *To Know as We Are Known: Education as a Spiritual Journey*, and respond to Palmer's point that academic environments that concentrated on fencing out spirituality were breeding grounds for a "pain of disconnection" among faculty, students, and administration.[9] While there was certainly no desire to see Keuka become any sort of fundamentalist bastion, I could not detect any significant animosity toward religion or spirituality per se. The group certainly reflected an openness to discussing various faith traditions, and they also claimed to have no problem with students who might wish to discuss such traditions and their values in the classroom, provided such discussions were appropriate to the topic and irenic in tone. The faculty also evidenced some of the common bifurcation in talking about "religion" and "spirituality," viewing the former's tendencies toward routinization and organization less favorably than the latter's drive toward personal fulfillment and individuality.[10]

Another critical component to the overall religious climate of the campus concerns Keuka's stress on "experiential education," attempting to combine the best of academic study and theory with practical, "hands-on" experience. As part of this curricular mandate, students are required to complete four, month-long "Field Periods" during their residency at the college. Field Periods are outside internships that are student initiated and faculty assessed, designed to mesh classroom learning with the realities of the modern workplace. One type of field period is the Spiritual Exploration Field Period, an internship that consists of working either with organizations that openly employ spiritual values (e.g., Habitat for Humanity) or in those internships that act to hone the student's own spiritual value-system. These particular field periods are fairly popular, indicating not only that many students think such combinations of faith and academics a normal part of college life but also that they are willing to put in the substantial commitment required (each Field Period requires 140 hours from the student). Additionally, Keuka's avowed stress on *experiential* education in general meshes well with the experiential nature of religion and spirituality. Keuka students are expected to be participatory in their educational journey, and this mindset can prove to be a fertile soil for the active demands of religion.

Thus, while Keuka's overt ties to the American Baptist Churches are largely more formal and historical than curricular, Keuka might fairly be described as largely "faith friendly," and I have been given a free hand in deciding how best to structure this particular class. Religion 103 is a core course, thus mandated to take a broad approach; and it is comparative in nature, covering the world's major religions as well as a selection of critical issues that all religions deal with (e.g., death and dying). It is offered at least once a semester, with an enrollment of approximately thirty-five students, and it is nearly always full.

The Attraction of Cinema as Narrative

In the summer before my first semester at Keuka College, I set aside some time to perform a thorough assessment of this particular class. I knew I had the nucleus of a good course—it had been well received at other colleges and universities—but I wanted to try to take the class to the next level. From researching the college, I knew Keuka's environment would be markedly different than previous institutions at which I had taught. Less confessionally religious, more rural, strongly concerned with combining theory and practice, Keuka had its own academic and organizational climate. I certainly wanted to challenge students, but I also wanted my course to be a good fit for this particular academic environment. Finally, having kept up with the "religion in the public square" literature, I sensed a new wind blowing in terms of openness among faculty and students toward discussing religion and spirituality in the classroom.

I had always thought that teaching introductory religion classes based solely on lecture was giving short shrift to the subject as well as depriving students of key learning opportunities. The world of spirituality is like a Yellowstone mud pot: its contents messy and often bubbling over, the temperature hot, with uncontrolled power lurking just below the surface. It might be a little "edgy" at times, but the subject begs for active engagement in the classroom. In a pure lecture format, however, students have little or no chance to interject questions, opinions, and insights into the mix (and once such a classroom moment passes it's often impossible to recapture). I had always made room for a significant amount of student-led discussion in this course, but I wanted to find a fresh pedagogy that would allow students to engage even more with the various traditions' attempts to take on the tough questions in life. I certainly agree with those who see religious classes as precisely the place where such dialogue on the big issues can take place, as long as the classroom is "open and safe."[11] After my "time in the desert," as I reflected on how to develop the course, I came up with a few broad—but fairly ironclad—parameters for the course's new iteration:

1. It had to take each religion seriously, and to do so it had to incorporate a fair number of primary readings from within each tradition.
2. It also had to take religious *narrative* seriously, which dictated that I find the best stories to illustrate both religious themes and each particular tradition.

3. It had to tackle the tough questions, ones that were inescapably *human* in nature, questions that have perplexed humankind for millennia.

4. It had to meet Keuka's mission regarding experiential learning, it had to get students somehow involved in looking at a tradition from the *inside*.[12]

5. It had to hold students' interest. Like most faculty (but *unlike* most students), I happily acknowledge there are worse things than being bored, but I *was* driven by the belief that religions are indeed fascinating, and ought to be presented in such a way as to reflect that luminescence.

After reflecting on the above criteria, it seemed only natural to make films a significant component of the course. Like most faculty, I had used movies in a piecemeal fashion in various courses, mostly to illustrate a particular point, but never as a consistent and evaluated component of a class. My graduate schooling was pretty much "old school"—using films to teach was considered a shoddy technique employed by lazy professors, or worse, a throwback to the era in which professors evaluated papers by writing "groovy" and "far out" in the margins. But Hollywood movies are not the pariah they once were.

In the educational field, there is a burgeoning industry on assisting the primary and secondary teacher on the use of film in the classroom.[13] Scholars have been forced to recognize the thousand pound gorilla that movies have become, and many educators are convinced that teachers must either employ films on their (the teachers') terms or risk losing a great pedagogical tool.[14] Paul Weinstein pulls no punches when he labels film and television as "the great history educators of our time."[15] For me, using films in class had many attractions: capturing student interest, prompting sharp questions on tough issues, getting students to reveal what they really think, and more than anything else, providing the enveloping presentation of story.

As a film buff myself, I had seen several television interviews with Steven Spielberg (whom I admire as a director), and paid close attention when he said what elevated a film to greatness. He insisted that it was the *story* that was the heart and soul of a movie; the actors, special effects, and even the director were to be secondary, a great supporting cast to the overarching narrative. I was already sympathetic to Alasdair MacIntyre's insistence that morals and virtue were inescapably linked to story and tradition,[16] and I likewise agreed that the power of narrative was due, in large part, to the fact that we humans are "storytelling animals."[17] I had also become fully persuaded early on that Martha Nussbaum was essentially correct in her insistence that ethical understanding ought to give a "certain type of priority" to the emotional pull and tug that comes with our examination of "particular people and situations, rather than to abstract rules."[18] And, although Nussbaum had primarily novels in mind, surely films (the really good ones, anyway) are examples par excellence of emotional and compelling storytelling.

Given the solid credentials of cinema as story, what could be more natural than to link narrative, religion, and film? To me, religions are inescapably about narrative. The story of Arjuna's painful dilemma in the Bhagavad-Gita; Siddhartha's fated journey outside the palace; Moses' journeys up (and down) a desolate Mt. Sinai; the parables of the New Testament; a vision quest of a Sioux warrior: all are written, learned, and passed down as story. The lessons and morals are only understandable as part of a narrative, and, as Wade Clark Roof suggests, there is even something "fundamentally religious about narrative structure" itself.[19] By the reflection and deliberation necessary, the writer is "ordering time" as a creator, and this meaning-as-story forces others into questions of hermeneutics.

Thus, I wanted to make films a substantial component of the course, but in a way that avoided any taint of the "slacker film class" familiar to all and taken by those students often looking for the academic path of least resistance. I confess that as a freshman I found myself in one such class at a large university in the Pacific Northwest, and the movies were sometimes drowned out by the sounds of snoring, stereos, and the slamming of the ancient wooden seats in the desks as students left—typically whenever they felt like it. It was a sham class, and even the teaching assistants did little more than go through the motions. But, as I reflect back on the reasons for that course's failure, it was not the concept of cinema-as-teacher that was at fault, but the films themselves. All documentaries, the movies were little more than other professors lecturing in other auditoriums to other students. We were pressed into becoming passive voyeurs from afar, not only lacking any opportunities for engagement but without even the presence of a live human being. There was nothing attractive about that pedagogy, and of course those films produced ennui like plants produced oxygen. I decided to take the next step.

Could Buddha Live in Burbank?

> Then we must first of all, it seems, control the story tellers. Whatever noble story they compose we shall select, but a bad one we must reject. Then we shall persuade nurses and mothers to tell their children those we have selected and by those stories to fashion their

minds far more than they can shape their bodies by handling them. The majority of the stories they now tell must be thrown out.

The Republic, book 2

Like most faculty, my campus mailbox is often stuffed with offers from documentary film companies, in my case touting every conceivable category of religious film. Many of them are probably fine accompaniments for certain types of courses, but they largely target students whose interest is already quite high in esoteric topics (I remember one film offer that promised to wow me on the various types of prayer shawls worn by certain monks). In addition, other such films seem perilously close to being mind numbing, especially when considering the average attention span of the modern freshmen. *Under a dismal gray sky, a hypnotic rain patters down in a jungle. A large brass gong sounds in a monastery, and a solemn voice slowly intones: "And this is Buddhism."* Yikes. Given my students and environment, I might as well hand out sleeping pills with the syllabi. So, not without some twinges of guilt, I ditched public broadcasting in favor of Hollywood. I faced up to the fact that many of the best storytellers in the country probably ate brie, drove their Hummers everywhere on congested highways, hated the New York Yankees, and had 900 as their zip code prefix. I then chucked all those documentary catalogs I had accumulated over the years, and headed down to the local video store. In retrospect, this crossover clearly was the watershed move: Caesar and I were now standing on the other side of the Rubicon.

But might this approach be akin to hiring wolves to guard the sheep? True enough, mainstream Hollywood films had a good shot at holding students' interest, might even enthrall them with seeing various traditions and human dilemmas from the inside, and would even address the tough questions of life—but at what cost? Was I in jeopardy of focusing on glitz and glamour at the expense of accuracy and objectivity? Would I be guilty of pawning off propaganda as truth, showing the present-day religious equivalents of *Reefer Madness* in the guise of teaching? Did I really want students thinking of the devil when they see either Al Pacino (*The Devil's Advocate*) or Max Von Sydow (*Needful Things*)? Was I in danger of becoming some sort of Jerry Springer of the academy?

Despite some misgivings at the first, I believe I have managed to avoid the Scylla of tedium *and* the Charybdis of falsity in teaching this course, probably due to a number of reasons. First, these films are never shown in abstract, but in close tandem with primary source readings. When such readings are in the hands of a competent professor, they act to counter any cinematic excesses nicely.[20] In my judgment, while movies can do a decent job at portraying a religion, and can be absolute dynamite for illustrating a religious theme or human dilemma, the *ultimate* religious narrative should consist of the tradition's own texts as much as possible.

Second, with proper professorial setup of the film's context and quality, students are forewarned (and forearmed) about any directorial hobbyhorses that might be in play, and at what spots the film may be wildly inaccurate (as opposed to reasonably speculative). Movies must be allowed ample room to explore the terra incognita beyond the known doctrinal world of religions; and certainly even lead the explorations when talking about the various issues dealt with by all religions (e.g., what happens when you die). Thus, the cinematic professor can maintain accuracy and proper care for the truth, while giving films the appropriate level of latitude to do what they do best: engage the viewers and provoke them to enter the dialogue.

Finally, and especially at a nonconfessional college like Keuka, and in a comparative religions course to boot, it's of course inappropriate to promote one certain religious faith or branch of a faith. A professor has to carefully evaluate all films that purport to teach about a certain tradition, and if they're far outside the mainstream of that tradition, either employ a healthy dose of contextualization beforehand, or choose another film. As long as films are reasonably faithful to a tradition's own texts (which themselves provide considerable leeway), and professors are alert (and honest) enough to state where such films may go beyond reasonably formed boundaries, Hollywood films need not offend any more than any other form of media. In addition (and we faculty probably need to hear this more often than we'd care to admit), students are far more savvy in watching films than we give them credit for, particularly when it comes to the films judiciously employed to teach on religious or ethical themes. In my experience, Spielberg's dictum has been right: the actors might be part of the hook that initially gets the audience, but they usually soon take a backseat to the issues raised by the film's story line.

Ultimately, I have found Hollywood films superb in raising the right questions and in the right fashion, giving excellent opportunities for the students—now aroused into thinking about these issues—to examine the traditions' own texts. As one student put it, "I love movies anyway, so it's actually fun to watch them, looking for the religious point of view. They got me to thinking about how different religions have to answer some of the same tough questions I do."[21] Again, in hindsight, this idea that films might join students and religions in common cause should raise few if any eyebrows. Both students and the major faith traditions grapple with the same "big questions," questions that deal in life and death, joy and suffering. As David Cawthon puts it, "The film is a most successful device for breeding understanding of human situations."[22] College students today have never experienced a world *without* AIDS; they have likely attended more than their share of funerals; and they are not as gullible or naïve as were pre-Watergate teens on believing the government's party line. Such phenomena may have helped create a veneer of cynicism, but mainstream movies—geared as they are to piercing such tough shells—have proved excellent vehicles to engage today's students. In my discussion sections that cover such issues and the films, students are alert, with their questions and opinions sharp and probative. I couldn't ask for more than that.

The Big Beyond on the Big Screen

Hollywood has a love affair with death as it does with sex, which merely (but importantly) points to the universality and inescapability of what lies ahead for all of us.[23] Religions of course also have to deal with death, with any tradition that wants to survive and grow forced not only to provide meaning for the act of dying but to give an answer for what awaits us after death.[24] As Harold Coward puts it, "The vitality of any religion is indicated by its ability to provide satisfying answers to our deepest and most difficult questions."[25] Theologically, coming to terms with death is a major part of constructing a theodicy, trying to make sense of how a beneficent, omnipotent divine being or universe can allow evil, a question Dean Kelley calls "the second oldest question in human awareness" (after bare human survival).[26] The inescapability and commonality of death does not detract from its profundity—far from it— and it remains one of the great endearing questions and mysteries. In covering the broad topic of death and dying in this course, I have chosen to focus on how various traditions view the afterlife, since such visions force students into more metaphysical and theological discussions (this is, after all, a course in *religion*!).

The first five weeks of the course are devoted to five critical topics or issues that religions must deal with: the identity of God, death and the afterlife, evil and the devil, free will and determinism, and the idea of apocalypse. I begin each topic by introducing the issue and what to look for in the film(s), then showing a lengthy clip from each movie (or movies) assigned for that topic. While viewing these clips, students keep "film journals," used both as prompts in class discussions and for aids in studying for course exams. On the next class day, I introduce the assigned reading, replete with historical and social contexts, and begin asking the students prompting questions about the various texts. On the last day devoted to each issue, the students take more of a leadership role in the discussion, and it is expected that their analyses will seek to compare the readings with the films.

The movies chosen for the Death and the Afterlife section are *Defending Your Life, Always,* and *What Dreams May Come.*[27] The accompanying readings are selections from *The Tibetan Book of the Dead; The Egyptian Book of the Dead;* the Bhagavad-Gita; chapters 7 and 12 in the book of Daniel (Hebrew scriptures); Matthew 26–28 and 1 Corinthians 15:1–11, 35–58 (New Testament); selections from the Qur'an (Suras 75:1–15; 69:14–35; 76:1–22; 56:1–39; 77:1–39); and "On Death," a selection from the *Chuang-tzu,* book 18.[28]

Defending Your Life (*DYL*) involves the death of Daniel (Albert Brooks) from a car accident, and his subsequent discovery that in order to progress to a new and better life in the universe he must have lived an earthly life uncontrolled by fear. Daniel finds himself in "Judgment City," a holding area for the newly dead, and is put on trial, with a prosecutor showing clips of Daniel's life, trying to prove that Daniel is dominated by fear and that he should be sent back to earth to try again. In his three-day trial, Daniel quickly becomes buried under the prosecutor's ample evidence that his life was dominated by various fears, and he soon becomes resigned to return to earth again, presumably to "get it right."

During his time in Judgment City, Daniel meets and falls in love with Julia (Meryl Streep), who clearly has lived a mostly fearless life, and he is crushed to learn that their destinies will likely be dramatically and eternally different—she to "progress," he to be sent back. In one last, valiant act, however, Daniel refuses to accept the court's verdict, risking his own life to be with Julia, and that act changes the court's opinion. Daniel is allowed to accompany Julia, demonstrating that indeed, love conquers all, even beyond the grave.

The film is a somewhat peculiar amalgam of staunch western individualism, transactional judgment, and reincarnation. In Judgment City, the individual takes full responsibility for his or her own life and actions—despite the presence of an advocate, the defendant stands alone before the tribunal. There is also little notion of the concept of grace or forgiveness, save for the curious admission that children who die need not face any judgment and are automatically moved forward. For adults, the tribunal's decision is based on a straightforward transactional squaring of the accounts, and whether or not one lived a more or less fearless life. In keeping with this calculus-like determination, the film does exude a certain sterility, despite some genuinely funny moments and an inspired performance by Daniel's advocate Bob Diamond (Rip Torn). Humans who fail to progress are sent back to earth—some many times—but even the universe's patience has limits: Daniel finds out that, eventually, failed humans are "thrown away."

Not surprisingly, students react first and foremost to the film's overriding theme of judgment of the individual's conduct, and any comparisons are usually made to those traditions with similar motifs. One student, in true Albert Brooks (or Woody Allen) fashion, wondered if such an afterlife would not inspire the very element (fear) it was designed to weed out? "I live a pretty good life, but not only would I not want to be judged, I don't think many of my friends would either. I thought about that part we read [in Islam] when you got your book in either your left or right hand [Sura 69:19–32] and thought 'OK, I guess I can live with that,' but if I had to worry about fear every moment that makes it different. I'd be paranoid." Another student saw the specificity of DYL as problematic: "I always thought the concept of judgment, at least in the Jewish writings we talked about [Daniel 12] were more general. You know, God cut you some slack because you had good motives, but the prosecutor nailed [the movie] Daniel for everything." Another student (one who seldom spoke in class, by the way) considered the criterion used for judgment as depressing. "Where is any idea of God's love in all this? What if a bad person was fearless, what then?" Not a bad point.

Still others picked up on the business-like context of it all, with the dead having nearly as many questions as they had before. "This is the least comforting of the three movies, because it left so many issues unanswered; at least in our readings you knew the requirements going in, you knew what God wanted you to do. How are we supposed to know that the whole thing's based on fear? I didn't think the people who worked in Judgment City were very genuine, it's like they didn't really care what happened to you. It was like a machine."

Finally, some students always comment on DYL's concept of paradise, admittedly made to look like Los Angeles so as to make people comfortable. "I liked the idea of being able to eat all the food you wanted [in Judgment City], but it didn't seem all that great overall. I expected more, either with angels and streets of gold or being able to meet your family members who had died before you." Even those who had previously commented favorably on reincarnation, saw DYL's variety as isolating: "You're all alone and lose the people you love and start over."

Always is loosely based on A Guy Named Joe, in which a WWII fighter pilot (Spencer Tracy) is killed and is recruited to help another budding pilot. In the remake (directed by Steven Spielberg), war is replaced by forest fires, and the Forest Service pilot Pete (Richard Dreyfuss) is killed while saving a fellow pilot's life. Pete is sent back to help a young pilot learn how to fight fires, but is dismayed to find out that his assigned protégé is falling in love with Pete's old girlfriend Belinda (Holly Hunter).

At first, Pete resists the fact that he cannot love Belinda anymore, and he refuses to guide his protégé properly, using his power to influence the pilot into a series of comic misadventures. Pete is then gently chided by his own guide, Hap (one of Audrey Hepburn's last performances), and he is told to see the big picture: we all take our turn on earth, then progress by guiding others. Unlike *DYL*'s judgment of fear, *Always* views humanity's attitude toward self and others as the critical salvific component. Pete finally gets it right, shedding his selfishness and letting Belinda go, resigned to the fact that he can no longer be a part of earthly life. In this movie, the romantic eros Pete has for Belinda gives way to a more agapic variety in which he simply wants her to be happy.

Students commonly pick up on the concept of spiritual guides and their perceived function: "I liked *Always*, and find it comforting that there might be guides to help me to make the transition back home. Although it's not quite the same, the Tibetan reading [*Book of the Dead*] seemed to function the same way, except it was to guide the dead person to progress further, not someone living." Other students were perturbed that Pete did not know his protégé: "We need guides to help us understand what's going on when we die, to interpret stuff for us, but I always thought it would either be an angel or someone I knew before."

Finally, students commonly discuss what appears to them as an overall loving message from *Always*. "The lawyer in *DYL* [Daniel's guide, Bob] was pretty nonchalant, but Hap in *Always* was very loving and welcoming, which is what I always imagined God would be like, sort of like the idea of God's grace and love [discussed in the class's Pauline reading: 1 Cor. 15], not that we can get away with everything, but that He [God] would just understand what we're going through. Hey, we're not perfect!" Another student liked Pete's metamorphosis, and simply thought it "God-like" to help others: "Isn't that what it's all about?"

What Dreams May Come (*WDMC*) is based on a novel of the same name by Richard Matheson in 1978, with its title coming from one of the more famous soliloquies in Hamlet: "For in that sleep of death what dreams may come, When we have shuffled off this mortal coil, Must give us pause" (act 3, scene 1).[29] The movie is a cinematic profusion of color in which Chris (Robin Williams) and his wife Annie (Annabella Sciorra) are faced with every parent's nightmare: the tragic death of their children in a car accident. And, as if that is not enough, a few years later Chris is killed in another car accident, leaving his wife a childless widow.

With help from a guide named Albert (Cuba Gooding Jr.) Chris discovers the afterlife is akin to a beautiful artistic masterpiece, one which he creates by his own imagination. But Chris is in for more pain. Not being able to bear her loss, and overwhelmed by feelings of guilt and despair, Annie commits suicide, and Chris then learns that suicides are permanently trapped in hell, mired in their own inescapable reality. Refusing (like Daniel in *DYL*) to countenance the idea of eternal separation, Chris undertakes a nearly Sisyphetic quest in an attempt to rescue Annie. Despite warnings from Albert and others that he is attempting the impossible, Chris becomes persistence personified, eventually breaking through to Annie, and they (and their children) enjoy a heavenly reunion. But the movie does not end in that realm, and both Chris and Annie decide to be reincarnated on earth "to make different choices," and to experience the joy of finding each other again.

For the most part, in her analysis of *WDMC*, Susan Schwartz is correct in seeing the significant South Asian religious influences on the film, and her exegesis of the film's debt to the novel and Matheson's own Eastern leanings is persuasive.[30] Albert's informing Chris that he is responsible for creating his own paradise (as Annie is for her hell) is indeed akin to the eastern idea of *Maya*, the belief that we live in a sort of virtual reality, with the mind *the* active artificer. I would also add, however, that such elevation of individual choice is not hard for westerners to stomach, and there are strong analogs in Western consumerism and autonomy. After all, Western culture's very "pro-choice" stance goes far beyond reproductive freedom; try imagining what things we do *not* like to choose for ourselves! And Schwartz's point that eastern teachings are the foundation to the moral of the film's tragedies—that human suffering may lead to wisdom—is well taken. But I would again add that the idea of suffering leading to wisdom could just as easily come from Job or Paul, suggesting that this idea may have more universal sources and appeal.

Ending in true Hollywood fashion, the film's triumphal result (Chris and Annie's paradisiacal reunion) is sunnier than the book's own ending,[31] and suggests not only that the producers wanted an audience, but the notion that love again trumps all (as in *DYL*). Of course it is simplistic to state with certainty that such triumphalism is a debt to the Western religious traditions in which God triumphs over evil and history itself, but it is certainly commensurate with it, and again, may reflect a more universal appeal. "Happy endings" may be what Hollywood likes, but they wouldn't make them if we didn't go see them.

WDMC is far and away the most popular movie of the trio, and many students interpreted Chris's ability to create a beautiful setting a just reward after a tough life. Chris and Annie were just plain, nice folks who had gotten a raw deal. "*WDMC* is comforting, knowing that your loved ones are in an OK place, safe, and at peace." "Chris and Annie had had more than their share of bad stuff happen, I'm glad they got to experience their own paradise, really good stuff" (echoes of the New Testament story of Lazarus and Rich Man [Luke 16:19–31]). Another student did not believe in reincarnation, but likened the end of *WDMC* to the end of the Christian biblical narrative when "God will dry every tear from their eyes" (Rev. 21).

One student's comment was echoed by many: "*WDMC* is the most comforting vision of the afterlife because I am a believer that heaven is what you make of it." In my judgment, this kind of resonance comes less from the idea that students have adopted an eastern mindset and more from the notion that they cherish their autonomy and would like their afterlife to reflect their own wishes and desires.

Many students easily pick up on the admitted eastern influences and tropes in the film, with many agreeing with the possibility of reincarnation, but some going further. "The whole thing that threw me at first is that Chris was dealing with multiple realities, and that he had to find the true one. [It] Reminded me of what Krishna told that Prince [Arjuna] about reality, that we could be fooled by what we think is real."

Finding Community in the Closing Credits

On a recent flight to the West Coast, my wife Allison found herself a somewhat unwilling participant in a drama that illustrated yet one more loss of community, albeit in an unexpected place. This particular airline rents DVD players and movies to individual passengers, allowing everyone to choose which movies they view, rather than be forced to watch some airline exec's idea of a great picture. For anyone who has been forced to watch yet one more Adam Sandler movie, this option might sound pretty good, and Allison was happy to select a few of her favorites. But as the DVD players began to snap open, and the passenger heads began to bend forward in their own tiny theatrical nooks, she found herself curiously regretting this new option. Gone was any sense of all the passengers being in this together, the camaraderie that springs up when good people jest about putting up with bad things (What? This movie again?). Absent was any notion of a group sharing the same emotion or experience, in a word, any sense of *community*. The god of individual choice had again triumphed, and my wife found herself surprised at her discovery that she missed the communal sense of the ritualistic shared experience.

Parker Palmer sees this lack of community and connectedness as running rampant in our modern educational system, and *the* scourge to what ought to be taking place in higher education. Teaching students to be manipulators and memorizers of atomized factoids, we create isolating spaces in which truth is hard to find, with students always pressed to "look outside" for reality. Gone is any true introspection, along with notions of responsibility for our world or ourselves.[32] What is needed, says Palmer, is the creation of learning environ-ments in which students mix it up with the material, where their passions are free to "warm up" the facts, to "make them fit for human habitation."[33] Texts ought to be employed in such a way that students can take an appropriate level of ownership of them, in a way that "allows them to enter and occupy the text," invited in by both text and professor, in a "hospitable, reassuring space."[34]

Using mainstream films as teaching tools can actually enhance a sense of connectedness amongst students. Through "looking outside" at the films, the students are freed to look within. The darkness of the classroom provides enough privacy and safety to experience deeply felt emotions, but as part of a larger, ritualistic, and communal experience. Each film day, at 1:25 p.m. the class becomes a small religious community, a little bit of sacred space in which they privately interpret a shared experience, one that allows them to talk about the real taboo topic of our time, death.[35] Grief and religion both need and seek community involvement, and if one type of symbolic interaction fails them, another must arise.[36] Unlike documentary films that often have "theses" but not narrative, mainstream movies are designed to seek out involvement, to get the audience engaged in their story. Students are only too happy to oblige.

In addition, the main actors (Albert Brooks, Richard Dreyfuss, Robin Williams) are not only believable as persons in their roles, they're accessible to the students, safe to approach, almost father-like. Thus, although the movie protagonists themselves needed guides in their death experience, they in turn become guides for the students, allowing the students to talk about death, their fears about it, and their belief (or disbelief) in how various religions deal with the afterlife.

A sense of humor doesn't hurt either. With the exception of WDMC, the movies' main characters often crack jokes and often make light of their post-mortem circumstances. Is this simple gallows humor, designed to mask the severity of death? Well, especially in DYL, there are definitely traces of this, but I think there's more to it than that. As Robert Wells points out, there is a fine line between courage and foolishness in the ability to laugh at one's upcoming death, and there is a long tradition of making light of the grim reaper.[37] And I've noticed that it doesn't take students long to get beyond the jokes. In DYL and Always they laugh at all the right places, but precious little of that laughter finds its way into either their film journals or the class discussions. When listening to their comments, and especially when I review their film journals (which are of course more private than open discussion), I am always struck at how profoundly moving these films can be to these students—again, not so much because of the Oscar quality of the work, but because of the eternal issues these films raise. "I don't consider myself a religious person, but this course and the way the films are used got me to think about religion in general, and what might happen when you die. I'm young enough I never thought about death much, but these movies sort of forced me to look at it from different angles. I did laugh at the guy in *Defending Your Life*, but not at what happened to him."

I have found that mainstream Hollywood films, despite their admitted foibles, can be excellent companions to the readings in this class, and superb vehicles to get students to really think about profound and troubling issues, such as death and dying. Surely Les Keyser is right when he says that effective teaching "must generate energetic visceral reactions if understanding is ever to take place,"[38] and these films do precisely that. When mainstream films are used to supplement (not supplant) the religious narratives that deal with death, a healthy and vigorous synergy is created that nourishes student learning and understanding.

NOTES

1. Unless otherwise noted, all quotes from students are from recorded in-class discussions in the course Introduction to Religion, at Keuka College, Spring 2005.

2. For one of the most recent surveys, see "Spirituality in Higher Education: A National Study of College Students' Search for Meaning and Purpose," found in *Chronicle of Higher Education* 51, issue 33, April 22, 2005, A1. Also see Conrad Cherry, Betty Deberg, and Amanda Porterfield, "Religion on Campus," *Liberal Education* 87, no. 4 (2001): 6–13. Peter Laurence also reports the same student interest in religions and spirituality, "Can Religion and Spirituality Find a Place in Higher Education?" *About Campus* 4, no. 5 (November/December 1999): 11–16.

3. Dean Kelley, *Why Conservative Churches Are Growing* (New York: Harper, 1977), 37.

4. In facilitating numerous student discussions, I have noticed that Keuka students exhibit the same preference for personal spirituality over organized religion that is evident both amongst their peers and within the general population. In the literature and in many forms of common usage, of course, "religion" often denotes the more formal, creedal, institutionalized faith forms; "spirituality" is defined as more personal, informal, and nonrational. See, for example, Robert Goss and Dennis Klass, *Dead but Not Lost: Grief Narratives in Religious Traditions* (Walnut Creek, CA: AltaMira Press, 2005), 54, or Laurence, "Religion and Spirituality," 14. Thus, it would be wrong to infer that someone who didn't attend regular religious services was "nonspiritual." When used in conjunction here, they refer to the general attitudes of openness to discussing either concept.

5. To see how viewing mainstream media can affect students' attitudes toward death, see Edward Schiappa, Peter Gregg, and Dean Hewes, "Can a Television Series Change Attitudes about Death? A Study of College Students and *Six Feet Under*," *Death Studies* 28: 5 (2004): 459–74.

6. See Philip Africa's thorough *Keuka College: A History*, and its placing the founding of Keuka College as within the dying embers of the famous "Burned-Over District" of New York (Valley Forge, PA: Judson Press, 1974), 19–37. Also see Whitney Cross's classic *The Burned-Over District* (New York: Harper Torchbook Edition, 1965) and Paul Johnson's *A Shopkeeper's Millennium: Society and Revivals in Rochester, New York, 1815–1837* (New York: Hill & Wang, 1978).

7. Data from surveys conducted in both 2003 and 2004 by the Office of Student Affairs at Keuka College. Since this figure includes *all* Baptists, the number of American Baptists is undoubtedly far lower.

8. National Survey of Student Engagement, *Institutional Report 2004: Keuka College* (Bloomington: Indiana University, 2004), frequency distributions, 6.

9. Parker Palmer, *To Know as We Are Known: Education as a Spiritual Journey* (San Francisco: Harper, 1993), x.

10. As a result of those conversations, four of the group decided to contribute an article on the place of spirituality and values in teaching. See Michael McKenzie, Kenneth R. Williams, Anne Weed, and Thomas X. Carroll, "Values, Transcendence, and Teaching: A Symposium," *Journal of General Education* 52, no. 1 (2003): 1–26. The authors see no overt conflict with religion or religious values on campus as long as they are neither polemical nor aimed at proselytism.

11. *Chronicle of Higher Education* 51, issue 33, April 22, 2005, A1.

12. I accomplish most of this objective with on-site visits to religious sites, a topic covered elsewhere in this book.

13. See Benicia D'Sa, "Social Studies in the Dark: Using Docudramas to Teach History," *Social Studies* 96, no. 1 (January/February 2005): 9–13. Not surprisingly, the Internet has tried to keep up; see http://www.teachwithmovies.org.

14. For a good academic summary on the effectiveness of using film as a teaching tool, see Debra H. Bailey and Bruce R. Ledford, "The Feature Film as an Instructional Medium," *International Journal of Instructional Media* 21, no. 2 (1994): 147–55. They and others see such films' effectiveness as strongly supported by current cognitive learning theory.

15. Paul Weinstein, "Movies as the Gateway to History: The History and Film Project," *History Teacher* 35, no. 1 (November 2001): 27.

16. See Alasdair MacIntyre's *Whose Justice? Which Rationality?* (Notre Dame: Notre Dame Press, 1988), 99, 349–69.

17. Alasdair MacIntyre, *After Virtue* (Notre Dame: Notre Dame Press, 1984), 216.

18. Martha Nussbaum, *Love's Knowledge* (Oxford: Oxford University Press, 1990), ix.

19. Wade Clark Roof, "Religion and Narrative," *Review of Religious Research* 34, no. 4 (June 1993): 298. Also see Wesley Kort's, *Narrative Elements and Religious Meaning* (Philadelphia: Fortress Press, 1975).

20. See Bailey and Ledford, "Feature Film," 148.

21. Anonymous comment, Student Course Evaluation, Spring 2005.

22. As quoted by Bailey and Ledford, "Feature Film," 148.

23. Typing "death" into the database search on Internet Movie Database (http://www.imdb.com) results in hundreds of related movies. One of the positive elements

of this sort of pedagogy is the vast amount of material from which to choose. It is indeed true that "sex sells," but death's fascination makes it a pretty close second.

24. This of course is rational choice theory as applied to religion. See Rodney Stark and Roger Finke, *Acts of Faith: Explaining the Human Side of Religion* (Berkeley: University of California Press, 2000), 36–38.

25. Harold Coward, *Life After Death in World Religions* (Maryknoll, NY: Orbis, 1997), 1.

26. Kelley, "Conservative Churches," 39. For the purposes of this discussion, it of course makes little difference whether a particular tradition lacks a "Western concept" of God (e.g., Buddhism); each tradition still must come to grips with the stark reality of death and give an account of perceived meaning behind it.

27. Due to the large number of films available on death and dying, I regularly employ other films on this topic. The three chosen for discussion in this chapter are employed most often. *Defending Your Life*, dir. Albert Brooks (Geffen Pictures Productions, 1991; Warner Home Video, 1999); *Always*, dir. Steven Spielberg (Universal City Studios, 1989); *What Dreams May Come*, dir. Vincent Ward (Universal Pictures, Polygram Films, 1998).

28. These readings are found in Robert E. Van Voorst's *Anthology of World Scriptures* (Belmount, CA: Wadsworth Publishing, 2002), and World Cultures Resource Series, a custom text assembled for my course by Harcourt Brace College Publishers, 2000.

29. Richard Matheson, *What Dreams May Come* (New York: Tor Books, 1998).

30. See her analysis in "I Dream, Therefore I Am: *What Dreams May Come*," *Journal of Religion and Film* 4, no. 1 (April 2000), available online at http://www .unomaha.edu/jrf/IDream.htm. This sort of "primacy of mind" motif is also found in Richard Matheson's *Somewhere in Time*, a novel in which the protagonist travels back in time by thinking himself back.

31. Compare Booth Tarkington's sad ending of his novel *The Magnificent Ambersons*, with the more upbeat version of the final film cut (over director Orson Welles's objections, by the way).

32. Palmer, *To Know*, 34–38.

33. Ibid., 36.

34. Ibid., 76.

35. For the modern college student, death has replaced sex as the taboo subject, one which is the "principal forbidden subject." See Philippe Aries, *Western Attitudes toward Death from the Middle Ages to the Present* (Baltimore: Johns Hopkins Press, 1974), 92. In an oft-cited quote, sociologist Geoffrey Gorer calls death "the pornography of the twentieth century," quoted in Robert V. Wells, *Facing the King of Terrors: Death and Society in an American Community (1750–1990)*, (Cambridge: Cambridge University Press, 2000), 283.

36. Compare Wells *Facing the King of Terrors*, 287, with Goss and Klass, *Dead but Not Lost*, 253–54.

37. Wells, *Facing the King of Terrors*, 281–82.

38. As quoted by Bailey and Ledford, "Feature Film," 147.

BIBLIOGRAPHY

Africa, P. *Keuka College: A History*. Valley Forge, PA: Judson Press, 1974.

Aries, Philippe. *Western Attitudes toward Death from the Middle Ages to the Present*. Baltimore: Johns Hopkins Press, 1974.

Bailey, Debra H., and Bruce R. Ledford. "The Feature Film as an Instructional Medium." *International Journal of Instructional Media* 21, no. 2 (1994): 147–55.

Cherry, Conrad, Betty Deberg, and Amanda Porterfield. "Religion on Campus." *Liberal Education* 87, no. 4 (2001): 6–13.

The Chronicle of Higher Education. "Spirituality in Higher Education: A National Study of College Students' Search for Meaning and Purpose." *Chronicle of Higher Education* 51, issue 33, April 22, 2005, A1.

Coward, H. *Life After Death in World Religions*. Maryknoll, NY: Orbis, 1997.

Cross, Whitney. *The Burned-Over District*. New York: Harper Torchbook Edition, 1965.

D'Sa, Benicia. "Social Studies in the Dark: Using Docudramas to Teach History." *The Social Studies* 96, no. 1 (January/February 2005): 9–13.

Goss, Robert, and Dennis Klass. *Dead but Not Lost: Grief Narratives in Religious Traditions*. Walnut Creek, CA: AltaMira Press, 2005.

Johnson, Paul. *A Shopkeeper's Millennium: Society and Revivals in Rochester, New York, 1815–1837*. New York: Hill & Wang, 1978.

Kelley, Dean. *Why Conservative Churches Are Growing*. New York: Harper, 1977.

Kort, Wesley. *Narrative Elements and Religious Meaning*. Philadelphia: Fortress Press, 1975.

Laurence, Peter. "Can Religion and Spirituality Find a Place in Higher Education?" *About Campus* 4, no. 5 (November/December 1999): 11–16.

MacIntyre, Alasdair. *After Virtue*. Notre Dame: Notre Dame Press, 1984.

———. *Whose Justice? Which Rationality?* Notre Dame: Notre Dame Press, 1988.

Matheson, Richard. *What Dreams May Come*. New York: Tor Books, 1998.

McKenzie, Michael, Kenneth R. Williams, Anne Weed, and Thomas X. Carroll. "Values, Transcendence, and Teaching: A Symposium." *Journal of General Education* 52, no.1 (2003): 1–26.

National Survey of Student Engagement, *Institutional Report 2004: Keuka College*. Bloomington: Indiana University, 2004.

Nussbaum, Martha. *Love's Knowledge*. Oxford: Oxford University Press, 1990.

Palmer, P. *To Know as We Are Known: Education as a Spiritual Journey*. San Francisco: Harper, 1993.

Roof, Wade Clark. "Religion and Narrative." *Review of Religious Research* 34, no. 4 (June 1993): 298.

Schiappa, Edward, Peter Gregg, and Dean Hewes. "Can a Television Series Change Attitudes about Death? A Study of College Students and *Six Feet Under*." *Death Studies* 28: 5 (2004): 459–74.

Stark, Rodney, and Roger Finke. *Acts of Faith: Explaining the Human Side of Religion*. Berkeley: University of California Press, 2000.

Schwartz, Susan. "I Dream, Therefore I Am: *What Dreams May Come.*" *Journal of Religion and Film.* 4, no. 1 (April 2000). Available at http://www.unomaha.edu/jrf/IDream.htm.

Van Voorst, Robert E. *Anthology of World Scriptures.* Belmount, CA: Wadsworth Publishing, 2002.

Weinstein, Pail. "Movies as the Gateway to History: The History and Film Project." *History Teacher* 35, no. 1 (November 2001): 27.

Wells, Robert V. *Facing the King of Terrors: Death and Society in an American Community (1750–1990).* Cambridge: Cambridge University Press, 2000.

PART IV

Death in Context

IO

Death and Dying in History

Albert N. Hamscher

The study of death and dying in the past, and the search for the reasons behind changes in attitudes and practices, provides an ideal vehicle to investigate belief systems, cultural values, geographical differences, the contrast between urban and rural settings, the influence of demographic patterns, and the now-conventional triad of race, gender, and social class. An investigation of the reciprocal relationship between death and culture invites students to engage in introspection about their current situation. Why do I believe and respond as I do, and how did this come to be? If there has been change in the past, what are the likely directions of change in the future, and what large forces might be responsible? Confronting these questions awakens students' curiosity because the subject of death is not one normally encountered in traditional university courses. In order to profit from this initial curiosity, and to keep student interest at a high level, a course on death and dying in history should be structured in such a way that the ordinary tasks of reading scholarly literature and discussing it in class are complemented by opportunities for a "hands-on" experience with historical artifacts. The local cemetery is an appropriate place for students to observe and explore trends in material culture. In a term paper, they can relate the findings gathered in fieldwork to the readings covered in the classroom. This article offers practical advice concerning both aspects of the educational agendum—activities in the classroom itself, and suggestions for a broad range of research projects that can be accomplished in the cemetery.

In the Classroom

In organizing the course, the approach I favor is to divide it into two distinct parts (conveniently separated by a midterm examination). In the first part, students read books and scholarly articles that provide a broad overview of the principal historical developments in attitudes and practices surrounding death and dying in Western civilization from the Middle Ages to the present day. It would be beneficial, of course, to consider the process of change in other cultures as well. But the expertise of the individual historian can be spread only so thinly, and I have learned by experience that attempting to accomplish too much can result in a course that is both superficial and confusing.

Even with the focus on Western civilization, a major challenge in this first part of the course is to select appropriate readings.[1] Unfortunately, there is as yet no comprehensive textbook on the subject of death and dying in history. But Philippe Ariès's short book, *Western Attitudes toward Death from the Middle Ages to the Present* is a useful point of departure.[2] Ariès defines attitudes toward death in four large chronological periods. The first, Tamed Death, encompasses roughly the fourth through the eleventh centuries. This was an era when people accepted death calmly with both a sense of resignation to the inevitable and an optimistic view of the afterlife. The dying person actively participated in simple ceremonies that were public in nature and attended by friends and family members, including children. The twelfth through the seventeenth centuries were the period of One's Own Death, when visions of the afterlife became more complex and concern about individual salvation emerged as the predominant motif in western culture. In the eighteenth and nineteenth centuries, the era of Thy Death, strengthened bonds of affection within the family made the death of loved ones more difficult to accept. In the twentieth century, western culture entered a dreary period of Forbidden Death, when natural death became a topic eliciting feelings of unease and denial; a period that witnessed the disengagement of the living from the world of the dead and from death itself.[3]

Ariès's brief survey is not a perfect solution to the absence of a comprehensive text. If he is attentive to nuances in Roman Catholic theology, to important changes in the physical design of cemeteries, and to a growing intimacy within the nuclear family, he is generally silent about regional differences, the traditions of various Protestant denominations and Judaism, and the broad range of social and economic forces—from the impact of war and pandemic disease to the consequences of urbanization and the expanding power of state institutions—that shaped collective views of death and dying over time. His book is more descriptive than analytical. Nevertheless, recent scholarship for the most part has confirmed and elaborated upon Ariès's central observations rather than challenged them. His discussion of cemeteries is especially helpful because it gets students thinking about this subject early in the course. Using the language of contemporary students, I urge them to consider Ariès's work to be a "template," a "platform" similar to a basic computer program to which they can add, delete, and emend elements as the course progresses. In order to keep students engaged in the remote past during the early stage of the course, I also assign T. S. R. Boase's *Death in the Middle Ages: Mortality, Judgment, and Remembrance*, an insightful and richly illustrated book that both elucidates Ariès's major points and provides additional material.[4] When considering the modern vogue of death avoidance, I also have students read Geoffrey Gorer's seminal article, "The Pornography of Death."[5]

A consideration of the views of Ariès, Boase, and Gorer takes about three weeks. In the following three weeks, students read works that review important developments in the United States in three broad chronological periods—the colonial era, the nineteenth century, and the twentieth century. Two anthologies of scholarly articles that accomplish this goal are David E. Stannard's *Death in America* and Charles O. Jackson's *Passing: The Vision of Death in America*.[6] Even though the articles in these volumes were written thirty years ago, I consider most of them to be classics in the field and the equals of most recent studies. Taken together, the articles explore in an interdisciplinary way pertinent subjects absent in Ariès's brief survey: the theological roots of Puritan attitudes toward the death of children; death in Mormon thought and practice; the religious and gender foundations of consolation literature; the origins of the rural cemetery movement; popular as opposed to elite perceptions of death and dying; the impact of urbanization on funeral practices; the influence of scientific thinking, notably Darwinism, on views of death, and so on. The articles in the Stannard and Jackson collections can be supplemented with still other readings that broaden the horizon of topics that merit attention—Jonathan Edward's famous sermon "Sinners in the Hands of an Angry God" (1741), for example, and Viviana Zelizer's study of the emergence of the life insurance industry.[7] This concentration on American history makes sense in a course offered in the United States. But teachers in other countries can locate interesting scholarship that illuminates their own cultural settings.[8] The essential point is that pausing to consider developments in a single culture highlights elements of diversity in the experience of different groups and regions. It also encourages discussion about what elements of the cultural response to death have changed slowly over time while others have evolved more rapidly.

By the conclusion of the first part of the course, students have a grasp of the most important developments in Western culture in general and the United States in particular, as well as a set of basic principles that they can apply to the material covered in the second part. The overarching aim, it must be emphasized, is not to expose students to every conceivable issue that might have some bearing on the subject—an impossible task in any case. Instead, the goal is to help them to understand the most significant trends, to identify multiple causes for change over time, and to assess evidence of different kinds (the various genres of written sources, both elite and popular; material objects located on a wide spectrum ranging from stained glass windows to tombstones, and so on). In brief, the study of even an unconventional subject introduces students to the historian's craft.

The second part of the course is less structured than the first. Each week, the students read a book or several articles on topics that received only cursory coverage earlier in the course or perhaps were not mentioned at all. Changing at least some of these readings each time the course is taught permits the teacher to remain actively engaged—repeatedly using the same material risks numbing an instructor's own enthusiasm—and to introduce recent scholarship that complements the older studies that began the course. The range of possible topics is quite large and can span the breadth of Western civilization. The principal criteria for selection should be the quality of the scholarship, its clear relationship to death and dying in the past (even if the authors did not write with this subject explicitly in mind), and topics that pique student interest ("I always wanted to know something about this issue"). Over the years, I have enjoyed success with works on suicide, genocide (both in the Americas and in Europe), death in literature, death and the medical profession, the cemetery as a historical source, and the cultural response to diseases perceived to be incurable, such as the Black Death in the fourteenth century, tuberculosis in the nineteenth, and cancer in modern times.[9]

Topics of contemporary interest—the business ethics of the funeral industry, for example, and debates about "death with dignity" and the "right to die"—are also acceptable so long as the teacher ensures that class discussions place them firmly within a historical context.[10] Indeed, addressing some contemporary issues not only enables students to ponder and comment on subjects that have a direct bearing on their own lives but it compels them to recognize that current problems have historical roots. What appears to them at first glance to be unprecedented is more often than not revealed to be an expression of deeply embedded cultural patterns of perception and behavior.

Learning this essential lesson is particularly important in a course that will enroll many students who are not history majors. Moreover, a consideration of some contemporary issues allows the teacher to invite guest speakers who can bring expertise to subjects that the historian ordinarily lacks. For example, a funeral director can comment on, and perhaps offer a rebuttal to, Jessica Mitford's biting critique of the modern "death industry," *The American Way of Death*.[11] A monument maker can describe the technical aspects of the craft and explain how they have changed over time. A colleague in anthropology can introduce students, even if briefly, to a culture very different from their own. A religious professional can provide insights into the place that death occupies in one or several faith traditions.

Four additional observations about pedagogy merit brief attention. First, as every teacher knows, it is easier to preach the virtues of class discussion than it is to initiate and sustain one. There will always be students, even those who have prepared properly for class, who are reticent to speak up. Although there is no perfect solution to this problem, what does often work is to invite the students to speak about themselves and their families, to offer an anecdote or an observation about death and dying rooted in their own personal experience. This approach can be fruitful even if the reading under consideration is purely historical in nature. A series of questions along the lines of How would the people discussed in the work before us have responded to your story? or How are you different from them, and why? eases students into a discussion of history and gives them a fresh vantage point from which to observe their current situation. History need not be, nor should it be, disengaged from the present. Second, although a teacher must by necessity offer a series of "mini-lectures" to move matters along, I resist the temptation to lecture for a long period. The subject of death and dying is inherently an interesting one, and even a discussion that begins slowly will pick up momentum if one gives it the opportunity to do so. Third, as might already be evident, I assign a substantial amount of reading—a book each week or the equivalent in articles. I confess that I could not do this in an ordinary history course. But a course on death and dying is so novel to the students, the subject so intriguing, that I enjoy a "seller's market." Enrollment is limited to thirty-five students—class discussion would be difficult with a larger group—and the course closes quickly. I inform students immediately that the course will entail considerable work. Knowing this from the outset, most students will do what is expected of them.[12] Finally, as a personal preference the course I teach meets once each week for roughly three hours (with some breaks). This schedule allows the group to consider a single subject at one sitting without the process of frequently recapitulating the material.

A history course requires some kind of paper in addition to essay examinations. Students have diverse interests and some will be comfortable with a conventional assignment—a comparative book review, for example, or a "reaction" paper that requires additional reading on a particular topic. Students adept with the internet can compile an annotated bibliography of web sites devoted to the study of death and dying in the past. This can be a useful exercise so long as scholarly integrity is the principal criterion for selecting sites. In order to make a well-informed selection, the student must have mastered the material covered throughout the course.[13] For most students, however, I have learned over the years that some form of fieldwork is appealing because this activity is not often encountered in a history course. They welcome the opportunity to try something new, especially when it can be accomplished in a venue close at hand, the cemetery. I frequently receive letters and photographs from former students keeping me abreast of their most recent visit to an interesting cemetery. Fieldwork is the most successful teaching strategy I have ever adopted.

In the Cemetery

Cemeteries can be a valuable source for investigating a broad range of subjects concerning the collective values and attitudes of generations past.[14] The inscriptions and images on tombstones, monuments, and other objects of funerary art provide important insights into views of death, the relationship between the living and the dead, religious beliefs, and gender and class distinctions. Ethnic influences are often evident, as is the desire of planners and local authorities to offer citizens opportunities for cultural enrichment and to instill civic pride and patriotism. The physical design of a cemetery can reveal as much about prevailing business practices as it does about the evolution of the landscaper's craft. Applying the techniques of the amateur archaeologist, students can receive a "hands-on" introduction to historical demography. Working either alone or in groups in the "comfort zone" of local history, students can study one or more of these subjects either by comparing one cemetery with another or by identifying change over time in a single location. The cemetery even offers the opportunity for creative writing that is grounded in historical fact. Written sources, such as local newspapers, cemetery registers, and the minutes of the meetings of city and county commissioners, can complement fieldwork.

The recognition that a cemetery is an outdoor museum, an archive fashioned in stone and bronze, awakens curiosity and opens numerous possibilities for historical research. One need not teach an entire university course on death and dying in history in order to include the study of cemeteries in classroom assignments. Research in the cemetery can be integrated into traditional courses of broad scope, and local findings can illuminate larger regional and national trends and developments. Cemeteries also have the advantage of being readily accessible to the student because even the smallest community has one or more close at hand. To be sure, cemeteries fall on a wide spectrum, ranging from the churchyards, domestic homestead graveyards, and potter's fields of the colonial era and the early nineteenth century, through the rural cemeteries of the mid-nineteenth century and the lawn cemeteries of the late nineteenth and early twentieth centuries, to the most recent of all, the memorial-park cemeteries that first appeared in the late teens and 1920s and then proliferated during the 1950s. But all of them—large and small, old and new—offer the opportunity for serious study. Some basic reading by interested students and teachers hard pressed for time is all that is necessary to begin the quest; the creative energy generated by teachers working with students, and by students interacting with one another, will compensate for the lack of specialized knowledge.[15] What follows are some suggestions for research in the American cemetery. The list is hardly comprehensive; all the better if it stimulates thinking about additional possibilities. As is the case with reading assignments in the classroom, teachers outside the United States can adapt these suggestions to their own particular situation.

A longstanding cemetery, one that was established a hundred years ago or more and still receives interments, is an ideal place for research because the student can trace change over time in a single venue. Walking through a cemetery venerable with age is literally taking a walk through time as one moves from the older sections (normally at the entrance) to the newer ones (at the rear or sides). If such a cemetery is unavailable, students might work in several cemeteries that were established at different times in order to create a rough chronological continuum. In either case, several kinds of research projects are possible.

The most obvious project is to chronicle changes in the symbols and inscriptions found on individual tombstones and family monuments, and then proceed to relate these changes to larger social trends. For example, the rural cemetery movement inspired many cemeteries established in the mid- and late-nineteenth century. Mount Auburn Cemetery, established in Cambridge, Massachusetts, in 1831, was the model. These cemeteries promote a close association between the living and the dead. Walking paths cutting through small sections of plots presume that there will be visitors. Standing headstones or a small monument erected on a family plot require weeding and other maintenance, chores that until recently were assumed to be the responsibility of family and friends. The inscriptions and symbols on stones and statuary are there to be viewed and read. They create a silent dialogue between the living and the deceased. The presence of benches allows the visitor to pause not only to recall memories of the departed but also to reflect upon larger questions of life and death. A landscape rich in trees and shrubbery creates an oasis of retreat from the bustle of everyday life. A tranquil, natural setting, even if shaped by the human hand, is intended to disclose divine revelation. The time-less quality of nature provides a frame of reference within which the brevity of a human life can be contemplated and understood. In short, the rural cemetery and its descendants rest on a foundation of what I will call "six Rs": *regret* over the death of a loved one; *remembrance* of earthly ties; *respect* for the dead body lying in a restful place; the hope for *reunion* in the afterlife; *religion* in the sense of a "natural theology" revealed in a landscape conducive to moral uplift; and a high degree of *romanticism* expressed in such hopeful symbols as fin-gers pointing heavenward, two hands shaking with the word "farewell," and weeping willows that represent resurrection as well as grief. The entire en-terprise reflects Ariès's characterization of the nineteenth century as a period of Thy Death, when deepened sentiments of affection within the nuclear family made the death of loved ones more difficult to accept, and their inter-ment in less than a respectful, safe, and inviting place for remembrance in-creasingly intolerable.

Of course, some features of cemeteries established in the nineteenth century have disappeared in the course of the twentieth: walking paths and benches became rare, and religious concerns as well as family affection and solidarity are expressed in different ways. But enough of the six Rs noted above remain for the student to find examples. One assignment that will engage students in a hands-on study of the past is to have them take photographs of several tombstones or monuments. I have found three photos to be sufficient, and they should record the venue and time of visit. The photos can be of stones or monuments crafted either in the same era or in different historical periods. In a paper, students describe and discuss the meaning of what they have discovered, and then relate their findings to larger themes that have been addressed in the course: the emergence of a theology of hope, for example, and the subsequent waning of religious preoccupations and the appearance of secular themes; or the progressive centrality of the nuclear family and its consequences in the realms of sentiment, emotion, and memory.

Still other issues explored in a course can find resonance in the cemetery. When do patriotic themes begin to appear and how are they expressed at different times? The subject of gender—in its broadest sense involving men and women—is also on display in the cemetery. Are men always predominantly recalled as "father and husband," women as "wife and mother," or has there been change over time? If change has occurred, when did it begin and what stages has it exhibited? Do changes in the content of inscriptions reflect broader developments in American society? If a locality has cemeteries that are used primarily by people of the same faith or ethnic group, how do these cemeteries differ from those that attract a larger and more diverse public? Are the symbols and inscriptions one observes essentially the same or are they different? What sentiments are expressed, and have they changed over time? Posing such questions can result in additional research and reading on the student's own initiative, often about his or her own religious background or ethnic group. The study of history then becomes highly personal and the teacher has contributed to making historical consciousness a vital part of the student's life.

Acting as amateur archaeologists, students can also explore important demographic developments that are mentioned in every general course on American history, such as the increase in life expectancy and the decline of child mortality over time, notably as the twentieth century progressed. For this project, students select a sample of tombstones and monuments from several historical periods. To make the sample somewhat random—one must bear in mind that the experience of conducting this research is more important than the application of sophisticated statistical methods—they can rope off several sections, each with fifty or a hundred stones (the larger the sample the better). Using the birth and death dates engraved on the stones, students can then calculate the duration of life spans in the different periods. The exercise requires the students to perform some very basic statistical operations—calculating averages, placing data in columns denoting life span—that provide an introduction to the use of quantitative techniques to investigate historical subjects. Observing, often with astonishment, how many people in the past died in infancy, childhood, and young adulthood is an experience that few students will forget. Additional calculations can yield information about birth rates, family size, and the frequency with which men and women remarried after the death of a spouse. In some cemeteries, inscriptions reveal the local impact of death in war and of epidemic diseases such as cholera and yellow fever.

Finally, students need not always study change over time in a cemetery, although at first glance this might seem to be a curious statement coming from a historian. The cemetery offers a splendid opportunity for creative writing. In this exercise, the student selects a tombstone—one that is a half-century or older is most suitable—and writes a fictional biography of the deceased. For this project to have legitimacy in a history course, the story the student tells must be firmly rooted in national, regional, and local events and developments. Was the person selected born in the locality of burial or did he or she move there from another place? If the person came from either a nearby town or another region or country, what circumstances accounted for the decision to settle in the place of eventual burial? Did the person work, and if so in what kind of employment? Were there events on the local or national scenes that had an important impact on this person's life and choices? Did the person marry or remain single, have children or not? If unmarried, why was this so, and if children figured in the person's life, what became of them and other members of the immediate family who either settled locally or lived in distant locations? Did the person have adventures that recall notable historical incidents? Answering these and similar questions draws the student into the realm of real events, developments, and trends because the story must have historical plausibility. When a student enters into the stream of history and is encouraged to experience the Industrial Revolution, immigration to a growing city, the hardships associated with the Dust Bowl or the Civil War, the anxieties associated with a strike at the local shoe factory—the possibilities are literally endless—the history recounted in textbooks takes on a human form. Empathy with the deceased results in an appreciation of the experiences of previous generations.

Thus far, the focus has been on what we might loosely call the "traditional" cemetery, one whose numerous inscriptions, sculptures, monuments, and symbols offer an irresistible invitation to interpretation. But what is the student to make of the most modern cemeteries, those of the memorial-park variety modeled on Forest Lawn Cemetery in Glendale, California (established between 1913 and 1917)? By 1935, more than 600 memorial parks had been established, mostly in the West, Midwest, and South. Many hundreds more opened in the two decades following World War II. The memorial park is immediately recognizable by the absence of many of the attributes described above. Its guiding principle is the efficient and profitable use of the land. Walking paths have been replaced by gently curving roads suitable for the automobile. Instead of small sections of plots, graves are grouped in several large sections often called "gardens" (Garden of the Apostles, Garden of the Good Shepherd, Christus, Devotion, and so on). Statuary is limited to a single piece in each garden called a "feature"—a large Jesus crafted of marble, a painted scene of the Last Supper, the Lord's Prayer engraved in stone, and so forth. In order to facilitate maintenance and mowing, markers of granite or bronze are flush to the ground; they commonly record only the most obvious vital statistics (name with birth and death dates). Detachable urns are set in the marker and when upright often contain artificial (thus reusable) flowers. Except for the open lawns, vegetation is generally sparse. Nature, in and of itself, is no longer a source of instruction and consolation. Benches, if any exist at all, are usually located away from the gravesites. Perhaps the most notable feature of the memorial park is the disengagement of the living from the world of the dead. Indeed, the dead themselves are the least intrusive element in the landscape. The dialogue between the worlds of life and death is muted.

At first glance, the memorial park is an unlikely candidate for historical research. Indeed, many projects suitable for the traditional cemetery cannot be accomplished well in the memorial parks. Most of these cemeteries have not been in operation long enough to reveal much in the way of change over time. The absence of standing tombstones and monuments limits the amount of information that can be gleaned about collective attitudes toward life and death. Nevertheless, if memorial parks offer few opportunities for original fieldwork, they can be included in class discussions or oral reports that center on some important developments in modern American life. Because at the time of their establishment memorial parks were for-profit, private entrepreneurial enterprises, they provide insights into business practices and consumer behavior. To be sure, the hallmarks of selling the memorial park to the public—the concept of "pre-need" sales, the establishment of perpetual care funds, sales in the home, and the advertising of services—were not new to the twentieth century. But the "commercialization of death" promoted by the operators of memorial parks combined these practices in a particularly effective way to appeal to a population that was increasingly mobile and eager for one-stop shopping for plots, markers, and the vault or liner. Payments for a plot in small monthly or annual installments made expenditure easier to bear. Should a client move far from the place of purchase, a plot and related services were guaranteed by another memorial park that was a member of a large, national association—an early example of "portability." There were other selling points as well. Infants could be buried free of charge in Baby Land (most memorial parks have such a section). The memorial park also tapped an egalitarian impulse: with only flat markers permitted, a pauper need not rest in the shadow of a prince's elaborate headstone or family monument. Although many of the decorations in a memorial park reflect an optimistic, nondenominational Christianity, all potential customers were eventually welcome: racial exclusion clauses, for example, disappeared during the 1950s. In brief, the memorial park was, and is, as much a part of the "American way of life" as of the "American way of death," and each can be studied with reference to the other.

For students sufficiently mature to confront directly the subject of death itself, the memorial park can be a vehicle to study the feeling of unease, of discomfort that characterized American attitudes toward natural death in the twentieth century, a development that Ariès hoped to capture in a memorable phrase—not only "forbidden death," but also "death denied," death as a "taboo," even "the reversal of death." The topic is too complex to address here in detail, but students might be encouraged to think about how the memorial park reflects the public's withdrawal, or at best, its distancing, from the subject of natural death. The absence of standing headstones and the paucity of other visible reminders of the dead, the reassuring religious images that pose no threat to complacency, the verdant lawns that invite thoughts of leisure and recreation, and the rarity of benches at grave site that encourage the visitor to pause and contemplate all bear witness to the disengagement of the living from the world of the dead and from death itself.

Research on the cemetery need not be limited to on-site fieldwork. References to cemeteries in written sources, such as articles in a community's newspapers and the minutes of the meetings held by its local governing authorities (both municipal and county), have a place in student projects concerning many aspects of local history. For example, the establishment of a cemetery in a community often served as a vehicle to express civic pride and to promote the cultural enrichment of its citizens. Evidence of a far less optimistic vision of the cemetery—the cemetery as a source of embarrassment—also exists. Few cemeteries escaped some measure of scandal, usually centered on the misuse of funds (a problem that plagued many memorial parks) or significant lapses in a cemetery's upkeep. The public discourse surrounding cemeteries offers students a novel vantage point from which they can view a community's successes and failures, its aspirations and its disappointments.

A cemetery's registers of interments can also be used in creative ways. Registers dating to the nineteenth century and the early decades of the twentieth century can often be found in state archives, county museums, and municipal repositories. Because cemetery superintendents usually recorded age at death, registers of interments can be used to advance the kind of demographic research mentioned above in connection with tombstones. But some registers also mention the cause of death. With this information, students can explore the impact of certain diseases on the local level—the great influenza epidemic of 1918 is one striking example—and also observe the unfolding of important technological developments, such as the appearance and proliferation of the automobile (a significant cause of accidental deaths as the twentieth century progressed). References to the birth places of the deceased can add local flavor to class discussions and projects concerning immigration and internal migration.

As a final, personal observation about pedagogy, every cemetery has its bizarre and unusual objects, its extraordinary examples of eccentric behavior. It is natural that teachers and students alike will be drawn to tombstones and monuments that attract immediate attention precisely because they appear to be out of place in their immediate surroundings. Funerary artifacts that are unconventional have their interest, of course, but they should not obscure the common experience of ordinary citizens. If culture can be defined as repetitive behavior, students should be encouraged to concentrate on the ordinary and the mundane. What most people did most of the time—what they considered to be socially acceptable behavior—is the key to understanding values and attitudes that were widespread in different historical periods.

NOTES

1. Unfortunately, some of the scholarship mentioned in the notes that follow is currently out of print. Putting together a course packet of photocopied material is possible, however, and university bookstores have become adept at identifying copyright holders and receiving with little difficulty permission to photocopy books and articles for teaching purposes.

2. Philippe Ariès, *Western Attitudes toward Death from the Middle Ages to the Present*, trans. Patricia M. Ranum (Baltimore: Johns Hopkins University Press, 1974).

3. For purposes of preparation, teachers might read Ariès's longer book, *The Hour of Our Death*, trans. Helen Weaver (New York: Alfred A. Knopf, 1981), which presents his views with greater detail and nuance than the shorter volume that is best suited for the classroom.

4. T. S. R. Boase, *Death in the Middle Ages: Mortality, Judgment, and Remembrance* (New York: McGraw-Hill, 1972). For teacher preparation, a recent collection of articles that provides important insights into medieval culture is Eldegard E. DuBruck and Barbara I. Gusick, eds., *Death and Dying in the Middle Ages* (New York: Peter Lang, 1999), a work that is also richly illustrated and has an excellent bibliography.

5. Geoffrey Gorer, "The Pornography of Death," in *Death, Grief, and Mourning in Contemporary Britain* (Garden City, NY: Doubleday, 1965), app. 4.

6. David E. Stannard, ed., *Death in America* (Philadelphia: University of Pennsylvania Press, 1975); Charles O. Jackson, ed., *Passing: The Vision of Death in America* (Westport, CT: Greenwood Press, 1977). For teacher preparation, see also James J. Farrell, *Inventing the American Way of Death, 1830–1920* (Philadelphia: Temple University Press, 1980).

7. Jonathan Edwards's sermon "Sinners in the Hands of an Angry God" is available in many editions and anthologies, including *Sinners in the Hands of an Angry God*, Pensacola, FL: Christian Life Books, 2003; Viviana A. Rotman Zelizer, *Morals and Markets: The Development of Life Insurance in the United States* (New York: Columbia University Press, 1979), especially chap. 4, "The Impact of Values and Ideologies on the Adoption of Social Innovations: Life Insurance and Death."

8. See, for example, Vanessa Harding, *The Dead and the Living in Paris and London, 1500–1670* (Cambridge: Cambridge University Press, 2002), which has an excellent bibliography of broad European scope.

9. A sample of books with which I have had success in the classroom: A. Alvarez, *The Savage God: A Study of Suicide* (New York: Random House, 1972); Christopher Browning, *Ordinary Men: Police Battalion 101 and the Final Solution in Poland* (New York: HarperCollins, 1992); Norman F. Cantor, *In the Wake of the Plague: The Black Death and the World It Made* (New York: Perennial/HarperCollins, 2002); Albert N. Hamscher, ed., *Kansas Cemeteries in History* (Manhattan, KS: KS Publishing, 2005); Sherwin B. Nuland, *The Doctors' Plague: Germs, Childbed Fever, and the Strange Story of Ignác Semmelweis* (New York: W. W. Norton, 2003); Richard L. Rubenstein, *The Cunning of History: The Holocaust and the American Future* (New York: Harper & Row, 1975); Susan Sontag, *Illness as Metaphor* and *AIDS and Its Metaphors* (New York: Doubleday, 1990); David E. Stannard, *American Holocaust: The Conquest of the New World* (New York: Oxford University Press, 1992); Elie Wiesel, *Night* (New York: Hill & Wang, 1960); and Leo Tolstoy, *The Death of Ivan Iliych and Other Stories* (New York: New American Library, 2003). Several of the older works are available in new, paperback editions.

10. Since 1987, as part of their Opposing Viewpoints series, Greenhaven Press has published several editions, each with changes in content, of *Death and Dying: Opposing Viewpoints* (most recently, Farmington Hills, MI: Greenhaven Press; San Diego: Thomson/Gale, 2008).

11. A classic that never fails to capture students' interest. Jessica Mitford, *The American Way of Death Revisited*, rev. ed. (New York: Alfred A. Knopf, 1998).

12. If assigning a substantial reading list is not feasible, teachers can devote some classroom time to oral reports by individual students on selected books and articles. This approach has the virtue of at least exposing the group to a range of subjects and interpretations.

13. Web sites on death and dying are common on the Internet. But their quality varies considerably and most deal with contemporary issues, such as the hospice movement and consumer awareness. Three sites of interest to historians are http://www. trinity.edu/mkearl/death.html (a sociology site with historical information and links to other pertinent sites); http://www.geocities.com/ppollefeys/main.htm (death and art); and http://www.cmp.ucr.edu/exhibitions/memento_mori/default.html (death and photography in nineteenth-century America).

14. A substantial portion of this section of the article was originally published as "Talking Tombstones: History in the Cemetery," *OAH Magazine of History* 17 (January 2003): 40–45.

15. The reading assignments throughout the course are sufficient to prepare students for research in the cemetery. For additional background reading, the most important work is David Charles Sloane, *The Last Great Necessity: Cemeteries in American History* (Baltimore: Johns Hopkins University Press, 1991), which is comprehensive in its coverage, is very readable, and has an excellent bibliography. Two works that are essentially picture books but offer perceptive insights are John

Gary Brown, *Soul in the Stone: Cemetery Art from America's Heartland* (Lawrence, KS: University Press of Kansas, 1994); and Kenneth T. Jackson, *Silent Cities: The Evolution of the American Cemetery* (New York: Princeton Architectural Press, 1989). Since 1980, the Association of Gravestone Studies has published an annual journal, *Markers*, which has many specialized articles on research in the cemetery. The contents can be viewed at http://www.gravestonestudies.org/markers.htm. Beginning with volume 12 (1995), each issue has a bibliography of "the year's work in gravemarker/cemetery studies." Web sites concerning cemeteries are generally of mediocre quality. An exception that contains useful information is "City of the Silent," http://www .alsirat.com/silence/. The works of Ariès and Farrell cited in the previous notes discuss cemeteries, as do some of the articles in the anthologies edited by Hamscher, Jackson, and Stannard. Four noteworthy specialized studies are Edwin Dethlefsen and James Deetz, "Death Heads, Cherubs, and Willow Trees: Experimental Archaeology in Colonial Cemeteries," *American Antiquity* 31 (April 1966): 502–10; Harriette Forbes, *Gravestones in Early New England and the Men Who Made Them, 1653–1800* (Boston: Houghton Mifflin, 1927); Blanche Linden-Ward, *Silent City on a Hill: Landscape of Memory and Boston's Mount Auburn Cemetery* (Columbus: Ohio University Press, 1989); and Richard E. Meyer, ed., *Ethnicity and the American Cemetery* (Bowling Green, KY: Bowling Green State University Popular Press, 1993).

BIBLIOGRAPHY

Alvarez, A. *The Savage God: A Study of Suicide.* New York: Random House, 1972.

Ariès, Philippe. *Western Attitudes toward Death from the Middle Ages to the Present.* Translated by Patricia M. Ranum. Baltimore: Johns Hopkins University Press, 1974.

———. *The Hour of Our Death.* Translated by Helen Weaver. New York: Alfred A. Knopf, 1981.

Boase, T. S. R. *Death in the Middle Ages: Mortality, Judgment, and Remembrance.* New York: McGraw-Hill, 1972.

Brown, John Gary. *Soul in the Stone: Cemetery Art from America's Heartland.* Lawrence: University Press of Kansas, 1994.

Browning, Christopher. *Ordinary Men: Police Battalion 101 and the Final Solution in Poland.* New York: HarperCollins, 1992.

Cantor, Norman F. *In the Wake of the Plague: The Black Death and the World It Made.* New York: Perennial/HarperCollins, 2002.

Dethlefsen, E., and J. Deetz. "Death Heads, Cherubs, and Willow Trees: Experimental Archaeology in Colonial Cemeteries." *American Antiquity* 31 (April 1966): 502–10.

DuBruck, Eldegard E., and Barbara I.Gusick, eds. *Death and Dying in the Middle Ages.* New York: Peter Lang, 1999.

Edwards, Jonathan. *Sinners in the Hands of an Angry God.* Pensacola, FL: Christian Life Books, 2003.

Farrell, James J. *Inventing the American Way of Death, 1830–1920*. Philadelphia: Temple University Press, 1980.

Forbes, H. *Gravestones in Early New England and the Men Who Made Them, 1653–1800*. Boston: Houghton Mifflin, 1927.

Gorer, Geoffrey. *Death, Grief, and Mourning in Contemporary Britain*. Garden City, NY: Doubleday, 1965.

Hamscher, Albert N., Kenneth S. Davis Professor of History, ed. *Kansas Cemeteries in History*. Manhattan, KS: KS Publishing, 2005.

Harding, Vanessa. *The Dead and the Living in Paris and London, 1500–1670*. Cambridge: Cambridge University Press, 2002.

Jackson, Charles O., ed. *Passing: The Vision of Death in America*. Westport, CT: Greenwood Press, 1977.

Jackson, Kenneth T. *Silent Cities: The Evolution of the American Cemetery*. New York: Princeton Architectural Press, 1989.

Linden-Ward, B. *Silent City on a Hill: Landscape of Memory and Boston's Mount Auburn Cemetery*. Columbus: Ohio University Press, 1989.

Meyer, Richard E., ed. *Ethnicity and the American Cemetery*. Bowling Green, KY: Bowling Green State University Popular Press, 1993.

Mitford, Jessica. *The American Way of Death Revisited*. Rev. ed. New York: Alfred A. Knopf, 1998.

Nuland, Sherwin B. *The Doctors' Plague: Germs, Childbed Fever, and the Strange Story of Ignác Semmelweis*. New York, W. W. Norton, 2003.

Rubenstein, Richard L. *The Cunning of History: The Holocaust and the American Future*. New York: Harper & Row, 1975.

Sloane, David Charles. *The Last Great Necessity: Cemeteries in American History*. Baltimore: Johns Hopkins University Press, 1991.

Sontag, Susan. *Illness as Metaphor* and *AIDS and Its Metaphors*. New York: Doubleday, 1990.

Stannard, David E., ed. *Death in America*. Philadelphia: University of Pennsylvania Press, 1975.

———. *American Holocaust: The Conquest of the New World*. New York: Oxford University Press, 1992.

Tolstoy, Leo. *The Death of Ivan Iliych and Other Stories*. New York: New American Library, 2003.

Wiesel, Elie. *Night*. New York: Hill & Wang, 1960.

Zelizer, Viviana A. Rotman. *Morals and Markets: The Development of Life Insurance in the United States*. New York: Columbia University Press, 1979.

II

Teaching Outside the Classroom

Kathleen Garces-Foley

The last time I took students in my Religious Approaches to Death course to a local funeral home, there was a moment I will never forget. On a dare, one student climbed onto the embalming table while three classmates whipped out their picture phones to capture the scene. The clash between the stark technological surroundings and the laughter of the students signaled a breakthrough in the site visit. Though lacking in decorum (among other things), the student's stunt changed the tone of our visit entirely and moved the students beyond the anxious reserve that marked their arrival to the funeral home. For the rest of the visit, they ceased to be observers and became participants in their learning. Lucky for us, the funeral director had a sense of humor and welcomed us back again.

Site visits are a wonderful tool for learning about death, but they are fraught with unpredictability. For many instructors, they simply seem to be more trouble than they are worth: How will the students get there? What if it's too emotionally difficult for them? What if the host is boring or the students don't ask any questions? Not only do site visits entail a considerable amount of advanced organization, stepping out of the classroom also requires the instructor to give up a good bit of control over the learning process. Site visits may not be appropriate for every death class at every institution, but I hope this chapter will prompt many readers to consider using site visits, for, when thoughtfully integrated into a course, they are more than worth the trouble.

In considering whether to use site visits, the place to begin is with the course learning goals. Obviously, if a site visit does not aid in the learning process, then it should not be used. For example, site visits are not easily integrated into a course on death in literature. On the other hand, many death courses seek to examine how death occurs in various social contexts and diverse responses to death, dying, and bereavement. Site visits can add a great deal to the study of death as a social phenomenon. I begin this chapter by discussing the pedagogical reasons for using site visits and how they can enhance the study of death from a "lived religion" perspective. The remainder of the chapter suggests practical ways to maximize the success of the site visit, from planning the trip to student preparation and follow-up. Lastly, I make specific suggestions for integrating the most common sites used in death courses, namely cemeteries and mortuaries or funeral homes.

Lived Religion

The study of lived religion is, very simply, the study of how real people live out religion in their daily lives. This approach to religious studies stresses the dynamic and negotiated nature of religious practice in its social context. Rather than something one can "turn to," religion is enacted or lived out. As Robert Orsi puts it, "People appropriate religious idioms as they need them, in response to particular circumstances. All religious ideas and impulses are of the moment, invented, taken, borrowed, and improvised at the intersections of life."[1] Death is a major intersection of life, and as such, provides a particularly useful lens through which to study lived religion.

In teaching the death course from a lived religion perspective, I ask students to pay close attention to social contexts in which death and life intersect. How people enact religion in the face of death is not simply a matter of performing inherited religious patterns; it requires wading through the array of voices, such as religious elites, funeral specialists, media experts, and family members, claiming the authority to define the appropriate religious response to death. Religion is not a static system of beliefs and rituals but contested terrain. The challenge of teaching from this perspective is to bring lived religion in all its complexity and materiality—texture, scents, sounds, and movement—into the classroom.

The problem with textbooks is that they necessarily oversimplify in order to relay complex ideas in a small number of pages. Instructors often play the role of "debunking" the neatness of such generalizations, in order to relay to students the great diversity of religious expressions. Textbooks are also incapable of relaying the material aspects of religion, which is why it is so beneficial to use the "tools of the trade" described in this volume: novels, audio and visual aides, film, and guest speakers. These tools help to bridge the split between the academic world and real world that is exacerbated by overreliance on textual sources. Site visits can accomplish the same thing but in a much more totalistic and intense manner.

In the classroom, we can light incense, listen to dirges, watch videos of funerals, and pass around a cremation urn, but these encounters with the intersection of death and religion are taken out of social context. By moving students beyond the classroom, we force them to step beyond the comfort of academic distance and encounter religion and death on their own terms. No doubt they will learn things that the teacher had not intended. Joyce Burkhalter Flueckiger writes, "When the site visit presents and/or requires unfamiliar body language and position, students may learn about cultured bodily ways of being in the world. They may learn as much about different modes of hospitality or child-raising as particular rituals or sacred text."[2]

Whether the whole class goes together or students go on their own, there is much to be gained beyond the specific learning goals related to a particular site. By stepping aside and relinquishing pedagogical control, instructors allow student to become the primary investigators of the experience. Writing for the *Spotlight on Teaching* special issue "Teaching with Site Visits," Grace Burford reassures us this loss of control is only temporary: "You will resume the seat of authority soon enough, and nothing someone else tells the students will permanently ruin their understanding of the subject at hand."[3]

Beyond the encounter with lived religion, on a site visit students gain useful skills that are rarely nurtured in the classroom. As they are pushed into unfamiliar situations, they have an opportunity to hone their observation and investigative skills as budding field researchers. Interacting with those at the site calls for open-mindedness, professionalism, respect of difference, and inter-cultural and inter-disciplinary communication skills. Though few students will go on to a career requiring field research, these skills will serve them well as lifelong learners.

Ethical Issues and Other Challenges

A site visit can be challenging for students (and instructors) not only on an intellectual level but also on ethical, emotional, and physical levels. Even without a site visit, most death courses push students beyond their comfort zones. It is not uncommon for syllabi of these courses to include a disclaimer warning students who are grieving or currently struggling with a life-threat-ening illness to reconsider taking the class. A warning is all the more appro-priate if a site visit is required, since being in close proximity to death may be too emotionally disturbing or physically revolting for some students. Beyond the emotional and physical strain, there are also ethical issues that can arise. Simply being in a particular religious site or seeing a dead body may violate a student's own religious commitments or sense of propriety. Should a student lose credit for not attending a site visit under these circumstances? And what are the ethical implications of asking students to do more than observe? The site host may require that students don special clothing like a head covering, segregate according to gender, or sit for a long period of time. Students may feel pressured to eat ritual food, such as *prasad* or communion, or to bow in front of a religious image as others are doing.

Before including a site visit in your course, consider the emotional, physical, and ethical challenges it raises. Presumably any instructor of a death course has a much greater comfort level with death than the students do, so it can be hard to understand why students are so disturbed by some experiences. Bearing in mind their apprehensions, I would not require a tour of the morgue or obser-vation of an embalming procedure. Given how little exposure most students have to death, requiring students to look at, smell, or touch dead bodies may be so upsetting that little more is gained from the experience than "shock value." On the other hand, I have no qualms about requiring a visit to a funeral home, which offers a safe and sanitized experience of death by comparison. One way to make the visit easier for students is to allow them a choice among several options that elicit varying levels of "discomfort." If all these options seem too troublesome to require, the site visit can be offered as an optional assignment.

Having given this disclaimer, the challenges of the site visit are not a reason to stay in the classroom. In fact, addressing these challenges in class can be a means of intellectual and ethical development. In preparation for the visits, have students dialogue about what is going to happen at the site. Have them consider the implications of their participation or their choice not to participate: What's wrong with wearing a T-shirt with a lewd image when visiting a religious site? Does wearing a hijab make one a bad Christian or a hypocritical feminist? What will they do when the funeral director wants to show them the embalming room? What will they do when they are offered *prasad* at the Hindu temple? If they sit in a meditation posture, are they being Buddhists? How will they feel if there is a family grieving at a gravesite? Is there a polite way to refuse to participate? This kind of dialogue will help to minimize the students' apprehensions, but more importantly it will empower them to act with integrity and respect in uncomfortable situations.

When students go individually on a site visit, their presence may not be noticed, but it is impossible for a whole class of college students to be inconspicuous. It is important to consider the impact of a site visit on those who will be at the site. It is courteous and often necessary to get permission from the site host; "funeral crashing" is never a good idea! Assuming we want to have good relations between our department or institution and the site, we should do our best to establish a rapport and not to overstep our welcome. Even if the site host welcomes the students, there may be individuals at the site who do not, such as the grieving family at the cemetery mentioned above. As part of their preparation, students should consider how it might feel to be "observed" or to have "outsiders" in your sacred space. They can strategize how to minimize both the disruption of their presence and how to bridge the divide between student and subject matter.

Given that a class site visit is unavoidably disruptive, thanking the hosts for their hospitality can become part of the learning experience. Many schools encourage service-learning projects that give something back to the community. For example, if students are going to visit a nursing home or hospice facility, rather than simply observe, they could spend time visiting and playing games with patients or put on a presentation. Easiest of all is for students to send a thank you note or, even better, a copy of a reflection paper based on the experience.

One final ethical consideration is whether monetary remuneration is appropriate. In dealing with established businesses or religious centers, money is rarely exchanged, but smaller organizations may be quite burdened by the extra work created by a class visit. For example, I once took a class to a Hindu temple during the scheduled class time in the middle of the day. Since the temple was normally closed at this time, the brahmin had to put in extra hours. In this case, he had hinted that a donation would be appreciated, so I came prepared, but I would weigh this added cost seriously before returning to this site again.

Limitations of the Site Visit

Site visits are not guaranteed learning tools. Like everything else we do in the classroom, they work best if they are thoughtfully integrated with the course goals and material. When they are tacked on as a "neat experience," they often fail to prompt students to a deeper or more critical understanding of religion and become mere sightseeing ventures. There is also the danger of students overgeneralizing from a single site visit. Flueckiger writes, "It is important to remind ourselves that religion is not static and thus what students observe in a single site visit needs to be contextualized in time and place, with a realization that institutions, communities, and individuals change."[4] Students may draw definite conclusions based on whether the visit is a good or bad experience. For example, if there is a site host, he or she may be perceived as authoritarian and belittling of students who ask questions. Jeffrey Carlson cautions that a negative experience may confirm a student's preexisting stereotype: "Now since they have in their minds attained a kind of 'credential,' they may feel unconstrained in voicing their previous stereotypes."[5] These problems can be minimized by including multiple site visits in the course. Regardless of the number, however, the visits will be more successful if they are well planned and students are prepared for what they may encounter.

The Successful Site Visit

Planning: Where, When, and How?

How a site visit is incorporated into a course will depend on many factors that the instructor may have little control over. Does your institution have policies related to off-campus learning? Some schools require written notification to hold a class off campus and many prohibit teacher involvement in carpooling for liability reasons. In addition to university policies, there is also the student culture to consider: Are these students able to attend a field trip outside of class time? Do they have transportation? Can they and will they carpool? In my experience, the smaller the school the easier it is for students to attend trips outside of class time. Some instructors will plan all-day trips that include a meal and several sites. At the large, state university where I now teach, most students work full time and many have children, so I would not add to their strained lives by requiring them to meet outside of the scheduled class time. In this case, I ask them to do individual or small group site visits on their own time and arrange a site visit during the scheduled class time. To make this latter strategy work, I pick a site close to the school so that we lose little time in travel, but a few students still complain about the inconvenience of losing their coveted parking space by leaving campus.

If it is possible to hold the trip outside of class time, this will greatly increase the number of potential sites. With this freedom, it is possible to scope out what is available in the community and get to know the religious and professional leaders who would serve as excellent hosts. There may be a special event coming up that fits well with the course, such as a traveling exhibit of relics. Ideally, you can choose a site that both fits well with the subject matter and has a host excited to interact with students. Phone calls and a personal visit will allow you to evaluate the usefulness of a particular site. Ideally, the site host would be informed of what the course is about and what you hope the visit will accomplish. Just as students have apprehensions, so do site hosts, unless they are frequent tour guides. They may ask for copies of the relevant readings from the course or even questions in advance. You may learn from these early conversations that the site host has an agenda to share with the students. For example, a funeral home director may be strongly opposed to cremations and relish the opportunity to "educate" students about the dangers of corrupt memorial societies. If students are prepared to think critically about their encounter with lived religion, they will learn a great deal even when confronted with propaganda.

Preparing for the Visit

Preparations for a site visit should begin well in advance. Integrating the visit means tying it together with the course material both before and after the visit. In the classes preceding the visit, the instructor can point out how the understanding of death gained from the readings will be enriched and possibly challenged by the upcoming site visit. Questions may arise that the site host can answer better than the instructor, and students should be reminded to ask these questions on the visit. Students should also be given clear guidelines of what to pay attention to on the visit; they will get much more out of the experience if they are looking for specific things. Some instructors ask every student to answer a set of questions. I like to have students prepare their own questions as they reflect on what they want to learn through this experience. Below, I give specific suggestions for assignments for visits to the cemetery and funeral home, which can be modified to fit with other sites as well.

Several weeks before the site visit is a good time to begin going over the practical details of the trip, details which will need to be repeated several times. Unless the students are used to site visits, they will have many anxieties, which can be alleviated with clarity and direction rather than a laissez-faire approach. As far as getting there, maps and a cell phone number to call if they get lost are very useful. Carpoolers should be directed to get organized in advance by sharing phone numbers and establishing a clear meeting place and time. Since last-minute changes in drivers and riders is common, having a class phone list or a Web site that everyone is expected to check before the trip will help to minimize confusion.

They will also need to know what to bring, what to wear, and what to expect. Encourage students to only bring what they need for the visit and leave large bags behind. Be clear about whether or not they are expected to take notes. Rather than telling students what clothes they should or should not wear, use the site visit as an opportunity to dialogue about why people wear special attire and act differently in a space they identify as sacred or professional. Students can reflect on what it means for them to adhere to the community standards or deviate from them. For example, will it affect the way they are treated at the nursing home if they wear an "Old People Suck" T-shirt? Should they care whether they offend someone at the site? Does their answer change if they begin to think of themselves as practicing field researchers rather than college students?

Most important is to give students a preview of what is going to happen at the site and what they will be expected to do versus what they may choose to do. Above, I have already noted some of the common ethical issues that arise on field visits. Anticipating these issues and having a class dialogue about them is a perfect opportunity to discuss the insider/outsider problem. Encourage students to share their concerns with you in private if not in class, and try to find a compromise that will allow them to participate with integrity.

On the Visit

Careful planning will help to make the visit go smoothly, but one should always expect the unexpected. Students may get lost, arrive late, and chatter among themselves while showing no interest in the site. If there is a site host, he or she may be rude or abrupt, have little interesting to say, have too much to say that is not interesting, or forget to show up. How teachers respond to the site-visit-gone-wrong will be an important lesson in itself if we take seriously the notion of training our students to be future field researchers or, at the very least, lifelong learners.

We can model a flexible, adventurous attitude that finds ways to learn even in uncongenial circumstances. Though I always provide incentives for students to ask questions, such as extra credit or assigning several students as discussion leaders for that day, I find it helps to ask the first question and model how to interact with the site host in a respectful and friendly way. Then it is time to step back and allow the students to be the leaders. Chattering students are usually quieted with a glare of daggers or a discreet warning. Rude hosts are best treated with undue respect and gushing compliments, and boring hosts may improve with some direction from the instructor of what the students would be interested to hear. Ultimately, it is impossible to gauge the pedagogical value of a site visit in the moment. Visits that I have found terribly disappointing received rave reviews from students, and they may have actually learned something, too.

Follow-up and Assessment

After a site visit, it is useful to have students reflect on the experience individually before discussing it in the next class meeting. Specific questions can aide this reflection: How did the visit correspond to your expectations? What surprises were there? What made you uncomfortable? How did it add to or challenge your understanding of death and religion? How did our presence affect those at the site? What do you wish had gone differently? Individual reflection can be as informal as a personal journal entry or as formal as a research paper that integrates the visit with textual sources. These questions can ignite the class discussion as well, as can sharing from journal entries in small groups or a quick write at the beginning of class.

At the end of the semester or quarter, students should evaluate the site visit as part of the overall course. With more time to process the experience, they may make quite different evaluations than immediately after. Students who found the visits too emotionally difficult often come to appreciate the uniqueness of the experience after the shock has worn off. Still, chances are that some students will not, and negative evaluations should be taken into consideration.

Ultimately, the instructor will have to decide if the visit was "worth the trouble" and how it might be used more effectively in the future. Did the trip aid in the learning process? Did it have other learning benefits beyond the course, such as encouraging students to be active learners wherever they are or enlivening a stagnant class? If the visit was a bust, consider the practical problems students encountered and the pedagogical shortfalls. Before rejecting site visits altogether, consider using a different site next time and new techniques for integrating this "real-world" experience into the course.

Visiting a Cemetery and Funeral Home

Cemetery

Cemeteries make excellent field sites and visits are easy to plan. As public spaces, cemeteries have regular hours when visitors are welcome on the grounds, which makes them especially hospitable to individual site visits, though they can also be used for group trips. The cemetery may be one of the few death-related sites that students have already encountered. This time, however, they are not at the cemetery as grievers or thrill-seekers but as field researchers with a clear assignment. In preparation for the visit, there are a number of excellent pieces on the history of the American cemetery that students can read, such as Colleen McDannell's "The Religious Symbolism of

Laurel Hill Cemetery," and many cemeteries, such as industry-leading Forest Lawn in Hollywood, now publish Web sites.[6] In contrast to the traditional cemetery, students can research the "green burial" movement recently imported from Britain to the United States.[7]

INDIVIDUAL VISITS. Before sending students to visit a cemetery on their own, get to know the local cemeteries and their unique characteristics. There is a wide variation in what students will find at a cemetery depending on how old it is and the cultural background of the local residents (living and dead). It is far more preferable for students to visit a cemetery that includes a mausoleum than one that is merely a well-manicured lawn with identical plaques, so you may want to provide a defined list of optional sites, with descriptions, addresses, public hours, and, if available, the URLs. Prepare written instructions of how you expect this assignment to be carried out. Professor Nan Chico of California State University, East Bay, has created a Web site called "Resources for Death and Dying Courses" that includes instructions for a cemetery site visit.[8] Chico recommends that his students go with a significant other and if they go with a classmate they must work independently on the assignment. The Cemetery Project assignment involves three parts. First, students look at photos that previous students have posted on the class Web site to help them decide where to go and what to look for. Second, on the trip they are asked to write down and take photos of at least thirty observations and note their own emotional reactions. To guide students' observations, Chico provides a list of seven specific things to make note of:

1. Two to three different epitaphs; religious symbols of images; styles of headstones; crypts, vaults, niches, both indoor and outdoor styles.
2. The marker of an infant (under 1); a young child; a teenager; someone close to your age; someone with your first name, and/or your last name; someone who was born or who died on your birthdate or in the year you were born; the very oldest person you can find; a family plot; a husband-and-wife plot; a headstone that mentions the cause of death; one that mentions occupation.
3. Two to three indications of ethnicity or national origin.
4. Anything that you don't understand (other than a marker with a foreign language): a symbol, a custom or practice, etc.
5. Anything that surprises you, for whatever reason.
6. A conversation with someone who works at the cemetery.
7. Five to six different things left on or near a grave by visitors (note the date of death).

The third part of the assignment is to write a paper that ties together the thirty observations with the course readings and Web sites. Chico gives this advice for a successful project, "If possible, go on a weekday during business hours, you are more likely to find cemetery workers to chat with, and might even see graveside ceremonies (from a distance). Allow plenty of time to look around for awhile, don't just start writing down the first thing you find."

CLASS VISITS. If the class is going together to the cemetery, it is best to arrange for someone who works at the site to give a tour in addition to allowing time for individual exploration such as described above. The site host can explain to students the legal and procedural issues surrounding burial and on-site funeral ceremonies. Hopefully the host will be able to share experiences of working with people from diverse cultural backgrounds and the challenges of living in an increasingly pluralistic society. He or she should also have insight into industry-wide issues, such as how cemeteries are responding to the increasing use of cremation. Many cemeteries have created scattering gardens to meet new consumer demands and have changed their policies around burying cremains. Learning about changing death rituals from a death industry professional, especially if contrasted with reading materials from consumer advocates, can be an excellent lesson in social change.

FOLLOW-UP. As described above, students should be expected to reflect on the visit individually and as a class. A written assignment can help them to analyze the experience in relation to the other course material. Here is a short essay question that can be done in class or as a take-home: "What does the structure, design, and use of the cemetery suggest about our culture's approach to death?" For a more complex and involved project, the class could compare observations and develop a regional map of the cemeteries and their unique characteristics. This project could be posted on the Internet with individual histories, descriptions of interesting aspects of the cemetery, and analysis included. There are also a number of Internet sites where cemetery images can be posted for anyone to learn from.

Funeral Home

Because a visit to the funeral home requires the attention of a staff person, it works best as a class trip. However, if there are many funeral homes in the area, it may be possible for students to schedule visits at several different sites so as not to overburden any single funeral home. With the increasing popularity of cremation, finding a funeral home with a crematorium will add considerably to the visit. When making arrangements with a funeral home, be specific about what you would like to see and learn about, but be prepared that the home may not be able or willing to comply. For example, funeral homes need to protect the interests of their customers, and may not allow you to view any rooms that have bodies in them or even to see cremains. Expect that they will have rules about photographing and tape recording as well.

I have been fortunate to find a funeral home near campus that gets little business, so is often available for a whole class visit. Best of all, we are able to get a behind-the-scenes tour if the facilities are not being used—in other words, if there are no bodies there. Unfortunately, never knowing when a customer may need their attention, the funeral staff cannot guarantee their availability until a few days before. Our back-up plan is to go to a larger, busier funeral home where staff can show us the chapel and casket room, but the embalming rooms and crematorium are off-limits.

There are many excellent resources on American funeral practices that students can study before the visit. Many teachers assign Jessica Mitford's classic, *The American Way of Death*. I highly recommend using the concluding chapters from two recent books: Gary Laderman's historical *Rest in Peace: A Cultural History of Death and the Funeral Home in Twentieth-Century America* and Stephen Prothero's *Purified by Fire: A History of Cremation in America*.[9] For up-to-date and brief statistics on current funerary practices, students can study relevant Web sites, such as that of the National Funeral Directors Association (www.nfda.org) or read online the Wirthlin report, *A Study of American Attitudes toward Ritualization and Memorialization*.[10]

For a glimpse at the marketing techniques and products offered by the funeral industry, students should take time to look through an online site such as the Batesville Casket Company, where you can choose music to accompany your shopping (www.batesville.com). This will familiarize them with catch phrases of the industry (e.g., "facilitating closure"), and educate them on why the industry continues to promote the traditional embalm-and-bury funeral. By way of contrast, I have students learn about those competing with the funeral industry, such as cremation societies, do-it-yourself funerals, and online casket suppliers. Lastly, examples of the industry in popular culture, such as the HBO series *Six-Feet Under*, may be the most comfortable way for some students to prepare to step into a funeral home.

ON THE VISIT. Students should arrive at the site visit with questions in mind. For example, a visit to the chapel can prompt discussion of funeral rituals and the director's experience working with customers from a variety of religious and cultural backgrounds. If at all possible, ask to visit the embalming room and the crematorium. Some students may find this too hard, but many will want to learn about the technological processes of embalming or cremation and the legal requirements surrounding the disposal of bodies. Having done some preliminary research into the funeral industry, students will know that it is undergoing significant changes directed by consumer tastes as well as by the family businesses being taken over by multinational corporations. Students should come prepared to ask the site host questions about industry restructuring and future trends in funeral practices. Students may enjoy hearing about the latest trends in Webcasting funerals or in theme-based funerals, and the director can provide an insider perspective on these ritual innovations that have not yet been studied by scholars.

FOLLOW-UP. One way to follow up the funeral home visit is by assigning a research paper that incorporates the visit with the preparatory readings and additional research on a specific aspect of the funeral industry or funeral rituals. For a more hands-on assignment, the class could develop and conduct an on-campus survey of ritualization preferences among college students and be prepared to explain the different options in the process. The results could be posted on the Internet with an accompanying analysis and comparison with those provided by the Wirthlin report.

For a creative and fun assignment, which also serves to evaluate what students have learned from the unit on funeral homes, have them write a scene between a funeral director and a family with nontraditional requests for the funeral arrangements of its newly deceased matriarch. Provide the basic facts about the family: religion, class, and ethnicity, and ask students to describe a *plausible* script of the negotiations and outcomes. These papers can be shared or even acted out and then evaluated by peers on the basis of accuracy and plausibility as well as creativity. Lastly, these papers can be sent to the host from the funeral home as a thank you gesture.

Conclusion

These suggestions are only a small fraction of the possibilities for integrating a site visit into a death course. In this limited space, I have not even touched on visits to morgues, spontaneous shrines, or established memorials. Once we begin to think about how religion and death intersect literally on the street, the possibilities multiply. It is not where you go that matters so much as why you go and how the visit is integrated into the course work. A well-planned site visit is often the most memorable and transforming aspect of the course on both an intellectual and personal level.

Perhaps the most important reason to consider using site visits is that they are a unique aspect of the college experience. Aside from those few students who go on to become professional researchers, most will have limited opportunity for this kind of directed, hands-on learning between college and Elderhostel vacations. If we want our students to become lifelong learners we need to show them how to push beyond the boundaries of their familiar worlds with open-mindedness and an adventurous spirit.

NOTES

1. Robert Orsi, "Everyday Miracles: The Study of Lived Religion," in *Lived Religion in America: Toward a History of Practice*, ed. David D. Hall, p. 3–21 (Princeton, NJ: Princeton University Press, 1997), 8.

2. Joyce Burkhalter Flueckiger, "Unexpected Learning Opportunities of the Site Visit," in "Teaching with Site Visits," *Spotlight on Teaching*, special supplement, *Religious Studies News* 19, no. 4 (October 2004): ii. *Religious Studies News* is a publication of the American Academy of Religion, and includes *Spotlight on Teaching* each May and October.

3. Grace G. Burford, "The Nuts and Bolts of Site Visits," in "Teaching with Site Visits," *Spotlight on Teaching*, special supplement, *Religious Studies News* 19, no. 4 (October 2004): v.

4. Flueckiger, "Unexpected Learning Opportunities," ii.

5. Jeffrey Carlson, "Site Visits and Epistemological Diversity in the Study of Religion," in "Teaching with Site Visits," *Spotlight on Teaching*, special supplement, *Religious Studies News* 19, no. 4 (October 2004): iv.

6. Colleen McDannell, "The Religious Symbolism of Laurel Hill Cemetery," in *Material Christianity: Religion and Popular Culture in America* (New Haven, CT: Yale University Press, 1995), 102–31. Forest Lawn Memorial Park, www.forestlawn.com.

7. On green burials, see http://www.memorialecosystems.com/index.html.

8. Nan Chico, "Resources for Death and Dying Courses," http://class.csueastbay.edu/faculty/NAN/dd/dd.htm.

9. Gary Laderman, *Rest in Peace: A Cultural History of Death and the Funeral Home in Twentieth-Century America* (New York: Oxford University Press, 2003); Stephen Prothero, *Purified by Fire: A History of Cremation in America* (Berkley: University of California Press, 2002).

10. Wirthlin Worldwide (2000), executive summary of the Funeral and Memorial Information Counsel Study of American Attitudes toward Ritualization and Memorialization. The 2005 version of this survey can be purchased from the National Funeral Directors Association, www.nfda.org.

BIBLIOGRAPHY

Burford, Grace G. "The Nuts and Bolts of Site Visits." In "Teaching with Site Visits,"
    Spotlight on Teaching, special supplement, *Religious Studies News* 19, no. 4
    (October 2004): v.
Carlson, Jeffrey. "Site Visits and Epistemological Diversity in the Study of Religion."
    In "Teaching with Site Visits," *Spotlight on Teaching*, special supplement,
    Religious Studies News 19, no. 4 (October 2004): iv.
Flueckiger, Joyce Burkhalter. "Unexpected Learning Opportunities of the Site Visit."
    In "Teaching with Site Visits," *Spotlight on Teaching*, special supplement,
    Religious Studies News 19, no. 4 (October 2004): ii.
Laderman, Gary. *Rest in Peace: A Cultural History of Death and the Funeral Home in
    Twentieth-Century America*. New York: Oxford University Press, 2003.
McDannell, Colleen. *Material Christianity: Religion and Popular Culture in America*.
    New Haven, CT: Yale University Press, 1995.
Mitford, Jessica. *The American Way of Death*. New York: Simon and Schuster, 1963.
Orsi, Robert. "Everyday Miracles: The Study of Lived Religion." In *Lived Religion
    in America: Toward a History of Practice*, ed. David D. Hall, p. 3-21. Princeton, NJ:
    Princeton University Press, 1997.
Prothero, Stephen. *Purified by Fire: A History of Cremation in America*. Berkley:
    University of California Press, 2002.

PART V

Literatures *of* Death and *on* Death

12

Literature, Textbook, and Primary Source: Constructing the Reading List

Sarah K. Pinnock

The subject of death and afterlife has a peculiar appeal. I find that my undergraduate students have both serious and sensational expectations from my course Death and Beyond. Many are questioning their beliefs and hope that the class will provide clarification or reassurance. These students are looking for information on their own religious tradition as well as a comparative survey. Numerous other students seek reconciliation with painful feelings of loss: the death of a parent, the suicide of a best friend, a fatal traffic accident, a family war casualty. They gravitate toward readings on grief, trauma, and spiritual recovery. There are those curious about paranormal phenomena, angels, Satanism, or near-death experiences. Other students want to learn about death as preparation for careers in medicine, counseling, social work, teaching, or other fields. They appreciate clinically and culturally based studies of how religions facilitate coping with death. Given this variety of interests, constructing a reading list for a course on death is a daunting task.

Aside from these divergent motivations, another unique feature about teaching a university course on death is the stigma attached to the title. Students tell me that they tend to describe my course on death euphemistically as their "religion class" to avoid the awkwardness of mentioning the topic to peers and family. At first, I was amused that the title of the course in itself could be a conversation stopper among students, but I became less so when the same thing happened to me repeatedly. I routinely endure uncomfortable silences after mentioning that I teach about death, and I should mention that as a religion professor, I am already accustomed to peculiar reactions when I mention my field. Evidently, according to popular wisdom, anyone who takes or teaches a course on death has a dark or morbid streak. This uncanniness is proven by the level of suspense found on the first day of class. Apparently, some students are disconcerted by the fact that their professor is not a venerable gray-haired sage, but a cheerful thirty-something woman. My teaching experience has proven to me firsthand how taboos about death pervade formal education and everyday life. This awe is ironic given that Americans are overexposed to death as entertainment on television, in the movies, and in news reports that draw their largest audience pool with stories about crime, murder, war, and terrorism. However, these secondhand images of death do not assuage the insecurity provoked by the potential and inevitable death of parents, friends, family, and oneself. Perhaps this explains the paradox of coexisting opposite reactions that I observe in class: fascination and aversion. Awareness of student reactions complicates the teaching process, but it has also provided me with a special sense of purpose. A course on death provides a rare outlet for discussing a sensitive and crucial subject.

From my experience, courses on death should be less focused on quantity of historical knowledge and more on personal engagement with death issues. To foster such involvement, students may be assigned to write their own obituary or describe their own funeral. Especially with a large class, I have found graded journals effective in eliciting analysis of the readings while incorporating student reactions on a personal level. Students are required to write a journal essay of two to three pages per week in response to the readings. They collect their essays in a folder or binder, as the journaling is cumulative over the semester. It is my practice to gather and grade the journals on at least three occasions for ongoing feedback. Instead of tests that emphasize memorization, I typically assign take-home essay exams or provide essay questions in advance of an in-class exam. My priority on integrating personal responses and critical thinking is best served when readings deal with the experiences of individuals in various cultural perspectives.

In this chapter, I shall argue that for teaching death, narratives are indispensable literature based on pedagogical and multidisciplinary factors. On my syllabus, I place a number of book-length experiential accounts—from various genres, including fiction, memoir, and autobiography—about people coping with death. One reason to use literature is to overcome student stereotypes and the defensive barriers that distance them from the reality of death. Narratives function to relieve the study of death of polarized reactions to the topic as either depressing or entertaining. Literature helps demystify the encounter with dying and shows how facing death can encourage people to live life to the fullest. It also debunks truisms about the comforting role of religion. Students often naïvely assume that belief in an afterlife takes the sting out of death, and they have an underdeveloped sense of how cultural differences affect dying or grieving. In religious studies, professors continually battle the misconception that belief is the essence of religion. A similar fallacy occurs in death studies, with the assumption that knowledge about the afterlife is the main topic of concern. Textbooks that survey death and religion can reinforce this error by accentuating what is common within a religion and neglecting distinctive cultural practices associated with death, such as sacrifices, vows, spiritual preparations, funerary rites, mourning, and memorials.

Before I turn to discussion of the advantages of literature for teaching death, using three books as examples, I shall briefly discuss my encounters with textbooks. I think that it's helpful to do so for two reasons. Firstly, and critically, dissatisfaction with textbooks serves as the backdrop for my pedagogical argument in favor of narratives. Nevertheless, I have undertaken the quest for a suitable textbook and wish to share what I have learned. Secondly, and affirmatively, I want to acknowledge the usefulness of death textbooks for aspects of course preparation, even in a narrative-centered syllabus.

The Use of Death Textbooks: An Ambivalent Report

My use of literature in my course Death and Beyond intentionally disrupts student expectations for a course centering on a textbook that gives an objective survey of religious beliefs about death. However, textbooks still play a role in my pedagogy. In designing my course, I have consulted textbooks in order to better understand the broad field of death studies, as well as to gather comparative historical and cultural viewpoints on religion. As a preliminary measure, I advise that instructors examine interdisciplinary textbooks on death studies. In my case, as a specialist in philosophy of religion, the insights of mental health practitioners, palliative caregivers, sociologists, and social historians are extremely eye opening and instructive. When I started teaching this course, I obtained a desk copy of the well-known and comprehensive textbook by Lynne Ann DeSpelder and Albert Lee Strickland, *The Last Dance: Encountering Death and Dying.*[1] This book surveys the field of death studies, dealing with divergent subjects such as US death attitudes, health care systems, terminal illness, grief, funerary practices, death and the law, and statistical risks of death in the modern world. As a scholar of religion, I cannot help being dismayed by the fact that there is only one chapter devoted to beliefs about afterlife in world religions with approximately two pages on each major religion. Another background resource that I recommend focusing specifically on death education is *Death and Dying, Life and Living* by Charles A. Corr, Clyde M. Nabe, and Donna M. Corr.[2] Compared to *The Last Dance*, which is more historical and social scientific, *Death and Dying, Life and Living* focuses on practical coping with death and gives illustrative vignettes about dying and grieving alongside counseling advice. The discussion of death education in the first chapter is particularly useful to spur reflection on how studying death contributes to personal growth. As the title indicates, the authors advocate enhancing life through confrontation with death, an aim that deserves critical examination in tandem with comparative religious perspectives on how death awareness enhances living.

Among death studies textbooks such as *Death and Dying, Life and Living*, there is a strong agenda to advocate a specific model of what counts as a "good death." Death pedagogy is presumed to play a potentially important role for dealing with death and to fill a lacuna in American society. Personally, I have largely come to agree with this pedagogic conviction, mainly because of the impact of my class on myself and my students. Quite by surprise, my experience teaching death classes has deepened my appreciation for the fragile beauty of life. It has also made me conscious of what it means to be ready to die by living life to the fullest and keeping focused on what matters most. I am a product of an educational system that encourages critical distance, which is perhaps why I have been so impressed with how teaching death has often unintentionally opened up unique personal avenues of communication with students. Repeatedly, I have had conversations about painful events, such as the suicide of a high school friend, a motorcycle accident, or the death of a parent, where students are seeking to come to terms with painful experiences. The study of death can have a personal impact from both sides of the podium, and this cause-and-effect relation deserves meta-level consideration.

On a critical note, my perspective on teaching death as a professor of religious studies has revealed some shortcomings in the aforementioned death studies textbooks. These books tend to deal with contemporary America in generic terms, discussing how "Americans" grieve, bury, mourn, or make end-of-life decisions. They presume a white Christian social norm, and they presume that Americans are largely in denial of death. Attention to ethnicity, race, gender, or class occurs in special sections devoted to "culture" or "religion." Diversity is commonly ignored when dealing with attitudes toward old age, suicide, death denial, death counseling, medical ethics, coping with death, and scientific approaches to healing. Yet it is obvious that America has many cultural groupings that disagree about what counts as healthy, respectful, or appropriate, and disagree about what counts as a "good death." Moreover, it is not taboo to openly discuss death among all groups in American society.[3] The history of immigration to the United States makes cultural plurality basic and large scale, but textbooks in the interdisciplinary field of death studies, founded in the 1970s, do not deal with this diversity adequately. I have found that a major advantage of a comparative religious perspective toward death is the working assumption that responses to death vary a great deal among ethnic and religious groups in America, and the study of global religious perspectives supplies additional complexity. In designing a course on death and religion, inevitably there is consideration of people from many nations, races, historical periods, and non-Christian cultures. Cultural relativity toward death should be recognized from the start.[4]

As I have searched for cross-cultural approaches to death for my syllabus, I have appreciated the anthology called *The Path Ahead*, compiled by the authors of *The Last Dance*.[5] Many selections in this reader address factors of ethnicity, nationality, and race, and it also exposes students to diverse disciplinary approaches. For instance, there are unique essays on religion and culture dealing with funerary practices among Hmong immigrants in the United States, hospital care for dying Native Canadian patients, low suicide rates among African-American men compared to white men, and the normalization of infant death among poor women in rural Brazil. Other excerpts on medical ethics, grief, hospice, death education, and coping with mortality also raise religious issues. The use of readings dealing with social work and health care foster reflection not only on the internal dynamics of religion but also on how religious practices have an impact on health and society. It is a growing edge of death studies in the United States to more adequately deal with religious and cultural diversity and to include more international perspectives. To this end, *The Path Ahead* is a reader that broadens the cultural scope of death studies.[6]

Doing research for my syllabus, I have perused numerous textbooks by religion scholars intended to give a comparative survey of perspectives on death. Such books are organized according to major religion, typically with one chapter on each religion. I have found that there are more edited books than single-author textbooks.[7] The advantages of edited books are that the authors are specialists, each religion is considered on its own terms, and an insider perspective is possible. Authors discussing Islam and Asian religions are less likely to be insiders, but this asymmetry is lessening. The advantages of a single-author book are thematic coherence and symmetry in the approach to each religion.[8]

My misgivings about survey textbooks are familiar to professors from many disciplines. There is the problem of providing a historical introduction to the subject matter that is concise yet detailed and readable. Background in religion is required for students who are not religion majors. To meet this need, textbooks on death spend much time on the origins of a religion and its sacred writings, yet this historical component can become weighty. In particular, death and religion textbooks tend to be oriented toward philosophical views of the soul and afterlife as opposed to focusing on rituals and material culture. Exposition of scripture and doctrine usually take priority over examining differences in social class or region. The standard textbook has chapters on Judaism, Christianity, Islam, Hinduism, and Buddhism, and often Chinese, African, Egyptian, or Greek religion. What is often lacking is account of pluralism within a given religion, as well as geographic, economic, racial, and cultural factors. Whether single- or multi-authored, textbooks with one religion per chapter usually oblige the instructor to give additional background for each religion to elaborate, which generates an excess of information for students to handle. On top of these drawbacks, this type of textbook validates the consumer style of knowledge acquisition that comes naturally to many undergraduates.

In the past few years, I have assigned a textbook on death and world religions to complement the death literature component of the course that is central. Overcoming my resistance to textbook format stems from two main factors: organizational convenience and student preference. University students are keen to obtain an overview of religious viewpoints on death that is not always satisfied by a sampling of case studies and literature on death experiences, even if that is the approach that seems most academically responsible to me. Moreover, I find a textbook useful to contextualize the narratives on the syllabus, precisely to show students how religious encounters with death have unique cultural contexts. Although it may seem counterintuitive, I strategically have the students read the survey textbook *after* reading literature on death experiences, so that they become aware of the fraught decisions that underpin generalizations about religious responses to death.

The textbook that I have used recently is *The Sacred Art of Dying* by Kenneth Kramer.[9] This book focuses on the quest for the meaning of life and death in world religions. The scope includes Abrahamic (Judaism, Christianity, Islam) and Eastern religions (Hinduism, Chinese religions, and Theravada, Zen, and Tibetan Buddhism), as well as Native American, ancient Greek, and Mesopotamian religions. The chapters are short and selective; they begin with sacred writings and mythical stories about deities or founding figures, and end with consideration of death rituals. Unlike most textbooks, there is no attempt to cover each era of history within a given religion. Instead, each section of the chapter covers a separate story or theme, which makes the book very readable. Each chapter includes a number of perspectives, often contrasting views within one religion, and these narratives open up multiple levels of interpretation. With such brief treatment of each religion, there is the danger of giving students a skewed impression. In using this book, providing a historical context is extremely important.

Somewhat ironically, one of the strengths of *The Sacred Art of Dying* is that the style of the book actually calls into question, and deconstructs, the possibility of an objective survey textbook that students expect. The text is more selective than encyclopedic, and more interactive than authoritative. It invites the class to examine the choices of the author in organizing each chapter and opens up methodological questions about approaches to the study of religion. In significant ways, the textbook shares my priority on interrogating religion on an imaginative subjective level as well as on an intellectual critical level that I apply to literary narratives. Kramer gives prompts for journal exercises at the end of each chapter, asking questions such as What does a person value most when faced with death? and What is the most sacred way of dying? In courses where there is a blend of disciplinary approaches and a preference for cultural case studies, this book does the job of giving a brief historical overview of world religions while raising practical questions about coping with death and methodological issues about religious generalizations.

Literature as Primary Source

Since the study of literature concretizes discussion about death and religion, it is appropriate to look concretely at books that have earned a place on my syllabi year after year. In the following pages, I shall discuss three texts that I have found particularly effective: *The Death of Ivan Ilyich* by Leo Tolstoy, *I Heard the Owl Call My Name* by Margaret Craven, and *Night* by Elie Wiesel. These books articulate in distinctive voices firsthand encounters with death and dying. Such narratives situate religion culturally without reducing death or religion to philosophical and theological abstractions. Approached as primary source literature rather than textbook, the stories foster a classroom discussion format consistent with my priority on creative personal engagement and critical thinking.

The Death of Ivan Ilyich

The Death of Ivan Ilyich is a novella written in the later part of Tolstoy's life, during a period of religious searching.[10] It has also become a classic text in death studies because of its perceptive depiction of illness, social norms, and religious transformation. The book begins abruptly with the announcement of the protagonist's death to his fellow civil servants in the law courts. They react with cold speculation on the financial consequences of his death and career promotions involved in replacing him. The reader sees the household mourning process through the eyes of Ivan's childhood friend and colleague, Pyotr Ivanovich, who observes the mixed reactions of the family and guests. Pyotr vacillates between sympathy for Ivan's suffering, relief that death happened to Ivan and not himself, and a barely acknowledged fear of dying. Meanwhile, Pyotr admires his sophisticated friend Schwartz, scheming to play cards instead of mourn Ivan and impervious to the disturbing impact of death. The upper-class government employees, Ivan's associates, display hypocrisy in coping with death, and the trappings of Orthodox rituals provoke awkwardness rather than soul searching. Even Ivan's wife is concerned mainly about financial details and maintains a superficial sense of decorum. *The Death of Ivan Ilyich* makes an excellent first book of the semester because it portrays social discomfort with death that extends into the classroom. I use the book to discuss the social awkwardness that students have witnessed in their own lives when dealing with a death—problems about what to say to the bereaved family, how to dress and act at a funeral, and how to hide one's own fears and discomfort. The book's negative portrayal of institutionalized religion confirms some students' perceptions of religious funeral ceremonies as awkward and artificial. Evidently, there are similarities between Tolstoy's Russia and today's America.

One might feel sorry for Ivan Ilyich as a dying man, until learning that he exemplified the pretentious and mercenary attitudes of his companions. He was always trying to secure a more lucrative and prestigious job, and his marriage was one of convenience. If confronted with a friend's death, Ivan would have behaved as coldly as Schwartz. However, Ivan falls ill just as his career seems to have reached its peak. Ironically, his illness derives from a ladder accident that occurs while decorating new living quarters to celebrate a job promotion. Ivan comes to see his former life as false: individualistic, materialistic, competitive, devoid of happiness, and fearful of death. His prestige is lost, as a dying man. To give a psychological perspective on Ivan's experience, I lead the class through Elisabeth Kübler-Ross's five stages of dealing with death, alongside Ivan's story.[11] In the novella, there are readily available examples of denial, anger, bargaining, depression, and acceptance, as Ivan consults multiple doctors, pretends nothing is wrong, blames his wife, pities himself, and finally dies in peace. It may seem peculiar that a work of fiction lends medical insight. However, in Bill Moyers's documentary on palliative care, *On Our Own Terms*, a clinician specifically mentions *The Death of Ivan Ilyich* as a must-read for doctors and caregivers in order to help understand the dying patient's experience.[12] Ivan's struggle sheds insight on the turbulent alterations in self-identity and values that accompany terminal illness. Through his powers of imagination, assisted by impending old age, Tolstoy vicariously works through the confrontation with death in the person of Ivan.

Further, the book is perceptive in dealing with not only social denial of death and the acceptance of terminal diagnosis but also in life philosophy. As his sickness worsens, Ivan becomes obsessed with the idea that his career success might have been inversely proportional to true happiness. He concludes bitterly that his life "was not the real thing but a dreadful, enormous deception that shut out both life and death."[13] Only his memories of childhood seem to embody goodness and "reality" for Ivan as a dying man, and he can hardly believe how long he deceived himself with false values. His servant Gerasim is the only comforting presence at his sickbed, in contrast with his wife, daughter, and friends. Gerasim treats death simply as he fetches things and holds up Ivan's legs to alleviate the pain. Even more than his service to Ivan, Gerasim's honest sympathy helps Ivan face up to the dishonesty of his peers (and himself) regarding death. The class difference between Gerasim and Ivan correlates with true and false perspectives on life, as Tolstoy envisions them. In his writings, Tolstoy displays admiration for the morality and spirituality of Russian peasants, to whom he attributes natural sincerity and compassion. The pity of the servant Gerasim is a foil for the superficial posturing of Ivan's wife, daughter, and contemporaries.[14]

The other figure who exhibits an honest reaction to Ivan's dying is his adolescent son, who shows emotion but lacks the maturity to support his father. Only a few hours before his death, Ivan stops regretting his error in missing "the real thing" and tries to find it. When he accidentally flails in the direction of his son's head, and his son kisses his hand and cries, Ivan has an epiphany. Suddenly he grieves for his son and his wife standing at his bedside, and he wants to relieve their pain on his behalf. His fear is gone, and his last words to himself are, "There is no more death."[15] In discussion, I ask the class: what heals Ivan? One answer is human touch. But there are also religious dimensions to his transformation, although God is nominally absent.[16] When Ivan takes the sacrament at his wife's request, he briefly feels hope, but the hope is connected with finding a cure, which amounts to bargaining for healing rather than accepting the truth. Yet in Ivan's last three days of incessant screaming, there is Christian symbolism of suffering followed by resurrection. His last word to his wife and son is "forgive," as Jesus forgives his tormentors from the cross. When in his weakness Ivan says "forget" instead, he accepts it "knowing that He [presumably God] who needed to understand would understand."[17] He endures the depths and is reborn into light, a journey which resembles a near-death experience in its visualization of moving from darkness into light, and its resultant transformation of Ivan's consciousness. Like a Christ figure, Ivan's agony is ultimately redemptive. Ivan finds bliss in the moments before death, and death is no longer the end. Tolstoy gives little credit to organized religion, either in the novella or in his religious writings; the religious reality that Ivan discovers is eternal life and love.

If you were faced with dying, like Ivan, would you revise your priorities? When I pose this question to students, I am raising issues about values that do not necessarily require death as a prompt. But like Ivan, many of us are not willing to face the eventuality of death, and Tolstoy is correct that the reference point of death can become a criterion for truthfulness. The university classroom is an appropriate place to examine logical consistency in values, even if the answers are individual. Also, I ask students to extrapolate from the book to reflect on whether, if after his epiphany Ivan miraculously recovered, he would live differently. Idealistic students propose that he would become a devoted father and husband, a merciful lawyer, and a philanthropist. I challenge them with Tolstoy's indictment of the deep hypocrisy of upper-class life where ambition and wealth corrupt, and honest simplicity is found only in the poor servant. On the other hand, cynical students claim that Ivan would slide back into his career and the only lasting effect of his epiphany would be sentimental appreciation of childhood or comforting belief in eternal life. I encourage them to think about the potential for awakening or conversion to new values, whether due to rational reflection on mortality, religious experience, or a serious illness. *The Death of Ivan Ilyich* serves as a case study that simultaneously raises issues about class values, social avoidance of death, care for the dying, institutional religion, and moral awakening.

I Heard the Owl Call My Name

I Heard the Owl Call My Name is situated on the Northwest Pacific coast of Canada among Kwakiutl indigenous fishing villages. The cross-cultural dimension of the book relates native perspectives towards death through a Christian lens.[18] The main character is a young Anglican priest named Mark whose bishop sends him to preside over a shabby church in a small native settlement called Kingcome by colonists. Mark is unaware that he is ill and has no more than three years to live. However, his bishop knows, and sends him to this difficult parish on purpose, in order to learn "enough of the meaning of life to be ready to die."[19] In Craven's narrative, the bishop's paternalistic intent, which might seem manipulative, benefits Mark who becomes integrated into the native community. The reader's expectations for a book about someone gradually preparing to die, as Ivan Ilyich did, are thwarted by the fact that Mark does not discover his illness until the last few pages of the book. Instead, the theme of death pervades the environment of the village as Mark encounters numerous actual deaths often caused by the harsh conditions and isolated location.

In native religion, the myth of the "swimmer" or salmon offers a parable of meaningful death. The female salmon struggles upstream from the sea to lay her eggs and then slips exhausted downstream, tail first, as she dies. Mark's native guide, Jim, takes him to watch the embattled swimmer in her last moments, along with Marta and Keetah. Marta, an elderly native woman, identifies Mark as one of the salmon people because he has a twin sibling, and twins are always considered swimmers in Kwakiutl folklore. To the surprise of his companions, Mark is able to recite a native prayer for the swimmer that he had read about before coming to the village; for the first time, Jim begins to drop his guard with the priest. Keetah, a young native woman, sees the swimmer's death as sad. But like Marta, Mark disagrees and sees the death of the swimmer as natural and good. Mark's attitude toward its death shows prescience, as he remarks: "The whole life of the swimmer is one of courage and adventure. . . . When the swimmer dies he has spent himself completely for the end for which he was made, and this is not sadness. It is triumph."[20] This sense of completion proves true for Mark's own life, where grief is counterbalanced by participation in community and harmony with nature. He learns from native religion to understand the integration of nature and culture, where the village is part of the river and animals symbolize human experience.[21] The myth suggests the inevitability of the life cycle, and even though Mark does make choices, there is no question that he is where he should be to fulfill his destiny.

Mark is instinctively respectful to native customs, which is why he does not resent the cool reticence of villagers or their non-Christian religious practices. During his first week in the village, Mark is not threatened when, after a Christian funeral he performs for a young boy, the tribe remains gathered in order to recite ancient burial rituals in the native language of Kwakwala. Later, the village elders trust him enough to ask for help to restore the old overgrown forest burial ground. In the past, the people buried the dead in open coffins suspended from the branches of trees, where the bodies of the dead were eaten by birds to help the spirit's rebirth remain in the human or animal realm.[22] Mark helps rebury grave objects and human remains in the ancient burial ground, since the tribe now uses underground burial stipulated by Canadian law. Another death custom banned by the government is the cannibal dance, or *hamatsa*, that took place during the Winter Ceremonies. Mark learns that the specially chosen hamatsa dancer would be ceremonially abducted by spirits and lived in the forest to undergo purification. When the hamatsa dancer first returned, he would claw other dancers, bite the flesh of onlookers, and perhaps draw blood. But through a series of rituals lasting four days, he was eventually cured of possession and restored to the community. The possessed dancer was rumored to eat human flesh, which horrified Christian colonists. Moreover, white legislators outlawed the custom of potlatches, a tradition of inter-tribal visitation and gift exchange sometimes held as a death memorial.[23] From his native friends, Mark hears rumors about how a potlatch squandered the wealth of the proud host, who would prove his wealth by giving extravagant gifts and feasts to guests who stayed for many days of festivities. Rather than understand the potlatch as a communal ritual reciprocated between tribes, colonists demeaned it as wasteful and senseless.[24] Mark views the old burial customs, the hamatsa dance, and the potlatch as lost traditions that grieve the native villagers. They mourn for the traditional ways, yet they do not resent him as part of white civilization.

To give students insight into contemporary native rituals, I show a documentary film about an Alaskan Athabaskan potlatch in honor of a young man who drowned.[25] I ensure that the class is well aware that the film depicts a different tribe, decade, and region of the Pacific Northwest coast. The minimally edited footage has a real-life quality that is instructive. Students who expect natives to paddle canoes and wear traditional garb are surprised to see them drive powerboats and wear baseball caps. The film de-romanticizes native religion as it shows the modern equipment and dress of everyday life in a working-class setting. Where in the past potlatch gifts consisted of wooden carvings and foodstuffs, today gifts include refrigerators, guns, and blankets. It is poignant to see the father of the deceased man and his relatives hitting sticks together and chanting verses expressing grief. The class discusses the benefits of having a memorial potlatch many months after the death. It honors the deceased with multiday festivities, and gives the family time to come to terms with the loss emotionally before the memorial is planned. In America, the funeral most often happens within a week of the death and there is usually no public follow-up event to commemorate the loss.[26]

In *I Heard the Owl*, the tone of village life is permeated by sadness. For the reader, this somber mood reflects Mark's terminal diagnosis, but materially, it stems from the poverty of the village of Kingcome as well as from cultural death. The village's remote location makes paid employment rare, and lack of accessible medical facilities raises mortality rates, especially for childbirth and emergencies. To encourage students to think about this problem in present-day conditions, I assign an article on palliative care for native Canadians.[27] This reading discusses how medical "interpreters" are needed on behalf of native patients to mediate conflicts about care for the dying, where native values conflict with medical science. Hospital care tends to isolate the patient, as opposed to native priority on an extensive network of visitors. The need to be evacuated to a hospital exacerbates this isolation. Moreover, native beliefs in spiritual causation are not tolerated by medical science, and the native preference for noninterference in medical treatment can seem ignorant or negligent.

Other sources of sadness stem from the inevitability of continued cultural deterioration in the future. The village children attend English school in a distant city, where they lose their native language and become enamored with technology and modern life. Native young people face many troubles. At one point, Keetah's sister brings her white fiancé from the city to the village. He cheats her uncle in the purchase of a ceremonial mask during a drinking binge, and later abandons her unmarried in the city, where she dies on the streets from a drug overdose. Also, Gordon, Keetah's boyfriend, who has always respected village customs, decides to pursue an urban career after his university studies. In the end of the novel, there is a slim hope for the village in Keetah's return from the city because of her engagement to Jim. But even young people who preserve the old ways see that they are dying.

The story ends with Mark's funeral conducted by an elder in the Kwakwala language. Marta remarks to herself that Mark is going "to the land of our Lord" while the old man Peter listens at night for Mark's spirit to return to the village in animal form.[28] *I Heard the Owl* plays gently with the irony that white man's presence, including the church, is a reason for cultural death in the village, yet the priest plays a constructive role. The final sudden twist in the plot has Mark die in a landslide during a boat trip with Jim. Mark has little time to face the journey toward death, compared to Ivan Ilyich. We can only assume that the bishop was correct: the village would prepare Mark for death. Although it is still nature that kills Mark, the cause is a natural disaster rather than disease. In the forest, nature is a destroyer as well as the symbolic continuity of the tribe. The final message is that life can be cut off at any point; therefore, people must make decisions according to their deepest values.

The blending of religions leaves unanswered questions for the class. Characters such as Mark and Marta meld the native belief in spirits that move between animals and humans with the Christian idea of divine being that existed before the white man arrived.[29] I pose the issue of pluralism to students: how can Mark find Christianity and native religion compatible? This question is difficult given that most of my Christian students assume the two religions to be mutually incompatible. Someone in the class will point out common ethical standards, such as caring and sharing. Another will suggest that native belief in spirits might be united in God's spirit. I am usually the one who observes that the function of religion is social, and the impact of both religions serves to unite the community. As a priest, Mark finds satisfaction in knowing that services at the church offer a gathering place, whether or not the people absorb Anglican doctrine. For the village, the continuity of memory, generations, and cultural practices exists where human and natural purposes overlap. For some Christians, understanding the world as God's creation evokes gratitude for nature and locates God's spirit in nature and human life. In some ways, native reverence for nature resonates with mystical aspects of creation spirituality developed by certain contemporary Christian thinkers.[30]

Night

I consider it important for the syllabus to include a representation of widely different conditions of death. The most important difference between the books by Tolstoy and Craven is their cultural setting. Ivan's upper-class Christian identity makes him part of the dominant sector of society, bringing his philosophical and familial struggles to the forefront of his death crisis. In contrast, Mark encounters the effects of colonization and poverty on the native peoples, and he reflects on their social subjugation and cultural grieving. Consistent with social context, Ivan had all possible help, although that did not make dying easy, whereas many native deaths could have been prevented with better medical care or living conditions. Life with the Kwakiutl shows that some social groups suffer in particular ways and are more at risk. To raise an extreme example of social victimization, I deal with anti-Semitism and the Holocaust in my course for students to reflect on how nearly six million Jews were cruelly exterminated under the Nazi regime.

In particular, I choose to include the Holocaust in my syllabus because of its visibility in American popular culture as the prime atrocity of the twentieth century, as well as because of its unique methods and magnitude.[31] The Holocaust has particular relevance to a religion course because Jews were targeted and because Christian European culture propagated the genocide with minimal overt resistance from the churches. According to Nazi ideology, the Jews were classified as inferior, expendable, and detrimental to civilization. The Enlightenment assumption that modern culture has progressed in rationality and political organization is called into question by the barbarities of Nazi violence.

To teach the Holocaust, I use the terse and gripping memoir *Night* by Elie Wiesel, which depicts the conditions of death for Jews in Nazi concentration camps through the eyes of a teenage boy, Eliezer.[32] The book traces the author's deportation from Hungary to the Polish concentration camp of Auschwitz, the forced march westward to Buchenwald in Germany, and the eventual liberation of the camp. The evolving relationship between Eliezer and his father, who stay together in the camps, can be followed to gauge the deterioration of social bonds and religious observances, for the death camps were not designed simply to kill but also to dehumanize inmates. Victims knew of the thousands of bodies gassed and burned daily, of the immediate threat that they might die from execution, selection, medical experiment, starvation, or disease. The humiliations of the camp were torture enough. Terrence Des Pres depicts *l'univers concentrationnaire* as a unique world, where victims were subject to excremental assault as they wet and soiled themselves, and permitted to use latrines infrequently despite incessant dysentery.[33] *Night* portrays the death factory setting and its traumatic impact. While teaching the memoir, I screen a documentary film about the concentration camps to show the shocking conditions uncovered after the camps were liberated.[34]

To comprehend religious responses to the Holocaust, I examine passages in *Night* dealing with Jewish ritual observances, while taking into account that few class members will be Jewish at my university. The opening chapters depict Eliezer's eagerness to study the Talmud and the mysteries of the Kabbala. He prays fervently and poses questions to God without answers, but the Hasidic Jewish mystic who is his teacher assures him that with enough dedication he could find the true answers in himself "when question and answer would become one."[35] Eliezer's devout childhood is interrupted by the Nazi occupation of his village in Hungary in the spring of 1944, when he is fifteen years old. Ironically, the beginning of Jewish persecution occurs during Passover, the week-long celebration of the Exodus of the Israelites from Egypt. Only days after commemorating the liberation from slavery led by Moses, the Jews are forced to wear a yellow star and live in fenced ghettoes. On the Sabbath, the holy day when work is forbidden, the Jews are rounded up for deportation. Waiting in line for the selection at Auschwitz, where the majority are sent to the gas chambers and the minority chosen for work, Eliezer's father whispers the Kaddish prayer used by mourners, but his son refuses, in protest at God's silence. In response to a camp inmate, Akiba Drumer, who claims that God is testing the Jews' moral strength, Eliezer objects; instead, he sympathizes with Job in the Bible who doubts God's justice. Some students misunderstand Eliezer's struggles with God as a weakness, as if his protest is disloyal to his faith. I explain that there is a long Jewish tradition of debate with

God, extending back to Abraham and Moses. In fact, struggle with God is a sign of deep faith, and more admirable and loyal to God than passive acceptance without questioning. I draw attention to the fact that later in the book Akiba Drumer, who previously gave confident theodicy explanations, loses his assurance and dies hopeless. In the camps, it is more pious to doubt God's goodness and mercy than to make them into a vehicle of God's plan.

The center point in the narrative, and the religious climax, occurs during the public hangings of a boy and two men, immediately before the observance of Rosh Hashanah and Yom Kippur. Watching the small body dangling on the rope for more than half an hour, a man standing near Eliezer asks, "Where is God now?" and a voice within him answers, "He is hanging here on the gallows."[36] Although this statement might be taken to indicate that God is present in the boy's suffering, this interpretation is not confirmed in the context of the narrative.[37] The soup tastes like corpses after the hanging, and later, during the winter march to Buchenwald, Eliezer prays to the "God in whom [he] no longer believed" that he not desert his father; but this prayer is not answered, since he feels the intense desire to be free of his father, dying of dysentery, shortly before the camp is liberated.[38] The degradation and devastation enacted in the camps is portrayed as a severe threat to Jewish faith, even a faith that accepts questioning of God.

After reading *Night*, which ends with Eliezar staring at his corpselike face in a mirror, students want to know whether Elie Wiesel ever recovered from the trauma that the book so vividly depicts.[39] Therefore, I invite the class to reflect on how Wiesel and other influential Jewish thinkers have responded to the Holocaust. For instance, I share the well-known argument made by Jewish philosopher Emil Fackenheim that there is a new commandment for Jews after the Holocaust: "The authentic Jew today is forbidden to hand Hitler yet another, posthumous victory."[40] This commandment entails the preservation of Jewish existence, including Jewish identity, traditions, and the Jewish state of Israel. Together we consider how contemporary Jews might consider Jewish survival and identification as even more important than adherence to specific religious beliefs. I recount how, over the course of history, Jewishness has not been defined by doctrine, comparable to Catholic and Protestant creeds, but has centered on household rituals, Hebrew texts, and communal identity. Within the community, there is a process of religious debate. In a moving essay entitled "Against Despair," Wiesel describes Jewish history as a drama of conversation with God in many moods, including joy, sadness, and even silence. Nevertheless, the relation to God is never broken even if the dialogue is difficult.[41] Fackenheim's commandment leaves room for secular Jewish identity, whereas Wiesel places the search for God at the center of Jewish endurance.

In teaching the Holocaust, it is relevant to mention other subsequent events that bear comparison in terms of massive civilian casualties or genocidal intentions, to name a few: Stalin's gulags, Cambodia's killing fields, ethnic cleansing in the Balkans and Sudan, and the Rwandan genocide. Ironically, although the Holocaust shattered European belief in the linear progress of European civilization, a new version of belief in progress prevails in Holocaust education in America, where students absorb the message that "never again" will such genocide occur. I raise skepticism about this truism using the example of the Rwandan genocide in 1994, where plenty of warning signs existed, yet the world watched as up to one million people were massacred in a three-month killing spree by Hutus against Tutsis.[42] Students are properly sobered to see staggering statistics about the millions killed in the twentieth century, whereas the U.S. has been relatively sheltered from the ravages of large-scale violence on American soil. The events of 9/11 have significantly changed this sense of security. In the wake of 9/11, I decided to assign a book on terrorism that compares extremists from Jewish, Christian, Muslim, Sikh, and Japanese movements and killing for religious reasons. In the popular American perception of world dangers, terrorism may even eclipse genocide in urgency because it could happen at any time in our own country.[43]

Conclusion

In focusing on literature as a resource for death studies, I have taken a controversial position in demoting textbook resources to a supporting role alongside literature. Yet always, there are competing objectives in teaching death that make the selection of readings a difficult choice. I regularly consider using new publications that might offer helpful additional perspectives. One book that I have used with misgivings is the national bestseller *Tuesdays with Morrie* by Mitch Albom.[44] The fact that the book strongly appeals to Americans reflects a feel-good mentality that seeks positive inspiration in death. When the book's popularity was at its height a few years ago, many of my students would rave about it, and ask me what I thought. My problems with the book reflect pitfalls of teaching a course on death in general; therefore, it is a fitting note on which to conclude this essay.

Tuesdays with Morrie is an easy read with a hopeful message. Morrie Schwartz is a sociology professor who dispenses wisdom from his sickbed, where he is in the last stages of amyotrophic lateral sclerosis (ALS), also known as Lou Gehrig's disease. Morrie is already receiving attention from the press for his "bite-sized philosophies" written while dying, when Mitch Albom chances upon an interview of Morrie with Ted Koppel of ABC's *Nightline*. Currently a successful sportswriter, Mitch studied with Morrie as an undergraduate at Brandeis University. He goes to visit his old "coach," and the idea for the book follows soon after, with short chapters on topics such as family, money, marriage, forgiveness, and of course, death. Palliative hospice care is implied by the fact that Morrie dies at home, but there is no discussion of the difficulties of medical care choices. Predominantly, the book contains saccharine observations about putting relationships first and accepting yourself.

Morrie is socially privileged and in command of his dying. He is receiving the best possible medical treatment and nationwide visits of condolence, including a second *Nightline* interview. The contrast with the three works of literature already discussed is significant. Morrie has always held the values that are so crucial to his acceptance of his immanent death, unlike Ivan, Mark, and Eliezar, who undergo a maturing process that is neither linear nor cheery. What we see of Morrie through the book is a sketch that paints the dying man in heroic colors, so that he becomes one dimensional. Somehow Morrie does not need to learn from death because he already had a life philosophy fully equipped. In my view, Morrie becomes a projection of Mitch's desire for reassurance. His dying is appropriated, even romanticized, to give Mitch life lessons.

It is intriguing that Morrie's philosophy, which Mitch admires, contains religious themes but seems independent of any commitment to a particular religion. Moreover, there is lack of reflection on ethnic and economic issues, compared to the grief in native culture in *I Heard the Owl* or the prejudice and violence in *Night*. We learn briefly that Morrie's parents were poor Jewish immigrants and that his mother died when he was young. In contrast with Elie Wiesel's account, there is no involvement of Jewish tradition in coping with dying. Morrie seems to take a New Age posture that adapts religious insights selectively from foreign cultures, at least according to Mitch's narrative. In the longest passage on religion, Morrie explains the Buddhist ideas of impermanence and nonattachment appreciatively, as helping him accept physical decline, but when Mitch asks if he believes in reincarnation, Morrie replies "Perhaps."[45] It is mentioned that Morrie has a meditation instructor visit the house, and Native American religious ideas are mentioned in passing. We are left unsure about Morrie's religious identity. To use a popular but dubious distinction, Morrie appears to be spiritual but not religious. As an account of one man's death in America, the book is superficial in religious, psychological, and social terms.

While Morrie plays the role of a dying sage, Mitch is the protagonist who struggles with death. Like Ivan Ilyich, Mitch is ambitious, competitive, well regarded, upwardly mobile, and negligent of relationships. Mitch benefits from Morrie's dying to discover the importance of family, of appreciating his wife, and of making contact with his estranged younger brother, who has cancer. Meanwhile, he keeps all the trappings of professional success as a sportswriter. When Mitch asks his definition of "the perfect day," Morrie describes eating his favorite foods, reading, swimming, visiting close friends, and going out dancing—activities that any healthy person could arrange. It seems that Mitch can learn to see his life as perfect if he is willing to stop and appreciate it. The message is, you can have it all.

Tuesdays with Morrie is a bestseller because it reflects mainstream American interests, primarily the concern with finding happiness. The book does not reveal as much about Morrie's dying as Mitch's self discovery. These are the clinching reasons why I do not place the book on my syllabus. Granted, a major purpose of death education is to prepare those who are not dying for death. But seeing Morrie's dying through Mitch's admiring eyes, we learn nothing deep about Morrie's coping process. More troubling, his dying experiences are immediately appropriated to serve Mitch's needs. *Tuesdays with Morrie* is a marketable product that feeds the insatiable consumer demand for tips on having a better life and minimizing negative factors. Death needs a positive spin, and gets it.

In reality, teaching a course on death requires acknowledgment that dying is complex. Even with a strong personal philosophy, formulaic answers fall short in the face of grief and loss. There is no fairness as to who lives and dies, and acceptance of death involves struggle. Moreover, it is important to communicate that there is more to death studies than examining the coping problems that face each individual. Millions of people die because of human decisions and humanly preventable causes. However, many Americans avoid such disturbing facts and are more directly concerned about assuaging personal fears with upbeat spiritual messages. Ideally, a university course should educate students about multiple conditions of dying, and explore socially conscious religious perspectives that do not simplify or sanitize death.

NOTES

1. Lynne Ann DeSpelder and Albert Lee Strickland, *The Last Dance: Encountering Death and Dying,* 5th ed. (Mountain View, CA: Mayfield, 1999). DeSpelder is a grief counselor and pioneer in death education; Stickland is an author on topics in thanatology, with a degree in religious studies. This book is the classic textbook in the interdisciplinary field of death studies that comes with its own instructor's guide.

2. Charles A. Corr, Clyde M. Nabe, and Donna M. Corr, *Death and Dying, Life and Living* 4th ed. (Belmont, CA: Wadsworth, 2003). Charles Corr is active in the

Association for Death Education and Counseling, in hospice work, and he has written books on helping children cope with death; Donna Corr is a nurse with experience in hospice care; Nabe is a death educator and an Episcopal priest.

3. The assumption that death is denied and avoided in industrialized Christian-dominated nations, such as the United States and Britain, is becoming more controversial. The assumption that death is taboo in the West is challenged by Tony Walter, "Modern Death: Taboo or Not Taboo?" *Sociology* 25 (May 1991): 293–310.

4. It is interesting that one result of cross-cultural comparison is idealization of non-Western practices, which may be praised, and even appropriated, for their ability to ritualize death in a more open, emotional, and communal ways. See, for example, Jenny Hockey, "The View from the West: Reading the Anthropology of Non-Western Death Ritual," in *Contemporary Issues in the Sociology of Death, Dying and Disposal*, ed. Glennys Howarth and Peter Jupp (New York: St. Martin's, 1996), 3–16.

5. Lynne Ann DeSpelder and Albert Lee Strickland, *The Path Ahead: Readings in Death and Dying* (Mountain View, CA: Mayfield, 1995).

6. Another reader that provides cross-cultural discussion of death focusing on religious distinctives is Colin Murray Parkes, Pittu Laungani, and Bill Young, eds., *Death and Bereavement across Cultures* (New York: Routledge, 1997). The most memorable essays deal with a high-caste Hindu death in Bombay and the death of a Tibetan Buddhist farmer in Ladakh, since they engage social class distinctions. Essays on Judaism, Christianity, and Islam place somewhat less emphasis on particular stories and give more of a historical overview.

7. Some recent edited books on world religions and death are Harold Coward, ed., *Life After Death in World Religions* (Maryknoll, NY: Orbis, 1997); Christopher Jay Johnson and Marsha G. McGee, eds., *How Different Religions View Death and Afterlife* (Philadelphia: Charles Press, 1991); John D. Morgan and Pittu Laungani, eds., *Death and Bereavement Around the World*, 5 vols. (Amityville, NY: Baywood, 2002–2005); Jacob Neusner, ed., *Death and the Afterlife* (Cleveland: Pilgrim, 2000); Hiroshi Obayashi, ed., *Death and Afterlife: Perspectives of World Religions* (New York: Greenwood, 1992); and Dan Cohn-Sherbok and Christopher Lewis, eds., *Beyond Death: Theological and Philosophical Reflections on Life After Death* (New York: St. Martin's, 1995).

8. Single-author textbooks with a comparative philosophical approach include John Bowker, *The Meanings of Death* (Cambridge: Cambridge University Press, 1991); Kenneth Kramer, *The Sacred Art of Dying: How World Religions Understand Death* (New York: Paulist, 1988); James P. Carse, *Death and Existence: A Conceptual History of Human Mortality* (New York: Wiley, 1980); Douglas J. Davies, *Death, Ritual and Belief: The Rhetoric of Funerary Rites* (London: Cassell, 1997); and John Hick, *Death and Eternal Life* (Louisville: Westminster John Knox, 1994), first published in 1976.

9. Kenneth Kramer, *The Sacred Art of Dying: How World Religions Understand Death* (New York: Paulist, 1988).

10. Leo Tolstoy, *The Death of Ivan Ilyich*, trans. Lynn Soltaroff, with introduction by Ronald Blythe (New York: Bantam, 1981). After Tolstoy (1828–1910) published his

two major works, *War and Peace* (1867) and *Anna Karenina* (1877), he became increasingly preoccupied with issues of religion and mortality, and this novella reflects his period of searching. In the decades before his death, Tolstoy wrote a number of religious reflections about the true meaning of life, including autobiographical writings preoccupied with death. Tolstoy rejected the Russian Orthodox Church (in fact, he was excommunicated in 1901) in favor of a simple Christian faith centered on nonviolence and love. See Leo Tolstoy, *A Confession and Other Religious Writings*, trans. Jane Kentish (New York: Penguin, 1987).

11. Elisabeth Kübler-Ross, *On Death and Dying* (New York: Macmillan, 1969).

12. *On Our Own Terms: Moyers on Dying* (Princeton: Films for the Humanities & Sciences, 2000). Interviews conducted by Bill Moyers in this four-part series originally aired on PBS, September 10–13, 2000.

13. Tolstoy, *Death of Ivan Ilyich*, 127.

14. Tolstoy himself was born into an aristocratic Russian family. Although he was directly acquainted with peasant life, he projects an idealized picture of peasant virtue.

15. Tolstoy, *Death of Ivan Ilyich*, 134.

16. In the only direct reference to God, Ivan accuses God of cruelty. Ibid., 118.

17. Ibid., 133. This indirect reference to God is isolated and unexplained.

18. Margaret Craven, *I Heard the Owl Call My Name* (1967; New York: Dell, 1973). Margaret Craven (1901–1980), an American journalist and a fiction writer, based this best selling novel on experiences in the Queen Charlotte Islands of British Columbia, Canada. The character of Mark was inspired by an Anglican priest working with native peoples, named Eric Powell, who was facing eventual paralysis from a spinal trauma. Craven describes her travels among indigenous peoples of the Northwest in her autobiography, Margaret Craven, *Again Calls the Owl* (New York: Putnam, 1980), 72–119.

19. Craven, *I Heard the Owl*, 144.

20. Ibid, 47.

21. Ibid., 19.

22. Ibid., 114.

23. Potlatches were outlawed by the Indian Act of 1915 and partially reinstated after 1951. For more on hamatsa and death rituals, see Bill Holm, "Kwakiutl: Winter Ceremonies," in *Handbook of North American Indians*, vol. 7, *Northwest Coast*, ed. Wayne Suttles (Washington DC: Smithsonian Institution, 1990), 378–86.

24. Craven, *I Heard the Owl*, 68–70.

25. *Hitting Sticks, Healing Hearts* (Manley Hot Springs, AK: River Tracks Productions, 1991). Produced in collaboration with KUAC-TV and Minto Village Council (58 min.).

26. In contrast, the Day of the Dead, held on All Saint's Day (November 1) and All Soul's Day (November 2), provides a vibrant current example of how bereavement is honored in public and private. Students are intrigued by the healing potential of this remembrance memorial, illustrated in *La Ofrenda: The Days of the Dead*, dir. Lourdes Portillo and Susana Muñoz (Los Angeles: Direct Cinema, 1989), an

excellent film covering the indigenous roots of the celebration, *calavera* (skull) art-work, home altars, and transnational rituals in Mexico and California.

27. Joseph M. Kaufert and John D. O'Neil, "Cultural Mediation of Dying and Grieving among Native Canadian Patients in Urban Hospitals," in DeSpelder and Strickland, *Path Ahead*, 59–74.

28. Craven, *I Heard the Owl*, 158–159

29. Ibid., 158.

30. The convergence of nature and God are proposed by Christian authors such as Matthew Fox, *Creation Spirituality: Liberating Gifts for the Peoples of the Earth* (San Francisco: Harper, 1991); and Rosemary Radford Ruether, *Gaia and God: An Ecofeminist Theology of Earth Healing* (San Francisco: Harper, 1992).

31. The Holocaust is the paradigm for "genocide"—a term coined by Raphael Lemkin during World War II and defined as the persecution and extermination of a racial, national, or ethnic group. Yehuda Bauer, "The Place of the Holocaust in Contemporary History," in *Holocaust: Religious and Philosophical Implications*, ed. John K. Roth and Michael Berenbaum (St. Paul, MN: Paragon House, 1989), 20.

32. Elie Wiesel, *Night*, trans. Stella Rodway (New York: Bantam, 1982).

33. Terrence Des Pres, *The Survivor: An Anatomy of Life in the Death Camps* (Oxford: Oxford University Press, 1976).

34. There are many documentaries of the concentration camps that may be used to educate students about the extreme conditions of death. I use either the classic film with poetic narration directed by Alain Resnais, *Nuit et Brouillard* [1955] (Monroe, CT: Reel Images, 1978), or the stark, silent newsreel footage taken at the 1945 liberation of the camps, *Memory of the Camps* (Alexandria, VA: PBS Video, 1989).

35. Wiesel, *Night*, 3.

36. Ibid., 62.

37. It is unfortunate that the foreword by François Mauriac refers to the hanged boy as a counterpart to Jesus Christ crucified (x). For discussion of Christian interpretations of this passage indicating divine suffering, see Sarah K. Pinnock, *Beyond Theodicy: Jewish and Christian Thinkers Respond to the Holocaust* (Albany: State University of New York Press, 2002), 89. To provide a Jewish perspective on divine suffering, I have assigned students a chapter on God's suffering, in Elie Wiesel, *All Rivers Run to the Sea: Memoirs*, trans. Jon Rothschild, (New York: Knopf, 1995), 103–5.

38. Wiesel, *Night*, 87, 101. I sometimes assign two short essays by Wiesel that offer students insight into his religious response to his time in the camps. Elie Wiesel, "The Death of My Father" and "Yom Kippur," in *Thinking the Unthinkable: Meanings of the Holocaust*, ed. Roger S. Gottlieb (New York: Paulist, 1990), 199–208.

39. It is interesting for students to hear Wiesel speak about his childhood, his religious searching, and what he did after camp liberation, in order to compare the account in the memoir and to gain an impression of his personality. Wiesel relates revealing anecdotes from childhood and Holocaust experiences in *A Portrait of Elie Wiesel: In the shadow of Flames* (Alexandria, VA: PBS Video, 1988).

40. Emil Fackenheim, "The 614th Commandment," in Roth and Berenbaum, *Holocaust*, 291–295.

41. Elie Wiesel, "Against Despair," in *A Jew Today*, trans. Marion Wiesel (New York: Random House, 1978), 155–67.

42. I would recommend the riveting account of the Rwandan genocide in Philip Gourevitch, *We Wish to Inform You That Tomorrow We Will Be Killed with Our Families: Stories from Rwanda* (New York: Farrar, Straus & Giroux, 1998).

43. See Mark Juergensmeyer, *Terror in the Mind of God: The Global Rise of Religious Violence* (Berkeley: University of California Press, 2000).

44. Mitch Albom, *Tuesdays with Morrie: An Old Man, a Young Man, and Life's Greatest Lesson* (New York: Doubleday, 1997). The author's second and most recent bestseller also deals with dying. Mitch Albom, *The Five People You Meet in Heaven* (New York: Hyperion, 2003).

45. Albom, *Tuesdays with Morrie*, 103–8.

BIBLIOGRAPHY

Albom, Mitch. *Tuesdays with Morrie*. New York: Doubleday, 1997.

———. *The Five People You Meet in Heaven*. New York: Hyperion, 2003.

Bowker, John. *The Meanings of Death*. Cambridge: Cambridge University Press, 1991.

Carse, James P. *Death and Existence: A Conceptual History of Human Mortality*. New York: Wiley, 1980.

Cohn-Sherbok, Dan, and Christopher Lewis, eds. *Beyond Death: Theological and Philosophical Reflections on Life After Death*. New York: St. Martin's, 1995.

Corr, C. A., C. M. Nabe, D. M. and Corr. *Death and Dying, Life and Living*. 4th ed. Belmont, CA: Wadsworth, 2003.

Coward, H., ed. *Life After Death in World Religions*. Maryknoll, NY: Orbis, 1997.

Davies, Douglas J. *Death, Ritual and Belief: The Rhetoric of Funerary Rites*. London: Cassell, 1997.

Craven, Margaret. *I Heard the Owl Call My Name*. New York: Dell, 1967/1973.

———. *Again Calls the Owl*. New York: Putnam, 1980.

DeSpelder, L. A., and A. L. Strickland. *The Path Ahead: Readings in Death and Dying*. Mountain View, CA: Mayfield, 1995.

———. *The Last Dance: Encountering Death and Dying*. 5th ed. Mountain View, CA: Mayfield, 1999.

Des Pres, Terrence. *The Survivor: An Anatomy of Life in the Death Camps*. Oxford: Oxford University Press, 1976.

Fox, Matthew. *Creation Spirituality: Liberating Gifts for the Peoples of the Earth*. San Francisco: Harper, 1991.

Gottlieb, Roger S., ed. *Thinking the Unthinkable: Meanings of the Holocaust*. New York: Paulist, 1990.

Gourevitch, Philip. *We Wish to Inform You That Tomorrow We Will Be Killed with Our Families: Stories from Rwanda*. New York: Farrar, Straus & Giroux, 1998.

Hick, John. *Death and Eternal Life*. Louisville: Westminster John Knox, 1976/1994.

Hockey, Jenny. "The View from the West: Reading the Anthropology of Non-Western Death Ritual." In *Contemporary Issues in the Sociology of Death, Dying and Disposal*, edited by Glennys Howarth and Peter Jupp, 3–16. New York: St. Martin's, 1996.

Holm, Bill. "Kwakiutl: Winter Ceremonies." In Suttles, *Handbook of North American Indians*, vol. 7, *Northwest Coast*, 378–86.

Howarth, G., and P. Jupp, eds. *Contemporary Issues in the Sociology of Death, Dying and Disposal*. New York: St. Martin's, 1996.

Johnson, Christopher Jay, and Marsha G. McGee, eds. *How Different Religions View Death and Afterlife*. Philadelphia: Charles Press, 1991.

Juergensmeyer, Mark. *Terror in the Mind of God: The Global Rise of Religious Violence*. Berkeley: University of California Press, 2000.

Kramer, Kenneth. *The Sacred Art of Dying: How World Religions Understand Death*. New York: Paulist, 1988.

Kübler-Ross, Elisabeth. *On Death and Dying*. New York: Macmillan, 1969.

Morgan, John D., and Pittu Laungani. *Death and Bereavement around the World*. 5 vols. Amityville, NY: Baywood, 2002–2005.

Neusner, Jacob, ed. *Death and the Afterlife*. Cleveland: Pilgrim, 2000.

Obayashi, Hiroshi, ed. *Death and Afterlife: Perspectives of World Religions*. New York: Greenwood, 1992.

Parkes, C. M., P. Laungani, and B. Young, eds. *Death and Bereavement across Cultures*. New York: Routledge, 1997.

Pinnock, Sarah K. *Beyond Theodicy: Jewish and Christian Thinkers Respond to the Holocaust*. Albany: State University of New York Press, 2002.

Roth, John K., and M. Berenbaum, eds. *Holocaust: Religious and Philosophical Implications*. St. Paul, MN: Paragon House, 1989.

Ruether, Rosemary Radford. *Gaia and God: An Ecofeminist Theology of Earth Healing*. San Francisco: Harper, 1992.

Suttles, Wayne, ed. *Handbook of North American Indians*. Vol. 7, *Northwest Coast*. Washington DC: Smithsonian Institution, 1990.

Tolstoy, Leo. *The Death of Ivan Ilyich*. Translated by Lynn Soltaroff. New York: Bantam, 1981.

———. *A Confession and Other Religious Writings*. Translated by Jane Kentish. New York: Penguin, 1987.

Walter, Tony. "Modern Death: Taboo or Not Taboo?" *Sociology* 25 (May 1991): 293–310.

Wiesel, Elie. *Night*. Translated by Stella Rodway. New York: Bantam, 1982.

———. *A Jew Today*. Translated by Marion Wiesel. New York: Random House, 1978.

———. *All Rivers Run to the Sea: Memoirs*. Translated by Jon Rothschild. New York: Knopf, 1995.

13

"Listen to the Dark": Death and Dying in Music, Film, and Literature

Amir Hussain

In this chapter, I discuss the uses of music, film, and literature in teaching courses on death and dying. While I describe material that I have found useful, I also discuss how to successfully incorporate these items into our courses. The approach that I take is that of one who has been concerned with effective pedagogy for the past decade.[1] Many of us want to increase student participation in class and thereby engage students with different learning styles (Fink 2003 provides excellent suggestions and examples). Instructors also want to increase the diversity of perspectives that are presented in their class. Finally, many instructors want to supplement their courses with audio and visual materials. This chapter will be of use to all these instructors.

I begin the chapter with a short discussion of the death and dying course that I have created and taught. I situate this course in the matrix of other courses on death and dying that are commonly taught in North American universities. Of particular concern in my course are cross-cultural approaches to death and dying, and an interest in how variables such as class, race, and gender intersect with the religious rituals of death.

I then describe an exercise where I ask the students to bring in a work that speaks to them about death and dying. Next, I turn to a discussion about how various pieces of literature (both poetry and prose) can be integrated into the course. After discussing literature, I move to the section on music. The use of music in the classroom allows students to bring in the songs that are most meaningful to them. This creates a tremendous empowerment and learning opportunity for students. It is useful in introducing the important roles that race, ethnicity, and language play in religion. The final section of the chapter will end with a discussion of the use of films in the course on death and dying. Two resources are included as appendices at the end of this chapter.

Like many instructors, I came to teach a course on death and dying due to a combination of my own personal circumstances as well as an interest in comparative religion. I provide some background information about my own life in order to provide a better context for my pedagogical approaches. I have taught courses on world religion for a decade: from 1997 to 2005 in the Religious Studies Department at California State University, Northridge; and from 2005 to the present in the Department of Theological Studies at Loyola Marymount University. These appointments have allowed me to blend my training in the study of religion with more theological approaches. In 1992, at the age of twenty-six, I became a widower when my wife died suddenly and unexpectedly. My own experiences with grief and loss led me to the academic study of death and dying, as I could not find many resources for young widowers or widows. My personal theological reflection as a Muslim on the death of my wife, a Christian, is included as the appendix "Shannon's Song." I share it with students in my course on death and dying so they are aware that the course is not only, or simply, an academic exercise for me. Also, my sharing of my own personal experiences invites students to share their experiences with me and with each other. In years of being involved with sessions at the American Academy of Religion (AAR) annual meeting on best practices for teaching about religion, one theme that continually arises is reciprocal exchange. If we are willing to share with our students, they become much more willing to share with us and with each other. For students, the course often offers them their first opportunity to think seriously about issues of death and dying.

There are a number of approaches that instructors take when designing courses on death and dying. The Syllabus Project of the AAR provides several syllabi for these various courses.[2] Some are oriented towards sociological approaches, others to medical and healing approaches. Some are concerned with the rituals of death, others with experiences of grief and loss. And yet other courses take a more theological or pastoral approach. My particular course was a basic introductory course entitled Death and Dying in the World's Religions. Naïvely, I assumed that students coming from a particular religious background would be more interested in learning about death and dying in traditions other than their own. What I discovered was that they often had little understanding of their own received traditions on death and mourning. As such, the death and dying course was as much a course on comparative religion as it was on particular issues about death. It is also a natural place to introduce issues of religious diversity.

When I designed my course, I wanted it to reflect not just diversity among different religious traditions but also within a particular tradition. I wanted students to be aware of factors such as race, class, gender, and ethnicity.[3] In the first half of the course, we examined the religious traditions of Hinduism, Buddhism, Judaism, Christianity, Islam, and Primal traditions. In the second half of the course, with some background in different religious traditions, we examined how these different traditions affect the lives and deaths of women, children, and men. We also examined some of the intersections of different religious traditions, as well as elements of class and ethnicity. Finally, we examined issues of the death penalty in America, particularly the religious reasons behind its reinstatement (the Mormon blood atonement asked for by Gary Gilmore, who was executed by firing squad in Utah[4]) and opposition and support from different religious traditions.

There was a break between the first and second meetings of the class (the class met once a week for 165 minutes) due to Labor Day. At the end of the first class, I asked students to address the following question: What object, film, song, piece of music, art, or writing helps you to understand death? I find this to be a very useful exercise, as it allows students to explore what is important in their own understandings of death and dying (before taking the course), and share their understandings with the class. This may be a poem, a work of literature, a song, a film, an object, and so on. This exercise immediately provides an opportunity for students to engage with each other and with the instructor. It allows students to learn from other students about what it is that they find meaningful in the area of death and dying. It also allows the instructor to learn more about her or his students, and the various backgrounds that they bring to class.

The second meeting of the class took place on September 10, 2001. I shared with my students the song "Magic and Loss" written by Lou Reed. The song, from the CD of the same title, was written in response to Reed watching two close friends die in the same year. Several students shared the tribute rap song "I'll be Missing You," performed by Puff Daddy, Faith Evans, and 112 in memory of murdered rapper Notorious B.I.G. Others brought in the music of another murdered rapper, Tupac Shakur. A few brought in personal readings that they had prepared on the deaths of friends, while others brought in Biblical verses that they had heard at funerals. Some students brought in works of fiction that they had read as children, including *The Outsiders, A Day*

No Pigs Would Die, and *Charlotte's Web*. One student brought in a video of the funeral scene from the popular British film *Four Weddings and a Funeral*. After these presentations, I showed the students part of the Bill Moyers video for PBS, *On Our Own Terms*, about death and dying in America.[5] It was a good way to introduce some of the issues that we would discuss for the rest of the course. The class ended around 10 p.m. Early the next morning, we saw the horrors of the terrorist attacks of September 11, 2001.

The next class was scheduled to be about Hinduism. Instead, it became an opportunity for students to talk about their reactions to the attacks. For many of the students who thought of death as something in the far distance, the attacks brought the reality of dying home to them. For others, it was a chance to vent their anger at what had happened. Since they knew me from the first class to be a Muslim, and had read the reflection I had given them on the death of my wife, they had a number of questions for me both personally as a Muslim as well as more generally about Islam. Daniel Smith-Christopher has edited an excellent resource that, post-9/11, provides resources for nonviolence and peacemaking in the world's religions. It includes two chapters about Islam and Muslims.

In teaching the course in the years after 9/11, I realized that many of my students are much more aware of death and dying than they were in the past. I have found the following piece by Mark Slouka to be the best at describing this shift:

> I believe, to put it plainly, that last year's attack was so traumatic to us because it simultaneously exposed and challenged the myth of our own uniqueness. A myth most visible, perhaps, in our age-old denial of death.
>
> Consider it. Here in the New Canaan, in the land of perpetual beginnings and second chances, where identity could be sloughed and sloughed again and history was someone else's problem, death had never been welcome. Death was a foreigner—radical, disturbing, smelling of musty books and brimstone. We wanted no part of him.
>
> And now death had come calling. That troubled brother, so long forgotten, so successfully erased, was standing on our porch in his steel-toed boots, grinning. He'd made it across the ocean, passed like a ghost through the gates of our chosen community. We had denied him his due and his graveyards, watered down his deeds, buried him with things. Yet here he was. He reminded us of something unpleasant. Egypt, perhaps.
>
> This was not just a terrorist attack. This was an act of metaphysical trespass. Someone had some explaining to do.[6]

Slouka's piece is an example of how various pieces of literature (both poetry and prose) can be integrated into the course. My course syllabus begins with the following line from *The Epic of Gilgamesh*: "The joyful will stoop with sorrow, and when you have gone to the earth I will let my hair grow long for your sake, I will wander through the wilderness in the skin of a lion." *The Epic of Gilgamesh*, perhaps the oldest surviving story in Western literature, speaks to us about certain understandings of death and mourning. For as long as we have been telling stories, we have been telling stories about death and loss. Literature may be used to illustrate various religious approaches to death and dying (e.g., Kaddish in the Jewish tradition), or it may be used to illustrate particular attitudes towards death (e.g., Dylan Thomas's poem to his dying father, "Do not go gentle into that good night"). Also, literature can be used to facilitate the discussion of various marginalized groups in religious traditions. For example, W. H. Auden's elegy "Funeral Blues," (recited in the film *Four Weddings and a Funeral*) can be used as a way to introduce issues of sexual orientation into the discussion of religious rituals.

For each week of the course that deals with a particular religious tradition, I have given students examples from the sacred texts or rituals of that tradition that dealt with death. This provides instructors an opportunity to present and discuss the literature from within texts sacred to a tradition. However, it is also important to mention the responses that are created by members of religious communities to death. In addition to the Dylan Thomas poem mentioned above, I also used his "A Refusal to Mourn the Death, by Fire, of a Child in London." Other works that I used were Anna Ahkmatova's "Requiem," and Paul Celan's "Death Fugue." Of course, instructors have their own favorite pieces of literature that they can insert at various points in their course, as appropriate. And student resources can be utilized here. Once teaching the course, I had a student who could speak German, and she read the Celan poem in its original to give us a sense of the rhyme and feel, as well as the performative aspect of reciting a poem rather than just silently reading it. In another course, a student who spoke Russian was able to read the Akhmatova poem in the original. Also, instructors might want to ask students to bring in pieces that are important to them from their ethnic and religious backgrounds, particularly if they can read them in the original languages. This helps to create diversity within the syllabus as well as encouraging students to speak out and make short presentations in class.

Alongside the use of literature, one can also incorporate music in the classroom. A very useful resource here is *Global Music Series: Experiencing Music, Expressing Culture* from Oxford University Press.[7] The series consists of several volumes on music in different cultures, with each volume containing a CD of some of the music used in the text. The use of music in the classroom allows students to bring in the songs that are most meaningful to them. This creates a tremendous empowerment and learning opportunity for students. It allows students to contribute to the course content, rather than simply receiving what the instructor has designed. As such, music, like literature, is useful in introducing the important roles that race, ethnicity and language play in religion. It also allows for the contrast between the formal music that may be used in certain religious services with the "informal" music that members of that tradition might sing. The use of music takes us away from what Kimerer Lamothe describes as the problem of textualization: "A privileging of texts as object, method, model, and goal of religious studies."[8] She continues: "Text-based methods assume as normative the experience of the body that scholars themselves cultivate in mastering the acts of reading and writing. They reproduce a belief that writing is the practice by which reason exerts its freedom over and against bodily experience and thereby secures a rational stance on 'religion.' "[9] In this way, the use of music allows us to counter the problem of textualization while also bringing "lived religion" into the classroom discussion.

The use of music also allows for an introduction to issues of class by contrasting formal pieces such as Sir John Tavener's "Requiem" with folk songs such as "Will the Circle be Unbroken" or hip-hop songs about the loss of loved ones (e.g., Everlast's "Graves to Dig"). Particular favorites in this respect are two songs by Vince Gill: "The Key to Life," written on the death of this father, and "Go Rest High on that Mountain," written on the death of his brother. These are useful in discussions of men's roles in death and dying, both for issues of masculinity and for the rituals associated with the death of men. Of course, the use of popular music also allows for the discussion of religious ideals versus the ways in which a particular religion may be lived out by its followers. While a tradition may celebrate the return of the deceased to God, the songs mourners sing may be songs of grief at the loss of their loved one.

The title of this chapter comes from a contemporary Christian religious song. I include it here as appendix 2 as it is not as well known as the songs mentioned above. The song is written by Jim Strathdee, a musician within the United Methodist tradition, and performed by him and his wife Jean. The song is based on an actual incident that occurred with Jim and his son Michael when Michael was a child. As an adult, Michael, who was also a very gifted musician, developed severe bi-polar disorder. In 2002, at the age of twenty-eight, he stood in the path of an oncoming train, ending his own life. Michael's parents, family, and friends were of course grieved over the loss. Years later, Jim was able to write a song about Michael and the loss to him of his only son. Songs like this one provide examples of how those that are left behind by a death come to understand that death.

Many instructors are also interested in incorporating films and video clips into their courses. I have created and taught a course on religion and film, and serve as the co-chair of the religion, film, and visual culture group of the AAR. As such, I have a great interest in issues related to religion and film.[10] The AAR Syllabus Project has a very useful Web page for incorporating film and video into courses.[11]

From a theoretical perspective, film is often useful in helping students to examine the construction of the category of "religion." Tim Murphy has written: "In order to teach religion effectively, which I take for granted means in a broad, comparative way, we are forced by the very findings of our own field to persuade our students that the taxonomic system which they inherit is not adequate to the larger world in which they live."[12] In an attempt to show students that religion is not simply about church, or that a religious film is more than *The Ten Commandments*, I often start with the music video for John R. Cash's "Hurt," directed by Mark Romanek in 2002. Since this is a short piece, it allows for repeated viewings even in a fifty-minute class. I will show the video once, and then show it a second time, asking students to pay attention on the second viewing to the camera angles and perspectives. Then a third time, I ask students to watch for the lighting. A fourth time, I ask them to watch for the editing. This allows students to learn the rudiments of camera angle, lighting, editing, and so on. I find this a useful way to introduce elements of film theory and filmmaking into a course on death and dying. John Hill and Pamela Gibson have edited a very fine collection on critical approaches to film studies that is accessible for instructors with limited knowledge of film theory.[13]

Many of my students know the original version of the song by Trent Reznor of Nine Inch Nails, and so the use of this cover version also raises issues of authorship as well as subject matter. They are watching a commercial video made by a director to promote a song from a CD by a singer, a song which is the cover of another musician's work. Since Cash's death in 2003, the video serves also as an elegy for him and his wife June Carter, who appears in the video and preceded him in death. Reznor wrote and recorded the original in 1994 before he reached the age of thirty. Cash recorded the song when he was seventy. The video therefore allows for a discussion of aging and how a song recorded by someone under thirty might be more relevant to the life of a senior citizen. This in turn allows for a discussion of issues of aging and approaching the end of life.

Many instructors regularly use the following films in courses on death and dying:

The Fisher King, directed by Terry Gilliam, 1991
Jesus of Montreal, directed by Denys Arcand, 1989
The Sixth Sense, directed by M. Night Shyamalan, 1999
Dead Man, directed by Jim Jarmusch, 1995
Santitos, directed by Alejandro Springall, 1998

For many instructors, particular films may be useful for certain traditions. So the Arcand film, *Jesus of Montreal*, is useful in discussions of how Christians understand issues of life and death, both of Jesus and their own. *The Fisher King*, by contrast, offers a brilliant meditation on loss and how one remembers those who have died. This theme is repeated in *The Sixth Sense*, analyzed by Adele Reinhartz.[14] Hollywood films (or other blockbusters like *Four Weddings and a Funeral*) may be particularly appropriate, as they are often easy to obtain. Also, since students may be familiar with the films, instructors can often show relevant clips rather than using class time to show the whole film. An outstanding resource is the online *Journal of Religion and Film*, which has peer-reviewed scholarly articles on a number of films, as well as reviews of others.[15] For those interested more in theological issues, particularly as applied to Christianity, the work of Robert Johnston is recommended.[16]

However, one should also venture beyond the commercial hits to expose students to new material. One example is Jim Jarmusch's *Dead Man*. One of the main characters in the film is a Native American named Nobody, who is played by Native American actor Gary Farmer. Gregory Salyer has an excellent analysis of this film.[17] There are also a number of international films that deal with issues of death and dying. This allows one to bring in cross-cultural examples. A favorite of mine set in the Southwest is the Mexican film *Santitos*, which deals with a widow searching for her lost daughter. Again, instructors may ask students to identify films from their own ethnic backgrounds. Often this allows for lively discussions of contemporary issues of death and dying in various cultures. Jolyon Mitchell and S. Brent Plate have edited an excellent collection that deals with global perspectives on film, along with other important issues.[18]

No matter the type of course on teaching on death and dying, using film, music, and literature can help to augment the material presented. Asking students for material that is relevant to them allows them to have more ownership of the course, and results in much higher student participation and involvement in class. It also allows instructors to do the type of comparative work necessary to help students understand more about religion. On this, Tim Murphy writes: "Without substantive comparison, the specific, *operational nature* of our inherited taxonomy cannot be understood. And finally, scholar-teachers must be equipped to see the various ways in which language and other kinds of cultural practices actively shape *a* world, and do not merely passively reflect *the* world." (emphasis in original).[19] Literature, film, and music, which students often use passively, can thus be used actively to help them learn more about their worlds, their neighbors, and themselves.

Appendix 1
"SHANNON'S SONG"

Easter 1998.

As a Muslim, I accept the Qur'an to be the very word of God, revealed to the Prophet Muhammad in the seventh century. It is in the words of the Qur'an that I find the themes that are important to me: love and mercy, peace, justice, and compassion. At this point in my life, one verse in particular is most meaningful (the translation from the Arabic original is my own):

> And God has put between you Love and Mercy.
> Truly in this are Signs for those who reflect. (Qur'an 30:21)

Many verses in the Qur'an speak of the "Signs of God," which are everywhere. Trying to understand or decipher these signs is one of the duties incumbent upon all Muslims. As I understand it, the verse speaks of the love and mercy that are found in human relationships, specifically, the relationship between married people (mentioned in the verse immediately prior). And the root or cause of human love and mercy is divine love and divine mercy, two of the attributes of God.

I did not truly begin to understand the many levels of meaning of this verse until I met my wife, Shannon L. Hamm. Shannon was born in Winnipeg and grew up in southern Manitoba, a member of the United Church of Canada. To say that Shannon was the most amazing woman that I had met would be an understatement. She was so involved with the world; she loved to travel, talk, dance, and, especially, sing. While I remember her as a singer, she was also a first-rate thinker, the recipient of many academic awards, and a truly gifted teacher, whether working with university students, abused women, mentally handicapped children, or head-injured adults. And she worked with all of these. Shannon and I were married on August 19, 1989. The service we designed included readings from both Christianity and Islam, including a longer passage from the Qur'an that contained the verse above.

Shannon challenged my world, the "know-it-allness" that only a twenty-three-year-old male can have. She taught me about peace and justice and the need to make a difference with our lives. Although she discovered her answers within a Christian framework, she helped me to find my own answers within a Muslim framework. This is important for me to say, because terrible misunderstandings persist about Islam as a religion of violence and Muslims as a violent people, stereotypes which are as destructive for Islam as they are for any other world religion.

As I read the Qur'an, I discovered its overwhelming emphasis on the mercy and compassion of God: the idea that reconciliation and forgiveness are preferable to retribution, that mercy takes precedence over wrath. In addition to the Qur'an, Muslims have the life of the Prophet Muhammad as an example. In reading about his life, I repeatedly encountered images of love and compassion, ranging from everyday acts like playing with his grandchildren, to acts of statesmanship in forgiving those who had persecuted him for the ethical monotheism he preached. And I discovered countless examples in the Muslim tradition of people who practiced mercy and justice, people such as Badshah Khan, who worked with Gandhi in using nonviolent resistance as a way to end colonial domination in South Asia.

I learned that these teachings of peace and justice were not foreign to Islam, but an integral part of it. To me, this was the secret of interfaith dialogue—not that we seek to convert each other but that we help each other find what is meaningful in our own traditions—that Shannon, as a Christian, could help me to become a better Muslim.

Transformed by my experience with Shannon, I began to do interfaith work, largely, but not exclusively, with the United Church. The challenge to work toward a just society led me to join a number of groups, including the World Conference on Religion and Peace, the World Interfaith Education Association, and Science for Peace. Again, I did all this within a Muslim framework, trying to follow the examples that I had been given from within my own tradition.

And then my world changed.

On July 7, 1992, Shannon died suddenly of a pulmonary embolism. At twenty-six, hers was the first death of someone close to me, and I had no words for it, no models for my grief. At that point, I did not stop believing but I did not know what to believe. I could not reconcile the ideas of a loving and merciful and all-powerful God with a God that would let Shannon die. At her death, Shannon was twenty-eight, the clinical manager of the Centre for Behavioral Rehabilitation, working with people with acquired brain injury. She was the classic example of a wonderful young woman doing important and ground-breaking work. And I could not imagine a God who would let her die, taking her away so quickly from such critical labors.

Of course, I have never been the same since. Shannon's death taught me many things, and in her death, she continues to be one of my teachers. I remember old conversations in different ways, thankful for a teacher who left me with answers to questions I had not yet learned to ask. And while there has been none of the communication with Shannon that I have so desperately sought since her death, occasionally I am blessed with some sense that she is still here. That her song is still being sung, in her own beautiful voice.

One of the times that I heard this song was while offering prayers in the lodge at the Dr. Jessie Saulteaux Resource Centre in Beausejour, Manitoba, in a gathering led by Stan McKay and Janet Sillman. The lodge that day held people from several traditions, and we all prayed together, as well as offered our own prayers in our own languages. Another time was at a United Church service in Toronto. July 7, 1996, was the fourth anniversary of Shannon's death, and it happened to fall on a Sunday. I had no idea what to do with myself that day. For no conscious reason that I can recall, I decided to go to the church that Shannon sometimes attended in Toronto, Trinity-St. Paul's on Bloor Street. I had never been to a church by myself for no reason before. The minister, Joan Wyatt, was on holiday, and the service was conducted by Michael Cooke, Juliet Huntly, and Sarah Yoon. And everything about that service was connected to Shannon, as if it were her memorial service. We sang one of her favorite hymns, there was a reading from a book she loved, the importance of meaningful work was stressed, and we held hands and danced for the closing hymn. Of course, the people conducting the service had no knowledge of Shannon, and I had never met any of them prior to that day's service. It was just one of those magical moments.

Despite such moments, I have also come to understand that my faith, my Islam, does not bring me healing. Instead, it does something infinitely more powerful. It allows me to live broken. It allows me to understand something of the gift that is life. As a believer, I know that at some point, Shannon, God, and I will meet again. And I will be asked what I did with this life I was given, what difference I made with that life.

And I have been so incredibly fortunate, to be given a life, and texts for how to live that life, and a teacher to help me read those texts and many more teachers since that first, best teacher. In the fall of 1997, I returned to San Francisco, a city that I had last visited five years before, only months after Shannon's death. Five years later, an important change came over me. As I sat down to a meal with one of my teachers, Professor Michel Desjardins of Wilfrid Laurier University, I realized just how many gifts I had been given. The Why me? question that I had been asking was still my question; its emphasis, however, was totally different. Instead of Why me? Why am I so cursed? Why did I no longer have Shannon around? now the question was Why me? Why am I so fortunate to be given so many teachers and friends?

What will I do with all that has been given to me? In my own poor way, I, too, will try to sing Shannon's song. I turned to my favorite complete chapter of the Qur'an (chap. 93), "The Morning," and found solace:

> By the morning.
> By the night when it is still.
> Your Lord has not forsaken you, nor is your Lord displeased
> And The Last will be better for you than The First
> And your Lord will give you so you will be content
> Did your Lord not find you an orphan and shelter you?
> And find you erring, and guide you?
> And find you needy, and enrich you?
> So do not treat the orphan harshly.
> Nor drive away the petitioner.
> And proclaim the bounty of your Lord.

These words were first given to the Prophet Muhammad and, through him, to all people, myself included. They are the words to Shannon's song. Help people. Work towards justice and mercy in this world. Proclaim the goodness of the Lord.

Let her song be sung.[20]

Appendix 2
"LISTEN TO THE DARK"

Words and Music by Jim Strathdee, 2006
From the 2007 CD *Stand for What is Right* by Jim and Jean Strathdee

> I was sitting by the window on a quiet winter night
> At the edge of town the moon was down the stars shone clear and bright
> Michael James, our three-year old, came in from our back yard
> Came up to me tugged on my sleeve, said, "Daddy come and listen to the dark"
> So out we went, sat side by side in that chilly desert air
> We listened to the stillness and the mystery that was there
> The night was big and we were small but cradled in the dark
> And not a word was spoken, the night we listened to the dark
>
> Our children born with wonder when they come fresh from God
> They don't know how but they just know the mystery deep and broad
> We do our best to teach them with our concepts, creeds and songs
> But sometimes they begin to feel that what they know is wrong
> Now, Jesus took them on his knee, blest them for who they are
> He said we must be like a child to enter heaven's door
> We spend our whole life trying to get back to where we start
> To know that God is big and real and present when we listen to the dark
>
> Now Michael's gone before us to that playground out beyond
> And we are left behind here to try and carry on
> An illness took him from us in the prime of his young life
> We seek to find the blessings in the midst of pain and strife
> But I await that glorious time, that starry winter night
> When I arise and spread my soul and take my final flight
> To follow Michael's mystery into that holy dark
> Once more to hear his gentle voice, say, "Daddy, come and listen..."

NOTES

My thanks to Professor Christopher Moreman for allowing me to be part of this volume, and for his helpful editorial suggestions. Thanks also to Professor Pat Nichelson for his help with developing the death and dying course that led to this chapter. On the death of her father, John R. Cash, Rosanne Cash described him as "a Baptist with the soul of a mystic." This chapter is dedicated to Jim and Jean Strathdee, Methodists with the souls of mystics, who carry on Cash's legacy of preaching the gospel through their music. It is also dedicated to the blessed memory of their son, Michael James Strathdee, 1974–2002.

1. I am thankful for the many workshops that I have attended on effective pedagogy. At California State University, Northridge, I am thankful to Professor Cynthia Desrochers and Kelly Kroeker who directed the university's Center for Excellence in Learning and Teaching. At Loyola Marymount University, I am thankful to Professor Patricia Walsh (of blessed memory) and Professor Jackie Dewar, as well as to Nick Mattos, who are responsible for the university's Center for Teaching Excellence.

2. See http://www.aarweb.org/syllabus/browse.asp.

3. Discussed in D. Field, J. Hockey, and N. Small, eds., *Death, Gender and Ethnicity* (London: Routledge, 1997).

4. On this, see the book written by Mikal Gilmore, Gary's brother, *Shot in the Heart* (New York: Doubleday, 1994).

5. Details are available at http://www.pbs.org/wnet/onourownterms/index.html.

6. Mark Slouka, "A Year Later: Notes on America's Intimations of Mortality," *Harper's Magazine* 305: 1828 (September 2002): 36.

7. See Various editors, Various Titles, *Global Music Series* (New York: Oxford University Press, 2003–2007).

8. Kimerer L. Lamothe, "Why Dance? Towards a Theory of Religion as Practice and Performance," *Method and Theory in the Study of Religion* 17, no. 2 (2005): 109–10.

9. Lamothe, "Why Dance?" 111–12.

10. I am thankful for conversations on religion and film with Michel Desjardins, Ken Derry, Frances Flannery-Daily, John Lyden, Brent Plate, Tony Michael, Rubina Ramji, Adele Reinhartz, and Susan Schwartz.

11. At http://www.aarweb.org/syllabus/films.asp.

12. Tim Murphy, "Cultural Understandings of 'Religion': The Hermeneutical Context of Teaching Religious Studies in North America," *Method and Theory in the Study of Religion* 18, no. 3 (2006): 213–14.

13. John Hill and Pamela Church Gibson, eds., *Film Studies: Critical Approaches* (New York: Oxford University Press, 2000).

14. Adele Reinhartz, *Scripture on the Silver Screen* (Louisville: Westminster John Knox, 2003).

15. Available at http://www.unomaha.edu/jrf/.

16. Robert K. Johnston, *Reel Spirituality: Theology and Film in Dialogue*, 2nd ed. (Grand Rapids, MI: Baker Academic, 2006).

17. Gregory Salyer, "Poetry Written with Blood: Creating Death in *Dead Man*," in *Imag(in)ing Otherness: Filmic Visions of Living Together*, ed. S. Brent Plate and David Jasper (New York: Oxford UP, 1999), 17–36.

18. Jolyon Mitchell and S. Brent Plate, eds., *The Religion and Film Reader* (New York: Routledge, 2007).

19. Murphy, "Cultural Understandings," 216–17.

20. An earlier version was published as "Shannon's Song," in *Stories in My Neighbour's Faith: Narratives from World Religions in Canada*, ed. Susan L. Scott (Toronto: United Church Publishing House, 1999), 101–6. Used by permission.

BIBLIOGRAPHY

Attig, T. *How We Grieve: Relearning the World.* New York: Oxford University Press, 1996.

Barnard, D., A. Towers, P. Boston, and Y. Lambrinidou. *Crossing Over: Narratives of Palliative Care.* New York: Oxford University Press, 2000.

Coward, H., and P. Knitter, eds. *Life After Death in World Religions.* Maryknoll, New York: Orbis, 1997.

Field, D., J. Hockey, and N. Small, eds. *Death, Gender and Ethnicity.* London: Routledge, 1997.

Fink, Dee L. *Creating Significant Learning Experiences: An Integrated Approach to Designing College Courses.* San Francisco: Jossey-Bass, 2003.

Gilmore, Mikal. *Shot in the Heart.* New York: Doubleday, 1994.

Heinz, Donald. *The Last Passage: Recovering a Death of Our Own.* New York: Oxford University Press, 1999.

Hill, J., and Pamela Church Gibson, eds. *Film Studies: Critical Approaches.* New York: Oxford University Press, 2000.

Hussain, Amir. "Shannon's Song." In *Stories in My Neighbour's Faith: Narratives from World Religions in Canada,* edited by Susan L. Scott, 101–6. Toronto: United Church Publishing House, 1999.

Johnston, Robert K. *Reel Spirituality: Theology and Film in Dialogue.* 2nd ed. Grand Rapids, MI: Baker Academic, 2006.

Lamothe, Kimerer L. "Why Dance? Towards a Theory of Religion as Practice and Performance." *Method and Theory in the Study of Religion* 17, no. 2 (2005): 101–33.

Mitchell, J., and S. Brent Plate, eds. *The Religion and Film Reader.* New York: Routledge, 2007.

Moyers, Bill. *On Our Own Terms: Moyers on Dying.* PBS four-part video series, 2000.

Murphy, Tim. "Cultural Understandings of 'Religion:' The Hermeneutical Context of Teaching Religious Studies in North America." *Method and Theory in the Study of Religion* 18, no. 3 (2006): 197–218.

Parkes, C. M., P. Laungani, and B. Young, eds. *Death and Bereavement across Cultures.* London: Routledge, 1997.

Plate, S. Brent, and David Jasper. *Imag(in)ing Otherness: Filmic Visions of Living Together.* New York: Oxford University Press, 1999.

Reinhartz, Adele. *Scripture on the Silver Screen.* Louisville: Westminster John Knox, 2003.

Slouka, Mark. "A Year Later: Notes on America's Intimations of Mortality." *Harper's* 305: 1828 (September 2002) 35–43.

Smith-Christopher, Daniel, ed. *Subverting Hatred: The Challenge of Nonviolence in Religious Traditions.* 10th anniversary ed. Maryknoll, New York: Orbis, 2007.

Various editors. Various Titles. *Global Music Series.* New York: Oxford University Press, 2003–2007.

Wheeler, Brannon, ed. *Teaching Islam.* New York: AAR/Oxford University Press, 2003.

14

Love Letters to the Dead: Immortal Gifts for the Lifelong Learner

Dorothy Lander and *John Graham-Pole*

How are you? Does the Great One (the goddess of the West) look after you according with your wish? Behold, I am the one you loved on earth.
— Letter from Mer-irtief to Neb-itief
(Little Stele, Cairo Museum)[1]

This fragment is from one of about fifteen surviving letters from relatives to their recently dead, often written on papyrus, pottery bowls or linen, between Egypt's late Old Kingdom (2700–2200 BC) and late New Kingdom (1550–1000 BC),[2] the earliest extant exemplars of an art form still espoused by grief counselors to the recently bereaved. It features in autobiography and research, including C. S. Lewis's *Grief Observed* and Elizabeth Kübler-Ross's *The Wheel of Life*.[3] Mary Jane Moffat's selections from the literature of mourning include those from writers who "address the beloved as if he or she is still alive and reunion is a possibility."[4] For this essay, we were inspired by Sharon Bajer's play *Molly's Veil*, based on the life of Charlotte Whitten, longtime mayor of Ottawa, whose personal papers were not to be made public until twenty-five years after her death.[5] When opened, they revealed the details of her thirty-year love affair with Margaret Grier—mostly through letters written for three years after her beloved's death.

Dying and mourning are holistic concepts, hard to teach through didactics, be our audience health-care students or professionals, families or community. Pedagogy must be woven with personal connection, fostering listeners'/readers' own reflections and self-expressions, and acknowledging the interplay between dichotomies—grief and joy, hope and fear, impotence and autonomy—along with the divine mystery that insistently intrudes.[6] Writing is best illuminated by personal story, exemplar, reflection and dialogue—a pedagogy of "reflective practice" rather than "technical science."[7] Arthur P. Bochner and Carolyn S. Ellis suggest a "contrast between humans as scientists and humans as poets.... All of us suffer loss sooner or later, and our capacity to make sense of and to work through pain is the foundation for rebuilding a life."[8]

Some bereavement literature speaks to the learning/healing power of recounted and written stories, memories, and dreams, which Rachel Remen applies not just to pedagogy but to personal and professional practice and research. "Stories allow us to see the familiar through new eyes. We become in that moment guests in another's life, sitting with them at the feet of their teachers. The meaning we draw may differ from that they themselves have drawn. No matter: facts bring us knowledge, stories wisdom."[9] As teachers of those whose lives and work bring them into intimate relation with the dying, we offer the art—or craft—of experiential portrayal, building narrative relationships between teller and listener. In praise of craft, Octavio Paz writes: "The handmade object is a sign that expresses human society in a way all its own: not as work (technology), not symbol (art, religion), but as a mutually shared physical life."[10] Whereas preservable "fine art" can become cult, handmade objects are useful *and* beautiful. We are "forbidden" to touch fine art or religious icons, but "made *by* human hands, the craft object is made *for* human hands." (emphasis in original).[11] Its transpersonal nature symbolizes healing touch, contrasting with the biomedical model of clinical history-taking from patient/family, standardized through the SOAP (subjective, objective, assessment, and plan) note, with which every American medical student has enduring acquaintance but which has little place in palliative pedagogy.[12]

The "immortal gifts" of our title captures this pedagogy inherent in the evanescent-preservable art continuum. Anthropologist Edmund Carpenter tells us: "The Eskimo word 'to make poetry' is the word 'to breathe;' both are derivatives of *anerca*, the soul, that which is eternal, the breath of life."[13] Memory immortalizes every act of human/divine artistic creation; every unique and intimate reminiscence is a work of healing immortal art. To cultivate this intimacy through experiential portrayal, we use autoethnography—of ourselves and those cared for—and reflexivity, that is, a person's *fixed* (demographic), *subjective* (life history), and *textual* (language) positions.[14] For us, then, *fixed* is John is emeritus professor of pediatrics, palliative, and arts medicine at an American university, and Dorothy is senior research professor in adult education at a Canadian university and a bereaved spouse; *subjective* is our personal relationship, starting as academic co-researchers in art and palliative care between Nova Scotia and Florida, and unfolding into our spousal relationship; *textual* is our letter writing to our beloved dead, our reflective dialogue, and first-name/first-person usage.

Our autoethnography draws on our arts-based research[15] in several cultures—hospitals, research and voluntary organizations, professional and student classes, families, homes, and communities.[16] Autoethnography informs lifelong pedagogy and encompasses formal and informal learning as *mourning*—from the Indogermanic for "re-membering." Scott Becker and Roger Knudson see mourning imaginally:

> Mourning entails moving into the mythopoetic space in which the living and the dead co-exist. . . . An ethical act of "re-membering" the dead . . . [has] several layers of meaning, including (a) to recall or recount; (b) to reattach the limbs of the body (suggesting forgetting is a kind of violent dismemberment); and (c) to grant the dead their autonomous membership in the living community. . . . Just as we remember the dead, so they remember us. . . . We are not responding to a ghost or a concept, but to a metaphorical "person," the source of which does not matter as much as the immediacy.[17]

Transitional experiences in William Bridges's before-after autobiography of his wife's death unfold through mourning/re-membering the broken connection in learning new ways of being. Like Dorothy, he experienced new love while in the "neutral zone" before a year had passed. Mourning contrasts with *grief*—from the Latin for "heavy"—the feeling of sadness accompanying broken connections.[18]

Parker Palmer links re-membering to teachers recovering from losing the heart to teach: they must go about "putting [them]selves back together, recovering identity and integrity, reclaiming the wholeness of [their] lives." Palmer explains, "When we forget who we are we do not merely drop some data. We *dismember* ourselves, with unhappy consequences for our politics, our work, our hearts." (emphasis in original).[19] Chris Hawes, after failing through poetry and play-writing to come to terms with his brother David's death, became a hospice writer in residence. Known as "the man who listens to stories," he finally got it:

> It is about a dialogue, a sharing, a learning: it's about listening to the dying. . . . It's about admitting we're frightened too, and that the dying are further up the road, and that they may, hopefully, be able to turn back for a moment and help us understand.[20]

Art's most important aspect in this pedagogy may be linking creativity to spirituality, treated in depth in Matthew Fox's book *Creativity*: "We are creators at our very core. Only creating can make us happy, for in creating we tap into the deepest powers of self and universe and the Divine self."[21] We have evolved from Freudian psychoanalysis, requiring emotional detachment for successful mourning, to recognizing the need for continuing bonds with the deceased.[22] Becker and Knudsen hold that "the road to the dead is a *via negativa*, a willingness to suspend belief and disbelief in favor of imaginative engagement . . . without any reasonable reaching after fact and reason."[23]

For Bochner and Ellis, autoethnography's power to inspire reflections extends its value beyond teaching and research to caregiving. The popular culture around what constitutes "good" death or mourning is reflected in the "canonical stories that circulate in one's society," often through TV and movies. Autoethnographies "show people struggling to resist or revise meanings that are not of their own making," and "allow another person's world of experience to inspire reflection on your own."[24] In *Final Negotiations*, Ellis's story of her loss of her partner, Gene, offers readers "companionship when they desperately need it. Maybe not *now*, but everyone's time surely will come."[25] Laurel Richardson's ethnography, *Last Writes*, portrays the intricacies of a long-term friendship at end of life; during her friend Betty's last few months, both Laurel and Betty give and receive care.[26]

Here, we offer our letters of mourning to show autoethnographic art as pedagogy, intending them as, in Bochner and Ellis's words, "an act of caring, of generosity, witnessing, becoming."[27] Our reflections on them unfolded as dialogue, often on hand-in-hand walks on our wooded Nova Scotia roads, to "show or enact communication [teaching and learning] as a living, breathing, active process."[28] They echo Dwight Conquerwood's praxis of co-performative witnessing: "what it means to be radically engaged and committed, body-to-body, in the field."[29] According to D. Soyini Madison, "We cannot be subjects without dialogue, without witnessing. Counterbalance is central in the give-and-take of dialogue and the meeting of two subjects whose subjectivities grow and deepen from their mutual encounter."[30]

John writes his mother, a single parent who died aged fifty-one when he was twelve, and Dorothy her husband, Patrick, who died aged seventy-five in 2004.

Dear Mummy,
  It's high time I wrote you! The last letter I actually posted would have been from boarding school—over 50 years ago. Yesterday I was

having a good cry while Dorothy, my wife, soothed me. There haven't been many people I've really trusted since you died. So I still miss you—I guess grief lasts a lifetime.

But—65 years young and happier than ever! And you'd be proud, and sure let me know it—like when I won that prize (Dombey & Son) for Latin or that little silver cup for the school handicap. I just retired after 40 years of doctoring. About 20 years ago I figured out my course was set—subconsciously—the moment I heard you'd died. Uncle Ken always tried to talk me out of it after we went to live with him, and I could never come up with why I was so sure—after all, I hated science in school! I know now it was no accident I chose oncology and pediatrics—your death made me declare a 12-year-old's war on cancer, and after my miserable adolescence I lost my heart to the first sick child I saw—though it was scary as hell. And at least the last 5 years I've been a hospice doctor. People often ask me how and especially why—and lately I've been figuring that out too. Another of those things I got into without knowing why. Here's the story.

I went to Barts [St. Bartholomew's Medical College, London University], like dad, and the year after I graduated ended up as Dr. Hamilton Fairley's intern—the first Oncology Professor in the NHS. I used to go to "The Blood Clinic"—a nickname for the weekly visits of patients with blood cancers, mostly leukemia. Forty years ago, hardly one was cured—most lived only a few weeks. But these were chemotherapy's early days, and Fairley was at the forefront. It was nothing for 60 patients to show up, a lot of them London stockbrokers and journalists, so pretty smart and informed. They figured out how to educate themselves and each other from the few resources out there, and there was something of a comrade-in-arms feel to where they waited to be seen by the specialists, or get their blood counts or chemo shots. They called themselves "The Blood Club," and obviously got to know each other well in their cramped surroundings—we'd call it a patient support group today.

But the docs didn't socialize with them at all, and there was one unbroken rule: no staff ever used the "C" word (= Cancer), let alone the "D" one (= Death), with a patient. Any such utterance was confined to quick asides in back corridors between social worker and wife of someone close to his deathbed. And the family members were encouraged to keep up this pretence; the thinking was, if you told a patient the truth you'd speed up their end. I saw this charade played out dozens of times—and it gave me an inkling why no one had warned me about you. Crazy thinking about it now, but you just didn't tell a 12-year-old his mother's dying—time enough afterwards.

The way it happened with me was—that second term after I went to Epsom [Epsom College, a private boarding school], *my housemaster, Mr. Berridge, summoned me into his study and told me to go home for the weekend. No explanation; Uncle Ken met me at Weston station and drove straight to the hospital. There you were, sitting up in bed in your pink crocheted bed jacket, Elizabeth, Mary, Jane* [my three elder sisters] *and Aunty Joan on either side of the bed. I sulked horribly—I can see now I must have known perfectly well something bad was happening, and was scared. But it took me years to get over being that way. So—I'm sorry I was mean to you, mummy.*

Because that was the last time I saw you—alive or dead. They sent me straight back to school in time for Monday morning French and Geography. And a month later I went through the whole scenario again— from Mr. Berridge's study to Uncle Ken at the station in his Ford Prefect. This time, though, we drove straight home to Ravenswood (I don't remember anything on the way), where he took me into the drawing room, sat me on the sofa with him in your armchair across the room—it seemed a hundred miles away—and told me you'd died three days ago. Fifty-three years later I still can't remember if he said anything else. Next thing I was walking down Bristol Road toward the seafront. That's all I remember—if my sisters or other uncles and aunts were at home, I don't remember seeing them, or even when I did get home. I "came to" sometime the next Monday back in Geography.

So, mummy, this is how I came to it—I must have chosen my career then and there. I did a year's residency in 1968 at Jenny Lind Children's Hospital in Norwich, and early on I looked after a 10-year-old—Audrey, I think—with a horrible cancer. But she lived most of the time I was there, because by then we were using chemo with children, which worked for a while. And I found out it was okay to make friends with my patients! She was in hospital most of the time toward the end and her mum and dad lived a good way away so couldn't visit much. I'd go and play card games and chat with her in the evenings. My boss got wind and worried I'd get too hurt when she died, but I knew it was all right. I held her hand and talked to her when she was dying. It was the best thing I'd ever done. I'd like to have held your hand, mummy, when it came your time but life doesn't work that way, does it?

So that's my story. You're the first to hear it—I haven't even read this to Dorothy yet. I'll write again or maybe I've said enough until we're together again.

Reflective Dialogue

D   Did you learn something new writing your letter?

J   Oh yes, I really got it—grief is lifelong one way or another. Though it's no longer acute—it's almost nostalgia for that childhood freedom and safety she supplied. Funny, I called her *Mummy*—absolutely a child's word. A grown-up wouldn't use it, so writing threw me back in time and I relived the experience . . . So cathartic. My poem, "Leaving Mother," speaks of the last time I saw her *joyful*—the end of summer holidays before that first school term.[31] We were walking in Weston Woods when she tired and my sisters and I "hoisted her four limbs between us, swung her with the abandon of children whose mother would never commit the treason of abandonment."[32] Twenty-five years on, I found my first good listener, and sorted things out—I made that twelve-year-old's subconscious decision to make war on cancer by choosing medicine. No one could talk me out of it—though uncle-doctor Ken tried his best. It's astounding what a huge and finally positive impact a seemingly senseless tragedy can have.

D   That reminds me of the Rumi poem that grief is a blessing.[33]

J   Making meaning of the existential purpose of loss—that idea can be a stretch for doctors. It's central to my teaching young students who mostly don't have the perspective life experience brings.

D   You seem to link grief to feeling safe, *held*. Here we are fifty-odd years later, and you still feel sad—guilty maybe?—about not holding your mother's hand that last time. Perhaps your not trusting people easily has something to do with feeling abandoned by your mother—by all those people who "couldn't" use the "C" word or the "D" word?

J   It was more than simply feeling "left out" and not knowing what was happening. I still feel some anger, maybe with her for not talking to me, though mostly with the whole culture that condoned this. But I see now it was really my fear and sadness about her being no longer *available*. Writing to her, I could take this stuff out and tell her I'm sorry—something I couldn't do as a boy brought up to hide all feelings! And with the perspective of age and "distance" I see how the good gets passed around. I didn't hold my mother's hand, but I did Audrey's.

D   So as a doctor you could translate your anger into compassion? Has it made a difference to how you tell someone their loved one is dying?

J   Oh huge. Backing up a minute, though, letter writing is an act of creativity—call it art or craft—and, like anything creative, implies self-expression, "getting it from inside to outside"—always good. Even fifty years on it's still therapeutic. Another epiphany I had is it's okay to "befriend" your patients—witness Audrey. Nowadays, I teach that flouting barriers between care giver and receiver is easier than blocking those feelings. It's also a huge gap in health professional education to know how to handle pain and distress in ourselves and our colleagues. So how's it changed my approach? Fundamentally! I had no guidance in med school. The first time I had to talk candidly to a family, indeed a patient, I was just on faculty back in London, with nobody "above me"' to tell me what to do. And the resources I found came from quite different places. For example, I'd done a lot of acting, where you get good both at dialogue and stagecraft.

D   How you enter a room?

J   Yup. My theater professor friend at Florida taught my students the importance of skilful, precise interaction, spoken and unspoken.

D   How might you hold your body when delivering bad news? I assume not like Uncle Ken who sat as far from you as possible.

J   No indeed. I think how one uses one's body is instinctive if you let it. It's self-evident that telling bad stuff requires sitting down and getting as close as acceptable to create the connection.

D   Like your example of six-year-old Joy who couldn't touch her dying brother because her Korean parents believed it "would hold his soul in the world."[34] Brings me back to the unfinished business of grief. Was there any resolution in making this first communication—structured communication, that is—with your mother?

J   Absolutely. A sense of closure came from going over the details so specifically. I had this vivid image of my mother's bed jacket—pink, handmade, probably crocheted—swimming up from the past. Crucial too, I found faith we'd meet again. I think personal faith is vital to teaching this subject.

Beloved Patrick:

In Sunday's paper, Silver Donald Cameron's First Word was head-lined "One Musician's Final Gift."[35] *Like you, Mary Louise VandeBerg gifted her body to science through Dalhousie's Anatomy Department. She died on Canada Day 2007 in her daughter's Nova Scotia home. I knew the procedure so well—after your heart attack you'd carried your donor card in your wallet for 7 years before you died, contact numbers pencilled on the back—so useful when I finally delivered on your gift. For you, it fit with two threads in your life: find value in anything you could—even your wasted body—and enrich human inquiry, however you could. Your body could teach especially about heart disease, diabetes and colon cancer.*

In your final months, whenever the nurses asked if students could attend you, you were happy they have their first try—so uncomplaining— at starting an intravenous infusion, tricky often for experienced nurses. You proudly gave your body to science, wanting to avoid dying in Christmas week, or when they had more than needed, and yours wouldn't be accepted. I gave the social worker your donor card the morning you died and heard another possible reason for refusal—dementia. Well, I could confirm you were lucid to the end; your last words—"too late" (for daughters Susan and Cathy, expected next day)—showed your certain knowledge of your death just before your last breath.

And I proudly attended the donor memorial service in Dalhousie's Memorial Gardens 18 months later; they buried your ashes in a collective grave, and offered prayers for you. During the service, several made trib-utes. One student said the bodies of our loved ones were "my first teacher." I'd tried to block pictures of students dissecting your precious body—only then did I let myself shape concrete images. We were especially moved by OT Student Jo-Anna Arseneau's tribute. At your eldest daughter Evelyn's request she emailed us the text. Here are some of her heart-warming words, which for me capture the meaning of your gift that keeps giving:

The selfless gift of your loved one . . . will help all the people we will help throughout our careers, a truly endless gift. . . . When we began studying the hand, we reflected upon the significance and the meaning behind this part of our body. In our everyday life, we speak and feel with our hands, hold others with our hands, and provide love and comfort with our hands. So despite efforts to try and distance ourselves from the people we were working with, humanity overrides and our hearts were touched.

This took me straight to those expressive listening hands of yours that I held the moment you died. Only Louise of your daughters was there, and as the morticians wheeled you past us, the sheet hiding you from view, she spoke her thought that we'd abandoned you to strangers: "I wish I could go with him and hold his hand." Octavia Paz's In Praise of Hands *broadens the craftsmanship concept that "teaches us to die and hence teaches us to live," to all handwork of self-expression and relationship.*[36]

My reading has kept your body's image front and center. Two things in Cameron's article struck me. First, I hadn't known Dalhousie students say a prayer before beginning dissection. I'm so comforted by the idea of students gathering around you in prayer. Second, I was taken with the picture of Peggy pinning a "vivid account of Mary Louise's life and character . . . to her mother's clothing before the body was taken away."[37] I wish I'd known students can, and like to, know about their donors. The OT student, Jo-Anna, said, "As students, we did not know your loved ones in the capacity that you have, nor did we know them in the traditional sense of what knowing a person might be. We don't know what names they held, where they came from or the things that they loved to do, but we do know that by their ultimate sacrifice and gift, they had a beautiful, kind and generous spirit." I wish I'd pinned [to your clothing] an account of your life and character—much more meaningful if they knew you loved jazz, that you were a master of spontaneous songs with altered lyrics to fit any occasion, were a longtime CBC radio/TV broadcaster in the city where they were studying. Maybe their parents danced to the music when you hosted High Society [Maritimes equivalent of Dick Clark's American Bandstand]. As they were dissecting your hand, I could envision you asking them your engaging questions about their own aspirations, and listening intently with your face—and your hands.

In Vincent Lam's novel, Bloodletting & Miraculous Cures, his work as an ER doctor validates his description of students' first encountering death.[38] The Dean's injunction—"distasteful incidents regarding cadavers have, in the past, resulted in expulsion"—and the anatomy demonstrator's declaration—"This fine cadaver is your first patient"—seem odious.[39] They reduce your body—and in a way, your life. I'd never use the word "cadaver" or "corpse"—it diminishes your gift and your humanity. Our language has made "over my dead body" a curse not a gift. And no mention of prayers before beginning. I learned their dissection manual was particular about the first incision beginning "at the top of the sternum, extending downward to the xiphoid," and I thought, "If only they were as particular about 'treating your [first] patient nobly.' "[40] But I hear in my "mind's ear" your challenging, clarifying question—a frequent response to my academic writing—"Are you really recommending a step-by-step manual for treating the patient nobly?" Preempting, as usual, a potential reader's/listener's question. For me, being "as particular" would focus on words and metaphors. For starters, I think it would change the relationship with your dead body, if the advice was—paraphrasing the student at your service—to treat your first teacher nobly. Calling your body a cadaver doesn't.

Richard Selzer talks about patient and caregiver both needing story and metaphor to illuminate their suffering.[41] *This could apply to the anatomy lab. Lam's students try to take meaning from signs written on their first teacher's body, in this case a tattooed crucifix in a heart. The manual called for an incision directly through the tattoo so they had to negotiate this conflict—learn the "bicipital groove" but still "respect a man's symbols."*[42] *I purposefully read Pauline Chen's* Final Exam *for its subtitle—*A Surgeon's Reflections on Mortality. *She reflects that one effect of separating death from life may be the sense of doctor immortality, which defines death as the result of errors: "Death is no longer a natural event but a ritual gone awry."*[43] *She laments this definition as "erasing the face of our patients and inserting our own fiercely optimistic version of immortality. . . . When we refuse to accept our own fallibility, we deny ourselves grief."*[44] *" 'Surviving' the illnesses and deaths of others creates the kind of illusory immortality that leads not only to professional arrogance but also to those selfless feats of medical heroism."*[45] *I want to believe medical practice and pedagogy has moved beyond Chen's experience of relegating the dead to "just another middle-of-the night operation" and "forgetting their humanity;" that the students who learned over you didn't erase your face but tried to piece together your "book of life . . . [beginning] with the epilogue and attempt[ing] to read backwards."*[46]

You know how attracted I am to Michel Foucault's ideas of how everyday practices are the effect of dominant discourses. Chen's book is a gold mine for tracing the history of public acceptance of anatomical dissection, a fairly recent phenomenon. Her scholarship ranges from early Christian beliefs about desecrating the bodies of Crusaders to the Renaissance lithographs of human anatomy, complete with artful poses.[47] *I think the effects of the 19th-century discourse that the "truth about illness and disease lay in the body . . . medicine could only ever be absolutely certain about disease once the patient had died and the body could be dissected" can be traced to the present.*[48] *Covering your dead body with a sheet and wheeling "it" down the corridor extends the view of patients as objects of scientific knowledge and practice to the human anatomy lab. I blocked images of students working on you because I shuddered to think of your being mined for science, with your humanity and life's value held of no account. Now I've come to this deeper understanding, I shall use the image of your precious body as a symbol to capture the attention of*

*caregivers and policy makers. You, meticulous recycler in life, would
appreciate this symbolic use of your dead body as a gift that keeps on
giving.*

Reflective Dialogue

J   Patrick spent twenty-seven years as a CBC radio/TV interviewer,
right? So, is it too fanciful to imagine him in his last hours interviewing
Death? What might be his opening question?

D   Well, when he interviewed Oscar Peterson, he asked what flashed
through his mind as his fingers raced over the ivories. So I see him
asking Death about the timing—timing's a big thing for interviewers
when they have just a few seconds to wrap up—*Why now when we had so
many wonderful plans?*

J   Your letter changes the whole idea of lifelong learning. Not just cradle
to grave but beyond. I always say I've learned more from patients than
medical mentors. I think Pauline Chen feels the same; her very first
patient had been dead over a year before she laid eyes or hands on her.[49]
And her dissection fears, like Lam captures in fiction, resound with me.
The lectures Chen attended preparing for her first day of dissection were
replete with tools to detach emotionally from the experience, with language the main tool in her kit, beginning with "the cadaver"—not a
person who'd had a life.[50]

D   Probably the students working on Patrick had only the information Chen had on her "cadavers"—a card with gender and approximate
age at death.[51]

J   No wonder the cult of death jokes grew up in anatomical dissection
rooms, to deal with embarrassment and barely suppressed fear of the
dead.

D   I wince thinking that Patrick could have been the subject of such
taunts.

J   I'm glad we're getting a bit more enlightened. Memorial services
are quite widespread in medical schools, honoring the dead as students' teachers. The spread of humanities programs has brought
telling and writing stories of the emotional impact of first intimate encounters with human life and death right into the dissection
rooms.

D   It was such a tribute, the medical student referring to the bodies of our loved ones as his "first teacher," rather than his first patient, as Chen does.

J   Words are potent, aren't they? We lose sight of the "MedSpeak" that pervades medical culture. It's terribly hard to get students to talk to their patients in "lay" language when they talk to each other in codes as unintelligible as "legalese" to nonlawyers. When I arrived in the U.S. as a new professor from England, I understood what Churchill meant about two countries separated by a common language—one medical culture doesn't even cross to another. Expected to teach residents and med students, I felt like a six-year-old unable to understand U.S. MedSpeak—quite different from England's version.

D   It's a funny thing, even though I know from adult education that writing is a reflective practice that churns up unexpected things, it took me by surprise when I wrote about Patrick's last words: you remember— "too late" (meaning for Susan and Cathy). I thought they were a kind of goodbye to those daughters who wouldn't see him again alive. But in writing, their deeper significance came to me—Patrick, always the inquiring mind, still learning and asking the hard questions, must have wondered about death itself.

J   When he was dying, did you, an educated and intelligent woman, understand everything the doctors told you?

D   It wasn't so much I didn't understand the *words*. I couldn't *read the codes* of what was *unsaid*. Both the surgeon and the oncologist drew pictures for us after Patrick's surgery, showing exactly where the tumor was in his colon, showing us they didn't get it all. I still have those scribbles. The oncologist's drawing showed the stages, with likely outcomes. Patrick's was C—60 percent chance. I just heard "chance," better than the top stage—D. But given his age—seventy-five—Dr. M. left it up to us whether to go with chemotherapy. Once that failed, and draining the ascites became a frequent necessity, he told us: "All bets are off." That felt like a body blow. I remember we walked out of the hospital gripping onto each other. But still I didn't "hear" the message to prepare for his death. In retrospect, though, I think Patrick did, and took concrete steps—always practical, he gave cash gifts to his daughters to avoid probate. But I chose to hear the oncologist's comments as clinical and statistical details, not—perhaps I couldn't—that Patrick was dying.

J   Well, the oncologist didn't say so directly. "All bets are off" is
euphemism—and you didn't use the "D" word with each other, did you?
[D: No.]. Even if you heard it with your heart, you chose the strong
resource of denial. Is that right in retrospect?

D   Yes and no. What about "tell all the truth but tell it slant" as in your
poem about the two surgeons' response to your telling an eight-year-old
straight out: "Joey, you're going to die."[52] So they told us—but they
told us *slant*. After all, right until the week before Patrick died, they were
trying second-line chemotherapy. Though I remember telling his
daughter Susan, when the nurse showed us the statistics on the drug's
success rate in terms of little blue men against colorless white ones,
"I wish there were more little blue men." I think you can know
and not know the truth simultaneously. Perhaps it got *told slant* just
for me because, alone, Patrick would have asked the straight questions
and insisted on the straight answers.

J   Yes. My poem ends: "Was I *too* candid? They'd thought so. For me,
I knew he knew. He knew I knew it: straight, no slant in that."[53]
Maybe your doctors knew Patrick knew it, but didn't know you didn't
know it! "We didn't get it all" and "All bets are off" are telling it slant,
you know now. They sound commonplace but they're so significant.
For all those little-blue-and-white-men statistics, it's the distinction between a cancer with every chance of being cured and one where all
bets are off. You see, they use the best drugs first, and if they definitely
fail—Patrick's tumor had spread to damage his liver—substitutes are
almost always much less successful.

D   It's just these kinds of clinical statistics that break my heart because they reduce Patrick to numbers—a specimen. That's why I was so
taken with Cameron's tale of Peggy pinning her mother's story to her
clothing.

J   So... how might the oncologist have done things differently, to hu-
manize his relationship with Patrick and yourself?

D   I don't want to demonize those doctors, who were clearly very drawn
to Patrick, and had him talking about his *life*—especially his CBC life.
And when the surgeon saw him last—he was moving to Virginia—he
gave Patrick a huge hug, and, more startling for me, Patrick returned it
warmly.

J   Gosh, can you remember how that felt to see two older men from
different cultures joined so intimately?

D   I was very moved. But this was a code I knew—no slant. Unconditional love between two humans, not doctor-to-patient. Elisabeth Kübler-Ross, who revolutionized how the world sees dying, says: "The only thing that truly heals people is unconditional love."[54]

J   The surgeon's hug seems like an act of real nobility. Isn't it a wonderful juxtaposition for those brown Semitic hands that had skillfully removed 180 centimeters of Patrick's colon to now embrace him? That's Paz's true art of handicraft.

D   Oh, lovely, use *and* beauty, not *either-or.*

Coda

D   Let's go back to the themes of gifts and learning in our title. Did our process of challenging cultural norms by writing to the dead along with reflective dialogue, do what the theorists and practitioners say it would do in terms of mourning and meaning-making?

J   Those folks, Rumi among them, ask us to learn from our greatest tragedies by seeing their gift. Let's try this. Take it back to your experience. Can you at this point after Patrick's death find any gift in his cancer, the way you have in the gift of his body to science?

D   Being with Patrick at the moment of dying is the greatest gift. It was a sacred time and space, giving me a glimpse of my own—what it means to have no time and space, and thus no fear. Fear's an utterly earthbound phenomenon. I wouldn't have got that without our reflective dialogue on my letter. One striking new image is of students remembering Patrick's life and his generous spirit as they dismember his tissues. Memory animated with dialogue is the art at the heart of the pedagogy of mourning as re-membering/dis-membering. Celebrating the hand's touch as the reciprocal care of the living for the dying, and the dying for the living, has shaped our thinking about "immortal art" on a preservable-evanescent continuum, which Edmund Carpenter calls "silent music and invisible art."[55] Your image of those hands that removed Patrick's tumor enfolding him in a goodbye hug is pure poetry—maybe it'll wend its way into a new poem! We've preserved the story of this evanescent experience as immortal memory—and as gift. Did something similar get jogged loose in our dialogue after your letter?

J   Yes, as teacher-practitioner, I've always tried to help students and colleagues handle hard truths around dying with integrity, recognizing the nuances, verbal and nonverbal, arising in these interactions. In our dialogue about my anger with the grown-ups taking care of me totally evading the truth, I saw clearly how formative those experiences were in setting me on course to find my power as physician-teacher.

D   Do you think mourning provided you with the creative materials for writing poetry, as the literature suggests, which is also a medium of "altruistic love" involved in teaching the art of truth-telling?

J   Yes, profoundly—but gradually, subconsciously over the forty-seven years since my first premed days. I never knew why I started writing poetry but I always knew bringing art into my hospital was linked with my drive to become a doctor of palliative art.

D   We didn't plan this paper this way. It's only coming to me now that we're wrapping up that we're engaging in the third level of dialogical learning—third-loop learning—which is "the learning that opens inquiry into the 'whys' " underlying reflective dialogue.[56] It's learning about our learning, which goes from single loop—*remembering* (our letters)—to double loop—*re-membering* (reflective dialogue)—to triple loop—*re-remembering*. Can we think at this level about this challenge to cultural norms about mourning, and teaching about dying—namely, communicating with the dead? This particular third level of learning opens inquiry not into the "whys" but into the "what ifs." As-if conversations give a special place to the subjunctive voice, so we can sustain our relationship with the dead, unlike the usual emphasis on confronting "reality" and accepting loss.[57]

J   Like "Mummy, you *would* be so happy to know I care for children" or "Patrick, what questions *would* you ask the students dissecting your tissues?" And, of course we often have "as if" conversations about Patrick when we cook in *his* kitchen. Because he was so meticulous in following recipes to the teaspoon, we often laugh at each other winging it through supper-preparation: "Patrick would turn in his urn!" It's like the down-to-earth quote from Mer-irtief's letter to Neb-itief we began with— "How are you?"

D   It makes the beloved's presence palpable. The subjunctive voice of "would turn in his urn" allows us a three-way chuckle with Patrick. I was comforted to find autobiography and in-depth research as evidence of the continuous bonds with the dead. Fifteen of [Luann] Daggett's eighteen interviews with the bereaved reported experiences of communicating with loved ones. I love the response of one man who wished he'd known about it so he "could have been on the lookout."[58] Almost by-the-by C. S. Lewis talks about the "*quality* of last night's experience" with his beloved H. I trembled with recognition where he says: "I never in any mood imagined the dead as being—well, so business-like. Yet there was an extreme and cheerful intimacy, an intimacy that had not passed through the senses or the emotions at all."[59] I'm surprised too there's no big emotional charge to the experience. I have only one experience of Western mourners exposed to the commonplace among indigenous people of talking to the dead, but it sure unleashed emotion. When my brother David, a United Church minister, assisted at Aunt Flo's funeral, shortly after he returned from a three-year placement in New Zealand, he included the Maori tradition of acknowledging the dead's presence in the funeral rites. He turned to the closed casket and spoke directly— conversationally. My Aunt Dorothy said later, "I was okay until David began to talk to Flo," in which "okay" meant sustaining the "stiff upper lip" expected of women of her generation. Looking back, there's some-thing almost comical in the unexpected set against the conventional.

J   Did anyone laugh, I wonder? In my experience, laughter is quite common at funerals, even if it seems unseemly. Actually, the Irish wake is a time of merriment. I'll tell you, you can feel free to laugh as much as you find it in you if I die before you.

D   And you can write me love letters and tell me jokes in the hereafter. For me, cultural norms about dying are instilled in us. Look at *Hamlet*— you were the First Gravedigger in last year's community theater pro-duction so it's fresh in my mind. Communication with Hamlet's ghost is filled with fear and trembling. And the cultural norm suggesting dis-loyalty in marrying soon after losing a spouse—"funeral baked meats did coldly furnish forth the marriage tables" (act 1, scene 2)—is very personal for me. So writing letters to my beloved Patrick, then laughing with him (subjunctively) *and* you in *his* kitchen turns this cultural norm on end.

J   Theory into practice, isn't it? Just what we've been posing all along about autoethnography: it's a teaching and research tool, but also for caregiving, including self-care. It's a hand-i-craft in Octavio Paz's terms because "it teaches us to die and hence teaches us to live."[60]

NOTES

1. "Letters to the Dead," in *An Introduction to the History and Culture of Ancient Egypt*, http://nefertiti.iwebbland.com/texts/letters_to_the_dead.htm.

2. Edward Wente, *Letters from Ancient Egypt* (Atlanta: Scholars Press, 1990), 210–19.

3. See C. S. Lewis, *A Grief Observed* (NY: Bantam Books, 1976), and Elisabeth Kübler-Ross, *The Wheel of Life: A Memoir of Living and Dying* (New York: Touchstone, 1997).

4. Mary Jane Moffat, ed., *In the Midst of Winter: Selections from the Literature of Mourning* (New York: Vintage, 1992), 159.

5. Sharon Bajer, *Molly's Veil* (Winnipeg, MB: Scirocco Drama, 2005).

6. Dorothy A. Lander & John Graham-Pole, "The Appreciative Pedagogy of Palliative Care: Arts-Based or Evidence-Based?" *International Journal for Learning through the Arts: A Research Journal on Arts Integration in Communities* 2, no. 1, article 15 (2006), available at http://repositories.cdlib.org/clta/lta/vol2/iss1/art15.

7. David Holman and Richard Thorpe, introduction to *Management and Language*, ed. David Holman and Richard Thorpe (London: Sage, 2003), 2.

8. Arthur P. Bochner and Carolyn S. Ellis, "Communication as Auto-ethnography," in *Communication as . . . Perspectives on Theory*, ed. Gregory J. Shepherd, Jeffrey St. John, and Ted Striphas (Thousand Oaks, CA: Sage, 2006), 118.

9. Rachel N. Remen, *Kitchen Table Wisdom: Stories that Heal* (New York: Riverhead Books, 1996). See also Diane Rooks, *Spinning Gold out of Straw: How Stories Heal* (St. Augustine, FL: Salt Run Press, 2001), and Tuija Saresma, " 'Art as a Way to Life:' Bereavement and the Healing Power of Arts and Writing," *Qualitative Inquiry* 9, no. 4 (2003): 603–20.

10. Octavio Paz and the World Crafts Council, *In Praise of Hands* (Toronto: MacClelland & Stewart, 1974), 21.

11. Ibid.

12. John Graham-Pole, "The 'S' in SOAP: Exploring the Connection," *Journal of Poetry Therapy* 18, no. 3 (2005): 165–70.

13. Edmund Carpenter, "Image Making in Arctic Art," in *Sign, Image, Symbol*, ed. Gyorgy Kepes (New York: Braziller, 1966), 206.

14. Bonnie Stone Sunstein and Elizabeth Chiseri-Strater, *Field Working: Reading and Writing Research*, 3rd ed. (Boston: Bedford/St. Martin's, 2007), 131–32.

15. 16. Dorothy A. Lander and John Graham-Pole, "Love Medicine for the Dying and Their Caregivers: The Body of Evidence," *Journal of Health Psychology* 13: 2 (2008): 201-12.

17. Scott H. Becker and Roger M. Knudson, "Visions of the Dead: Imagination and Mourning," *Death Studies* 27, no. 8 (2003): 694.

18. William Bridges, *The Way of Transition: Embracing Life's Most Difficult Moments* (Cambridge, MA: Perseus, 2001), 171, 224.

19. Parker Palmer, *The Courage to Teach* (San Francisco: Jossey-Bass, 1998), 20.

20. Chris Hawes, "Writing in Residence," *British Medical Journal* 303 (1991): 527.

21. Matthew Fox, *Creativity: Where the Divine and the Human Meet* (New York: Jeremy P. Tarcher, 2002), 28.

22. See Becker and Knudson, "Visions of the Dead"; Luann M. Daggett, "The Experience of After-Death Communication," *Journal of Holistic Nursing* 23, no. 2

(2005): 191–207; and Nigel P. Field and Michael Friedrichs, "Continuing Bonds in Coping with the Death of a Husband," *Death Studies* 28 (2004): 597–620.

23. Becker and Knudson, "Visions of the Dead," 694.

24. Bochner and Ellis, "Communication as Autoethnography," 116, 119.

25. Carolyn Ellis, *Final Negotiations: A Story of Love, Loss, and Chronic Illness* (Philadelphia: Temple University Press, 1995), 111.

26. Laurel Richardson, *Last Writes: A Daybook for a Dying Friend* (Walnut Creek, CA: Left Coast Press, 2007).

27. Bochner and Ellis, "Communication as Autoethnography," 117.

28. Ibid., 112.

29. Dwight Conquerwood, cited in D. Soyini Madison, "Co-Performative Witnessing," *Cultural Studies* 21, 6 (2007): 826.

30. Madison, "Co-Performative Witnessing," 829.

31. John Graham-Pole, "Leaving Mother," in *Quick: A Pediatrician's Illustrated Poetry* (San Jose, CA: Writers Club Press, 2002), 25.

32. Ibid.

33. See Lander and Graham-Pole, "Appreciative Pedagogy of Palliative Care," 10.

34. See Lander and Graham-Pole, "Love Medicine."

35. Silver Donald Cameron, "One Musician's Final Gift," *Sunday Herald*, September 9, 2007, 2.

36. Paz, *In Praise of Hands*, 24.

37. Cameron, "One Musician's Final Gift," 2.

38. Vincent Lam, *Bloodletting and Miraculous Cures* (Toronto: Anchor Canada, 2005).

39. Lam, *Bloodletting*.

40. Lam, *Bloodletting*, 34.

41. Richard Selzer, *The Doctor Stories* (New York: Picador, 1998).

42. Lam, *Bloodletting*, 42–43.

43. Pauline W. Chen, *Final Exam: A Surgeon's Reflections on Mortality* (New York: Random House, 2007), 95.

44. Ibid., 119.

45. Ibid., 195.

46. Ibid., 195, 13.

47. Ibid., 21.

48. Sarah Nettleton and Roger Burrows, "From Bodies in Hospitals to People in Community: A Theoretical Analysis of the Relocation of Health Care," *Care in Place* 1, no. 2 (1994): 95.

49. Chen, *Final Exam*, 3.

50. Ibid., 8. "We must view this dead human body not as 'one of us' but as 'one of them,' a medical case to be understood but not embraced. . . . It was as if such separation would provide me with a greater sense of objectivity . . . and thus an enhanced ability to care for my patients" (Ibid.).

51. Ibid., 13.

52. Graham-Pole, *Quick*, 90. "Tell all the truth but tell it slant" comes from an Emily Dickinson poem by the same name ("Tell All the Truth but Tell It Slant" [1868] in *The Complete Poems of Emily Dickinson*, ed. Thomas H. Johnson [Boston: Little, Brown & Company, 1960]).

53. Graham-Pole, *Quick*, 90.

54. Kübler-Ross, *Wheel of Life*, 15.

55. Edmund Carpenter, "Silent Music and Invisible Art," *Natural History* 87, no. 5 (1978): 90–99.

56. William Isaacs, "Taking Flight: Dialogue, Collective Thinking, and Organizational Learning," *Organizational Dynamics* 22, no. 2 (1993): 30.

57. Lorraine Hedtke and John Winslade, "The Use of the Subjunctive in Re-Membering: Conversations with Those Who Are Grieving," *Omega* 50, no. 3 (2005): 197.

58. Daggett, "After-Death Communication," 197.

59. Moffat, *Midst of Winter*, 199.

60. Paz, *In Praise of Hands*, 23.

BIBLIOGRAPHY

Bajer, Sharon. *Molly's Veil*. Winnipeg, MB: Scirocco Drama, 2005.

Becker, Scott H., and Roger M. Knudson. "Visions of the Dead: Imagination and Mourning." *Death Studies* 27, no. 8 (2003): 691–716.

Bochner, Arthur P., and Carolyn S. Ellis. "Communication as Autoethnography." In *Communication as . . . Perspectives on Theory*, edited by Gregory J. Shepherd, Jeffrey St. John, and Ted Striphas, 110–22. Thousand Oaks, CA: Sage, 2006.

Bridges, William. *The Way of Transition: Embracing Life's Most Difficult Moments*. Cambridge, MA: Perseus, 2001.

Cameron, Silver Donald. "One Musician's Final Gift." *Sunday Herald*. September 9, 2007, 2.

Carpenter, Edmund. "Image Making in Arctic Art." In *Sign, Image, Symbol*, edited by Gyorgy Kepes, 206–25. New York: Braziller, 1966.

——. "Silent Music and Invisible Art." *Natural History* 87, no. 5 (1978): 90–99.

Chen, Pauline W. *Final Exam: A Surgeon's Reflections on Mortality*. New York: Random House, 2007.

Daggett, Luann M. "The Experience of After-Death Communication." *Journal of Holistic Nursing* 23, no. 2 (2005): 191–207.

Dickinson, Emily. "Tell All the Truth but Tell It Slant" (c. 1868). In *The Complete Poems of Emily Dickinson*, edited by Thomas H. Johnson, 507–8. Boston: Little, Brown & Company, 1960.

Ellis, Carolyn. *Final Negotiations: A Story of Love, Loss, and Chronic Illness*. Philadelphia: Temple University Press, 1995.

Field, Nigel P., and Michael Friedrichs. "Continuing Bonds in Coping with the Death of a Husband." *Death Studies* 28 (2004): 597–620.

Fox, Matthew. *Creativity: Where the Divine and the Human Meet*. New York: Jeremy P. Tarcher, 2002.

Graham-Pole, John. *Quick: A Pediatrician's Illustrated Poetry*. San Jose, CA: Writers Club Press, 2002.

———. "The 'S' in SOAP: Exploring the Connection." *Journal of Poetry Therapy* 18, no. 3 (2005): 165–70.

Hawes, Chris. "Writing in Residence." *British Medical Journal* 303 (1991): 527.

Hedtke, Lorraine, and John Winslade. "The Use of the Subjunctive in Re-Membering Conversations with Those Who Are Grieving." *Omega* 50, no. 3 (2005): 197–215.

Holman, David, and Richard Thorpe. Introduction to *Management and Language*, edited by David Holman and Richard Thorpe, 1–12. London: Sage, 2003.

Isaacs, William. "Taking Flight: Dialogue, Collective Thinking, and Organizational Learning." *Organizational Dynamics* 22, no. 2 (1993): 24–39.

Kübler-Ross, Elisabeth. *The Wheel of Life: A Memoir of Living and Dying*. New York: Touchstone, 1997.

Lander, Dorothy A., and John Graham-Pole. "The Appreciative Pedagogy of Palliative Care: Arts-Based or Evidence-Based?" *International Journal for Learning through the Arts: A Research Journal on Arts Integration in Communities* 2, no. 1, article 15 (2006). Available at http://repositories.cdlib.org/clta/lta/vol2/iss1/art15.

———. "Love Medicine for the Dying and Their Caregivers: The Body of Evidence." *Journal of Health Psychology* 13: 2 (2008): 201-12.

Lam, Vincent. *Bloodletting and Miraculous Cures*. Toronto: Anchor Canada, 2005.

Lewis, C. S. *A Grief Observed*. New York: Bantam, 1976.

Madison, D. Soyini. "Co-Performative Witnessing." *Cultural Studies* 21, no. 6 (2007): 826-31.

Moffat, Mary Jane, ed. *In the Midst of Winter: Selections from the Literature of Mourning*. New York: Vintage, 1992.

Nettleton, Sarah, and Roger Burrows. "From Bodies in Hospitals to People in Community: A Theoretical Analysis of the Relocation of Health Care." *Care in Place* 1, no. 2 (1994): 93–103.

Palmer, Parker. *The Courage to Teach*. San Francisco: Jossey-Bass, 1998.

Paz, Octavio, and the World Crafts Council. *In Praise of Hands*. Toronto: MacClelland & Stewart, 1974.

Remen, Rachel Naomi. *Kitchen Table Wisdom: Stories that Heal*. New York: Riverhead Books, 1996.

Richardson, Laurel. *Last Writes: A Daybook for a Dying Friend*. Walnut Creek, CA: Left Coast Press, 2007.

Rooks, Diane. *Spinning Gold out of Straw: How Stories Heal*. St. Augustine, FL: Salt Run Press, 2001.

Saresma, Tuija. " 'Art as a Way to Life:' Bereavement and the Healing Power of Arts and Writing." *Qualitative Inquiry* 9, no. 4 (2003): 603–20.

Selzer, Richard. *The Doctor Stories*. New York: Picador, 1998.

Stone Sunstein, Bonnie, and Elizabeth Chiseri-Strater. *Field Working: Reading and Writing Research*. 3rd ed. Boston: Bedford/St. Martin's, 2007.

Wente, Edward. *Letters from Ancient Egypt*. Atlanta: Scholars Press, 1990.

PART VI

Life After Death

15

Life After Death: An Overview of Contemporary Beliefs for Teachers

Paul Badham

This chapter was originally written and published in the journal *Dialogue* as a guide for teachers in Britain responsible for teaching Philosophy of Religion to advanced level students.[1] These "A" Level examinations are taken at age eighteen in Britain. The chapter explores the wide range of beliefs held in contemporary society giving both the case for extinction on naturalistic grounds as well as spelling out the importance for world religion of belief in life after death. It explores the case for dualism in the writings of leading British philosophers. It looks at resurrection in Judaism, Christianity, and Islam as well as the importance of the law of karma in the religions of the East. It outlines the philosophical arguments for life after death in Christian philosophy and examines the empirical evidence for reincarnation with special reference to the Tibetan and Pureland traditions of Buddhism. The chapter ends with an examination of near-death experiences and their possible significance.

What Do People Believe Today?

A survey of "contemporary belief in life after death" by Douglas Davies found the following range of beliefs about what happens when we die:

> Nothing happens. We come to the end of life—29 percent
> Our soul passes to another world—34 percent

Our bodies await resurrection—8 percent

We come back as someone else—12 percent

Trust God, we are all in God's hands—22 percent[2]

The Case for Extinction

Those who believe that after death nothing happens normally take for granted a "naturalistic" understanding of what it means to be human. This says that we are essentially embodied creatures whose mental and spiritual existence is totally dependent on our material body and brain and whose only possible existence is on this earth and in this time. We have evolved from and are part of nature. We are born, reproduce ourselves, and die like all other animals. Philosophy of language teaches us that we learn to understand and use "person words" like "I," "you," or "Mary" to refer to ourselves and other embodied people. Hence it is literally meaningless to talk of a person surviving bodily death any more than it would make sense to talk of an immaterial table living on after the actual table had been wholly burnt up.[3]

The Case for Dualism

Those who believe in life after death can accept most of this naturalistic picture as accurately describing what our everyday experience of life teaches us but they reject the conclusions drawn from it and the idea that naturalism is the whole truth. They accept what science shows about the intimate relationship between all our thinking, feeling, and willing and some quite specific brain states. But they argue that the same facts can be equally well explained by a doctrine of mind-brain interaction which can also explain further facts about how the mind in turn can affect the brain. They also argue that though language was originally learned in relation to everyday experience, it can be developed to cover further insights.

Richard Swinburne believes that dualism is "inescapable" if we are really to explain human existence and experience.[4] First, he points out that though the mental life of thought, sensation, and purpose may be caused by physico-chemical events in the brain, it is quite different from those events. Second, he draws attention to the fact that "conscious experiences are causally efficacious. Our thoughts and feelings are not just phenomena caused by goings-on in the brain; they cause other thoughts and feelings and they make a difference to the agent's behavior." Third, he suggests that "though a human soul has a structure and character which is formed in part through the brain to which it is connected ... [it] acquires some independence of that brain."[5] Keith Ward adopts the same position: "Of course the soul depends on the brain ... but the soul need not always depend on the brain, any more than a man need always depend on the womb which supported his life before birth."[6] Such views provide a philosophical backing for the perspective for which John Hick argues in his "soul-making theodicy."[7] One purpose in life is to "school an intelligence and make it a soul."[8] A soul is not something with which we start life, but it may be something with which we end.

This hypothesis appears to be supported by the claims made by many resuscitated persons, that at the moment their hearts stopped beating, they found themselves outside their bodies looking down with interest on the attempts made by the medical teams to revive them. What makes these claims evidential is that their observations seem to be extraordinarily accurate, and to accord with what would have been seen if they genuinely were looking down from above.[9]

A second argument for the emergence of the human soul is the view that rational thought, scientific inquiry, and responsible decision making all depend on the view that human persons are genuinely free agents. A materialist understanding of the mind threatens that freedom because the human brain is a physical organism, and as such is subject to the laws of physics and chemistry. One such law is that physical causes always precede physical effects, and hence explaining natural phenomena by reference to future goals is inappropriate. But almost all human researchers think of their own work as responsible and goal directed, and think they are doing something more than simply giving a report on their own past brain states. When Jacques Monod declared that his goal in writing *Chance and Necessity* was to show that there was no such thing as purpose, his argument depended on exempting himself from its remit.[10]

A third argument for dualism is the claim that people have religious and parapsychological experiences that are inexplicable within a materialist framework. Research into religious experience shows that between one-third and one-half of all people questioned say they have had an *awareness of a power of presence different from everyday life*. Among committed believers, experiential knowledge of God through prayer and worship is central to living faith. Yet, no one imagines that we experience God through our senses. No one literally "sees" or "hears" God, so if divine-human encounter is real, it must be that God makes the reality of his presence felt other than through neural pathways, direct to the mind and not via sensory stimuli. This can only happen if the soul exists as a substantive reality.[11]

Similar issues arise with the experience of telepathy, by which I mean the transfer of information from one mind to another mind without the use of the neural pathways of the brain. A vast amount of experimental evidence in its favor has been gathered in universities throughout the world, but perhaps more convincing is the fact that most of us experience what may be telepathy in our everyday lives, with phenomena like the sudden feeling that we ought to contact someone moments before they phone or e-mail us.[12] What such experiences show is that our conscious awareness is not solely limited to information that reaches our brains through the senses, and hence, brain and mind are not identical.

Immortality and Resurrection?

Traditionally, Jews, Christians, and Muslims have believed in both the immortality of the soul and the resurrection of the body. According to the Vatican, "The Church affirms that a spiritual element survives and subsists after death, an element endowed with consciousness and will, so that the 'human self' subsists though deprived for the present of its complement of its body. To designate this element the Church uses the word 'soul,' the accepted term in the usage of Scripture and Tradition."[13] Historically, this view was held by all Christians, but because of the unease some philosophers feel about the concept of the soul, the Church of England Doctrine Commission has suggested it might be better to speak of "the *vastly complex information-bearing pattern*" (emphasis added) which constitutes our identity as being preserved in God's memory between death and resurrection.[14]

As far as belief in resurrection is concerned, this used to be taken literally as saying that we would get our old bodies back, but today it is normally understood as claiming that God will create for us a new form of embodiment suitable for a wholly different life in heaven. This is a logically possible belief in that modern physics allows for plural spaces or other dimensions of being, but there is no evidence for it other than the belief that it is something an all-powerful God would wish to bring about. Christians also base it on the belief that Jesus Christ was raised from the dead into a radically transformed life and that what happened to him, then, will happen to us all at the end of time.

Why Believe in Life After Death?

Five kinds of arguments tend to be put forward in favor of these beliefs. They can be classified as the following:

1. Religious: The claim that in this life it is possible to enter into a living relationship with God which God values and hence that God will wish to hold us in being through death.

2. Philosophical: John Hick argues in his *Evil and the God of Love* that to believe in an all-powerful and all loving God requires that old age disease and death do not have the last word, otherwise there could be no possible solution to the problem of evil. Hence belief in life after death becomes an essential element in making sense of belief in God.

3. Moral: Immanuel Kant argued in his *Critique of Practical Reason* that for morality to make sense, it is necessary that virtue and happiness should ultimately go together and this requires the postulation of immortality.

4. Historical: Belief in the resurrection of Jesus has led Christians to believe that what happened to him then will happen to them later. The evidence for Jesus' resurrection is primarily the amazing change in his disciples and their total conviction that he had appeared to them. We know they were convinced themselves because they persuaded others to share their belief and they died as martyrs (witnesses) to it. All the first Christians were Jews, yet they stopped observing the Sabbath and switched to observing the day of Christ's resurrection.

5. Scriptural: Some Jews argue that because the Torah speaks of God as being in living relationship with Abraham, Isaac, and Jacob, so they, and by analogy us, must live after death. Every book in the New Testament mentions the resurrection of Jesus, and the Qur'an speaks constantly of the importance of "the hereafter."

Philosophical Objections

All these beliefs assume the existence of God and collapse without that belief. An atheist can argue that the claim to a relationship with God is a delusion, that the problem of evil has no answer, and that morality does not make sense. She might also argue either that there is inadequate evidence for the resurrection of Jesus or that his resurrection was unique to him, and that in any case no authority attaches to the scriptures unless one believes them to be, or contain, revelation from God.

What about Eastern Religions?

Hinduism, Buddhism, and Sikhism believe in life after death on quite a different basis from Judaism, Christianity, and Islam. For them, the foundation is not belief in God but belief in the law of *karma*. What we are now is the product of what we have been in the past, and what we will be in the future is shaped by how we behave now. The law of karma cannot be restricted to this life. This is because there are enormous differences in the quality of life that people experience in the here and now and these differences go far beyond what they could be said to have merited through the way they have so far lived in their present lives. Here, for the law of karma to be fair, we must have had previous lives. The classic understanding of this is the doctrine of reincarnation in Hinduism and Sikhism and of rebirth in Buddhism. In all cases it is hoped that ultimately we will escape from the cycle of rebirth and become one with the ultimate *(moksha)* or enjoy the deathless state of *pari-nirvana*. In Hinduism, it is believed that our essential self *(atman)* is unchanging and eternal passing from one life to the next. Buddhism rejects this is in its no-self *(anatta)* doctrine which repudiates the idea of an atman as the core of our being on the grounds that our identity is in a constant state of flux. Some modern Buddhists, particularly in the West, interpret the no-self doctrine as implying that death means extinction and that *nirvana* should be understood as blowing out the candle. However, the doctrine of karma and rebirth is so central to Buddhism that other scholars take a different line and point out that in Sanskrit *anatta* is literally *an-atman*. What is being repudiated is the idea of an unchanging self, not a continually changing and developing self as implied in Western ideas of an emergent soul being developed by the way we live.

How Good Is the Evidence for Reincarnation?

The popular understanding of reincarnation is that it takes place on earth and that it is evidenced by children who claim to remember previous lives.[15] Professor Ian Stevenson, who researched this phenomenon for forty years, has argued that the evidence is very much stronger than is generally supposed in the West.[16] However, this is a controversial issue, and other scholars highlight the objection that all the apparently well-attested cases come from areas where the community supports the belief and where standards of evidence are not high. There is also the problem that Professor Stevenson always conducted his work using translators and normally followed up cases which were several years old and where the stories may well have "improved" through constant retelling. Moreover, in all reported cases there are anomalies in the stories told. For example, children may seem to "remember" a lot about the living conditions of "their" former lives, but then fail to recognize their mothers or wives. There is also the puzzle that acquiring some correct memories of someone else's life does not make one identical with that person. If a child born after my death could "remember" forty correct facts about my life, I don't think that this would be enough to justify my widow treating that child as being me!

There is also the difficulty that only a tiny handful of people have any memories of a past life. Some have suggested that hypnosis might enable us to "recover" such memories, and some striking success stories were reported by using this method. Unfortunately, however, it has subsequently been discovered that in the cases most carefully investigated, what was being remembered was not a real "previous life" but instead either hidden memories from childhood, say, relating to a book read many years earlier, or simply creations of the individual's imagination. So, the problem remains that most of us have no memories at all of a previous life and so the question has to be asked of what meaning we attach to the claim that "we" have all lived before if we remember nothing at all of that earlier life?

Tibetan Buddhism

Belief in claimed memories of previous lives as evidence for reincarnation is extremely important and apparently well evidenced in Tibetan Buddhism. This is because succession to very important positions such as being the *Lama* or spiritual leader of an historic monastery or major denomination (including the position of the Dalai Lama of Tibet) is dependent on a young child correctly identifying objects which belonged to the last Lama in that succession. If a child can do this, he will be taken from his family and educated in the traditions of his faith so he can fulfill this important role. The evident spiritual charisma of the present Dalai Lama might be thought as offering support for the validity of such beliefs.

The Pure-land Tradition

In China and Japan, many Buddhists follow the Pure-land tradition. This is actually the most popular form of Buddhism in Japan. According to this tradition, rebirth takes place not in this world but in Buddha's Pure-land, an idyllic world described in the Pure-land sutras in terms very reminiscent of the Christian heaven. This understanding of reincarnation is less problematic for those who see the continuation from this life to the next as requiring the continuing existence of the self-same self because it presupposes that we move on to a new life in a new world. This might be thought not dissimilar from contemporary Christian interpretations of *resurrection* as meaning that we will be re-created for new life in heaven.

Near-Death Experiences

Many people who have been resuscitated after their hearts have stopped beating and their lungs stopped breathing reported that they "left" their bodies and observed the resuscitation attempts from above. What makes such reports fascinating is that their observations seem remarkably accurate in relation to the facts otherwise unavailable from the position of their bodies. Those who have near-death experiences (NDEs) almost always think that the experiences prove that at the moment of death the soul leaves the body, and they believe that if they had not been "brought back," they would have gone on to a new life.

NDEs do not of course prove life after death because, of necessity, what all the experiencers have in common is that they did not finally die. Moreover, many doctors and scientists believe that naturalistic explanations of such phenomena can be given. Dr. Susan Blackmore, for example, sees all such experiences as generated by the dying brain and accountable through such factors as shortage of oxygen, increase of carbon dioxide, or by-products of the medication terminally ill people have been given, or through a massive release of the body's own pain protection mechanism of endorphins.[17]

However, all naturalistic explanations are open to objection. Other research has shown that there is simply no correlation between the presence of such factors and the having of a near-death experience. In particular, if near-death experience really was a product of oxygen starvation, then one would expect the observations to be hopelessly confused, as happens when people suffer from shortage of oxygen in other contexts, such as in mountain climbing or while flying planes.[18] So far, no consensus has been reached, though the evidence does seem to me to support the evidential character of near-death experiences because of the accuracy of the descriptions given. Such reports are of immense importance to our view of the relationship between mind and body. For, if a single "out-of-body experience" is correctly described as actually being just that, then the naturalistic identification of mind and brain is false.

If consciousness can leave the body and observe from a different vantage point, then the soul is a reality and life after death a real possibility.

NOTES

1. Paul Badham, "Life After Death," *Dialogue: A Journal of Religion and Philosophy* 21 (2003): 41–45.

2. In Peter Jupp and Tony Rogers, *Interpreting Death: Christian Theology and Pastoral Practice* (London: Cassell, 1997), chap. 11.

3. Linda Badham, "Problems about the Resurrection of the Body," in *Philosophy of Religion: An Introduction with Readings*, ed. Stuart Brown (London: Routledge, 2001), 133–37.

4. Richard Swinburne, *Is There a God?* (Oxford: Oxford University Press, 1996), 77.

5. Richard Swinburne, *The Evolution of the Soul* (Oxford: Oxford University Press, 1986), 1–2.

6. Keith Ward, *The Battle for the Soul* (London: Hodder & Stoughton, 1985), 149–50.

7. John Hick, *Evil and the God of Love*, rev. ed. (New York: Harper & Row, 1978).

8. Ibid., p. 295, citing *The Letters of John Keats* edited by M.B.Forman (1952), p. 334–5.

9. Paul and Linda Badham, *Immortality or Extinction?* 2nd ed. (London: SPCK, 1984), 74.

10. Jacques Monod, *Chance and Necessity* (New York: Knopf, 1971), 30.

11. Paul Badham, "God, the Soul and the Future Life," in *Death and Afterlife*, ed. S. Davis, p. 36-52 (London: Macmillan, 1989).

12. See Rupert Sheldrake, *The Sense of Being Stared At* (New York: Crown, 2003).

13. The Vatican, "Letter of the Sacred Congregation for the Doctrine of the Faith (Man's Condition After Death)," May 17, 1979, in *The Christian Faith in the Doctrinal Documents of the Catholic Church*, ed. J. Neuner and J. Dupuis, rev. ed. (London: Collins, 1938/1983), 691.

14. This is the view taken by the Church of England Doctrine Commission in their report, *The Mystery of Salvation* (Harrisburg, PA: Morehouse, 1995).

15. For discussion and references, see Paul and Linda Badham, *Immortality or Extinction?* chap. 7.

16. See, for example, Ian Stevenson, *Twenty Cases Suggestive of Reincarnation*, 2nd ed. (Charlottesville: University Press of Virginia, 1974).

17. Susan Blackmore, *Dying to Live* (Buffalo, NY: Prometheus, 1993).

18. Mark Fox, *Religion, Spirituality and the Near-Death Experience* (London: Routledge, 2003).

BIBLIOGRAPHY

Badham, Linda. "Problems about the Resurrection of the Body." In *Philosophy of Religion: An Introduction with Readings*, edited by Stuart Brown, 133–37. London: Routledge, 2001.

Badham, Paul. "God, the Soul and the Future Life." In *Death and Afterlife*, edited by S. Davis. P. 36-52. London: Macmillan, 1989.

———, and Linda Badham. *Immortality or Extinction?* 2nd edition. London: SPCK, 1984.

Blackmore, Susan. *Dying to Live*. Buffalo, NY: Prometheus, 1993.

Church of England, Doctrine Commission. *The Mystery of Salvation*. Harrisburg, PA: Morehouse, 1995.

Fox, Mark. *Religion, Spirituality and the Near-Death Experience*. London: Routledge, 2003.

Hick, John. *Evil and the God of Love*. Rev. ed. New York: Harper & Row, 1978.

Jupp, P., and T. Rogers. *Interpreting Death: Christian Theology and Pastoral Practice*. London: Cassell, 1997.

Kant, Immanuel. *Critique of Practical Reason*. Edited by Mary J. Gregor. New ed. Cambridge: Cambridge University Press, 1997.

Monod, Jacques. *Chance and Necessity*. New York: Knopf, 1971.

Sheldrake, Rupert. *The Sense of Being Stared At*. New York: Crown, 2003.

Stevenson, Ian. *Twenty Cases Suggestive of Reincarnation*. 2nd edition. Charlottesville: University Press of Virginia, 1974.

Swinburne, Richard. *Is There a God?* Oxford: Oxford University Press, 1996.

Swinburne, Richard. *The Evolution of the Soul*. Oxford: Oxford University Press, 1986.

The Vatican. "Letter of the Sacred Congregation for the Doctrine of the Faith (Man's Condition After Death)." May 17, 1979. In *The Christian Faith in the Doctrinal Documents of the Catholic Church*, edited by J. Neuner and J. Dupuis, 691. Rev. ed. London: Collins, 1938/1983.

Ward, Keith. *The Battle for the Soul*. London: Hodder & Stoughton, 1985.

16

Why an Investigation of Paranormal Experience Should Be an Essential Component of a Course on Death

L. Stafford Betty

When I took over our "death course" from an older colleague ten years ago, its formal title was Death and Aging in a Technological Society. I felt compelled to teach the first half of it as a social science, so we looked at issues like demographic profiles of older Americans, signs of teenage suicide, the funeral industry, bereavement patterns among minorities, the ethics of euthanasia, the child's grasp of death, wills and advanced directives, how to define death, even cryonics. These are legitimate subjects in any course on death, especially one slanted toward the social sciences. But I found myself uninterested in what I was teaching. What I wanted to talk about was the *meaning* of death, not the facts surrounding death. Eventually I found the vision to design the course I *wanted* to teach, not the one I inherited. Its title, predictably, was The Meaning of Death, and I've been teaching it ever since. It is this course I will be talking about here, and I should tell you at the outset that it takes a hard look at the question of an afterlife. For it is that question, whether you believe in one or not, that largely determines the meaning of death—and for many, the meaning of life.

So what do I do with those sociological issues I used to teach? I work them in as I can, especially those with moral implications such as euthanasia and physician-assisted suicide. But for the most part I leave them to my colleague in social work who looks at death in a more conventional way through one of the standard textbooks on death. While she does that, I explore in depth the various beliefs about death and afterlife in the world's major religions and look at evidence for the truth or falsity of these beliefs. And where does one go to find such evidence? *Is* there really such evidence? Surprisingly, there is a great deal. But it is found far away from the beaten track. Any serious investigator seeking to know what *really happens* at death will be forced to turn to psychical research, or what is more often called today "the paranormal." What I mostly want to describe here is the way that a study of paranormal literature—including the near-death experience, deathbed visions, medium-istic phenomena, and reincarnation cases—helps us get a handle on the af-terlife question. And the students? Judging by the numbers who sign up for the course, they enjoy this approach very much. Some claim it changes their whole outlook on death—and life. "If only I had known this earlier." I have heard that remark more than once.

The Course

Tim is a man about twenty-five who tells me after class that he and his wife have just lost their first child, who lived less than a day. He goes on to say that this baby is the twenty-ninth significant death he's experienced, a dozen in his large family alone. By the end of the quarter, Tim declares a major in religious studies. Jerry is a man in his early thirties who sits in the back row and never says anything until I call him—which I start to do with regularity after he makes the highest grade on the midterm. At the end of the class, he writes on the bottom of his term paper: "I do not exaggerate when I say: I have received more from this class than any other in my college career. I only wish I had enrolled in it earlier." I will never see Jerry again as he pursues a major in business. Cara is one of twenty-five nurses in the class, and she's taking it because she deals with dying people all the time. But she gets a bonus she didn't expect. She e-mails me after the class is over: "I've always known that my 'calling' as a nurse has been in hospice, which is why I enrolled in your class in the first place. I also have always had a profound interest in life after death, the paranormal, and so forth. . . . Your class was an incredibly eye-opening expe-rience for me." Finally, there is the unknown student I hear about in an indirect way. A counselor friend I eat lunch with tells me he has a client who is a student of mine. The student had never shown affection to his mother and never received much either. Now all that is changed, and his mother does not quite know what to do with all the love he is showing her. A family's life changes because of a course one young man took on death.

What is there about this course that makes these things happen? I'll take a little of the credit, but without the six books I use—without the *approach* I use—none of the above could have happened. What are those six books, and what is there about them that unleashes so much healing and inspiration? We read them in the following order: Tolstoy, *The Death of Ivan Iliych*; Mitch Albom, *Tuesdays with Morrie*; Hiroshi Obayashi, *Death and Afterlife: Perspectives of World Religions*; C. S. Lewis, *A Grief Observed*; Maggie Callanan and Patricia Kelley, *Final Gifts*; and Helen Greaves, *Testimony of Light*.[1] In addition we use shorter readings and quite a few films. I have structured the course with the following themes in mind:

1. Aging: The Beginning of Death (Film: *Strangers in Good Company*)
2. Death in Fiction (Tolstoy)
3. Coming to Terms with Death (Albom)
4. Death in the World's Religions (Obayashi)
5. Arguments For and Against Life After Death (five readings on reserve by Pascal, Lucretius, Bertrand Russell, Philip Larkin, Ian Stevenson)
6. A Theology of Death (Lewis)
7. What It's Like to Die (Callanan and Kelley)
8. Life After Death (Greaves)

Let us look at the logic of the course as it unfolds, moving increasingly away from this world and toward the next. The film on aging that begins the class is solidly situated in this world; but by the time we get to the last book we have left it altogether. In conjunction with this movement is the ever-increasing dependency on paranormal experience. We get a faint whiff of it at the end of *Ivan Iliych*, but by the end of the course we almost wallow in it.

Let us follow this progress book by book, heading by heading.

(1) *Strangers in Good Company* is an award-winning feature film that both celebrates and soberly exposes old age. Seven elderly women are forced to spend a weekend without any food or medical supplies in a remote cabin in the Canadian woods when their charter bus breaks down. Their resilience is alternately inspiring and funny, but their vulnerability and fear of the worst keeps them on edge. This exquisitely sensitive film is the perfect opener.

(2) *The Death of Ivan Iliych* plunges straight ahead into the theme of the course: the question of meaning. Ivan is a man who has never given a thought to life's meaning, but now he is dying. A successful judge, he represents everything that conventional people think they want: status, admiration, material comfort. But he is a conceited, hollow, unloved, and in the end, lonely

man; Tolstoy powerfully pulls the reader into the horror of this man's death as he gradually realizes the truth about himself. Does Ivan represent most of us? Tolstoy thinks so. We discover through Ivan the way we do not want to die. The question arises naturally: then how *do* we want to die?

(3) *Tuesdays with Morrie* tells us. Here is the perfect foil to Ivan: a man who did most of the right things and dies a beautiful death surrounded by loving family and friends. Morrie is a real, not a fictional, character, a professor of sociology who taught at Brandeis, and through the author Mitch Albom gives his "last class." "No books were required," Albom writes. "The subject was The Meaning of Life. It was taught from experience."[2] Morrie describes how he comes to terms with Lou Gehrig's Disease, an unforgiving, ravaging disease of the neurological system. But the best part of the book is his teaching about love. "Love each other or perish,"[3] he says, quoting the poet Auden. And he shows us how to do it. And he makes us *want* to do it. This book is simply written and is cherished by all my students, from the dullest to the brightest.

(4) Morrie was not a religious person, though he begins to pray and to think about what might follow death as his sickness progresses. Obayashi's *Death and Afterlife: Perspectives of World Religions* is of course explicitly religious. It's a collection of essays by various experts on the religions covered—in particular their beliefs about what happens at death and what follows. This is the least inspirational book of the six for most students, though it is packed with essential, sometimes fascinating information. It's the best book on the subject that I've found so far, though I can imagine better. Stay away from Kenneth Kramer's *The Sacred Art of Dying*. The title might grab you, but the treatment of religious views on death is sometimes shallow and misleading.

(5) We devote one class period to philosophical, poetic, and empirically based reflections on the possibility and desirability of a life after death. The pieces by Pascal, Lucretius, Russell, and Larkin are short and lapidary—little gems that stimulate thought about death and afterlife. The longer piece by Stevenson, the world's leading authority on children's memories of previous lives, is an in-depth empirical study of a woman who woke up one day speaking a language from another time and place. This deeply ambiguous essay, which need not be interpreted reincarnationally, introduces the student to the world of paranormal scholarship.

(6) After the midterm, we turn to C. S. Lewis's little masterpiece about his wife's death. *A Grief Observed* chronicles the stages of grief that he went through, his temporary loss of faith, his grappling with the problem of evil (Why does a good God permit so much pain and suffering?), and his solution to the problem. Since a majority of my students are at least nominally Christian and most have some kind of belief in a transcendental world, this book,

brilliantly yet simply written, hits home. Very few have ever wrestled with the problem of evil, and thus their religion has come cheaply. In class I try to help them confront the dilemma not only intellectually but existentially; then I work through with them the classic "free will defense," which Lewis uses to recover and deepen his faith.

(7) Two hospice nurses, Maggie Callanan and Patricia Kelley, wrote a study of what it's actually like to die. Dozens of cases are presented. "Beautifully written, illuminating and reassuring . . . *Final Gifts* is truly a gift to us all," says the jacket, and I agree. If ever there was a book that all of us should read when we or our loved ones are close to death, this is it. It places much emphasis on what holds the dying back, on the visions that they report and that we often wrongly dismiss as "confusion," and on the reasons we should not fear death. I ask my students the first day of class how they would want to die, and almost all say they want to die suddenly, preferably in their sleep. *Tuesdays with Morrie* and *Final Gifts* make many change their minds. Death is a dreadful experience, yes, but also a precious one. It is a time for reconciliation and even for joy; one gets the impression that death is not to be missed, and that the lucky ones are the ones who know what they are going through, not the ones who die without a warning. *Final Gifts* is not a religious book, but the visions of the dying support a religious interpretation of death. These nurses clearly do not believe that death is the end. The evidence they present practically rules it out. I will come back to this impression below.

(8) We finish with what I call "the bomb." *Testimony of Light* is ostensibly a report of what the world beyond is like; Frances Banks, an Anglican nun for twenty-five years who taught Alan Paton (author of *Cry the Beloved Country*) while stationed in South Africa, is the alleged source of the report. She's been dead for a month when she starts communicating through Helen Greaves, Banks's "channel" and good friend while both were alive. I tell my students that I think there is a fifty-fifty chance Banks is really coming through her friend telepathically, and a fifty-fifty chance the whole thing is being spun subconsciously out of Greaves's imagination. (It is a great mistake to think that all books like this are a hoax.) "Read it as fiction if you like; that's perfectly legitimate," I tell my students. But about half the class do not take it as fiction once they have finished. Either way, this book is an amazing account of what allegedly lies ahead for all of us, from the saintliest to the wickedest. I have read quite a few books in this genre and find some of them ridiculous and possibly fraudulent, but not this one. It is the best of its kind—with the classic collaboration between Geraldine Cummins and F. W. H. Myers (*The Road to Immortality*) a close second.[4] A few students, usually fundamentalists, despise the book. But a different kind of student went out and bought twelve copies

to give to all his friends. Many students do not quite know what to think. I see the book as a fit conclusion to the course. It certainly gets people thinking about the meaning of death—and of life. The main theme of the book is that what we do with our lives is important and has everything to do with the quality of our experience after we die. *Testimony of Light* gives powerful incentive to live the life that Morrie and Tolstoy would have us live. Whether taken as fiction or revelation, it leads to thoughtful reflection on the incredibly precious thing that life on earth is. It is one of the main reasons that my "death course" is so popular.

A Deeper Look at the Paranormal Component of the Course

Why devote so much time to paranormal experiences in a course on death, even in a course emphasizing afterlife? Isn't it enough to look at the extensive teachings on death and afterlife in the world's religions? From the resurrection teachings of the West to the reincarnational teachings of the East—isn't that enough? It is—if all you want to do is learn about the religions. But what if you want more? What if you want to discover which, if any, of these teachings *is true?* In a more conventional death course, the type I described above, the teacher wants to get across to her students *the truth* about teenage suicide, the funeral industry, bereavement patterns among minorities, and so forth—not just provide a collection of contending opinions on these subjects. Indeed, all education should be concerned with truth. Why, then, should we feel apologetic about pursuing the truth about death and afterlife? We should not. This is not to say that we will be completely successful, that we will ever approach certainty on these questions. But we should at least make the effort and see where it takes us. But how do we best enhance our chances of getting at the truth about this ever mysterious dimension of reality? By checking with scripture? For some that is enough. But the scriptures of the world religions do not speak with one voice; indeed they sometimes contradict each other. For many of my students, and certainly for me, scripture, while suggestive, does not provide the final answer. The best way to get possibly authentic glimpses into a world beyond ours is by studying what we call these days "the paranormal."

What topics or fields of investigation does the paranormal comprehend? Many more than we have time for in my course. But the ones we make time for are the following: reincarnational memories, deathbed visions, the near-death experience, and material channeled through mediums. I will show below why each is relevant to our quest for truth.

Reincarnational Memories

Ian Stevenson has left us close to a dozen books on children's memories that come from a world not their own.[5] Stevenson's subjects are very young children who remember what feels to them like a past life. Their memories of this life are as vivid, lifelike, and—most startling—accurate as any child's ordinary memories. In particular they remember their past death.

Stevenson has investigated over 3,000 cases of the reincarnation type. Some are stronger than others. Let's consider the typical features of an ideally well-developed case.

A child of two, three, or four—let's place her in India and call her Devi—begins talking about a former life in a different village. Devi gives her former name, Sita, and the name of the village. She also names and describes her mother, a favorite sister, and an influential teacher from that life. She tells how she misses life in that village and especially her two children, who were little more than toddlers when she died after being bitten on the toe by a krait. She tells her parents she is homesick and wishes to visit her former home, which is never talked about and has never been visited by anyone in her family.

One day she runs up to an apparent stranger outside her home and, speaking with great joy, calls him "Teacher." The man is startled, and Devi's mother runs up to apologize. But the little girl insists she is Sita and knows him and that he was her teacher back in the other village. By now Devi's parents, both Hindu, begin to wonder if Devi might really be a reincarnation of someone named Sita who lives in a distant village. Her parents begin to talk about their case, and someone brings it to the attention of one of Stevenson's associates living in India. The associate does some preliminary work, ascertains the case is genuine, and identifies a family in the alleged former village matching Devi's description. He even hears about the young mother who died by snakebite some six years earlier. Stevenson, who travels regularly to South Asia to investigate new cases and follow up on old ones, is notified, and he makes plans to visit Devi in a few months. But he does not inform the families—neither Devi's nor Sita's—of his plans.

When he arrives in the district, his associate takes him to see Devi. He asks the child to talk about her past life, and he writes down everything she says. She describes her home, a small temple across the street dedicated to Rama, a vegetable vendor who had a parrot that could recite one line from the Vedas, and many other particulars. He gets permission from Devi's parents to take her—she is just shy of her fourth birthday—to the alleged former village. He stays overnight in Devi's home, and the next day they set out in an automobile, the first Devi has ever ridden in. It takes two hours to cover the thirty-four-km distance over rutted lanes, and on the way he jots down more of Devi's memories. She shows tremendous excitement.

When they get to the village, the party gets out of the car, and Stevenson asks Devi to lead them to her former home. The child does not hesitate, and they wind their way through narrow lanes, with a curious crowd beginning to gather. "Here is my home," she exclaims, "but it used to be white." Stevenson's associate points out that this is not the house he visited her former family in, but Stevenson notes the temple directly *across* the street. The residents of the house are unknown to Devi and tell Stevenson's associate they've been renting the house for five years. Then they agree to lead the party to the landlord's home.

When they arrive there, Devi recognizes an uncle and runs up to him, telling him she is Sita. He is amazed but remembers the earlier visit from Stevenson's associate. He tells the party to wait and sets out at a run. He returns with a dozen people around him, and Devi/Sita squeals in delight. First she runs to her mother, then turns to her two children, now much bigger than she is, and begins to talk to them using terms of endearment that her husband, also present with his new wife, recognizes. It's clear she knows most of the people her uncle brought along, and most become convinced that Devi is indeed Sita. They also verify that her former home was white, that she died of snakebite, and that the vendor with the parrot still makes his rounds. Someone produces a family photograph, and she points to and names most of the faces. She asks about her favorite sister, but she has married and moved to a different town. When it's time to go, Devi/Sita begs to stay with her old family, but she's carried away waving and shrieking.

In the following months she asks repeatedly to be taken for another visit. But once she starts school, the old memories begin to fade, and so does her interest in a visit. Eventually she learns to regard her present mother as her "true mother." Stevenson visits Devi seven years later and finds her a normally developing girl with only the vaguest memories of her former life.

What do we do with a case like this? If it were unique, it would certainly arouse curiosity, but it would not convince. What is so convincing about Stevenson's research is the sheer number of cases he has meticulously collected. Described in bland academic prose, published by the University Press of Virginia for consumption by scholars, they are no easy target for debunkers. Dr. Albert Stunkard, a professor of psychiatry at the University of Pennsylvania Medical School, said of Stevenson: "I know there are a lot of people who disagree with him, but most of their criticism is done without reviewing his work. He's an incredible methodologist, hard to fault. He's very convincing, but I'm not convinced. Which is not to say that his research isn't valid."[6]

And that is the response of many of my students when we discuss the research that Stevenson is so famous for. Further, I do not assign a typical case for my students to read; instead we look at one of Stevenson's "unusual cases" (involving an adult, not a child), one that raises more questions than it answers.[7] I do this out of respect for my students' religious beliefs, which are usually not reincarnational. This case is just as easily explained by some sort of spirit possession as by reincarnation. In other words, the subject and the other personality (who speaks a language not known by the subject) might be two different persons, not one person with two different bodies. It is even remotely possible that the subject's strange, unaccountable linguistic ability could derive from a multiple personality disorder (MPD), an interpretation bypassing paranormality altogether. Personally, I am convinced that the subject's abilities cannot be accounted for conventionally, but that is not the point. The point is to show the students the facts of the case, provide alternative interpretations, and let them draw their own conclusions.

Deathbed Visions

Nowadays many, if not most, of our loved ones die slowly. They suffer from cancer, emphysema, heart disease, AIDS, or some other gradually debilitating disease and slowly slip away. *Final Gifts* provides an in-depth look at this kind of dying. For me, and I think for the authors, the most striking feature of many such deaths is the visions that the dying have of previously deceased relatives or friends. It is usually the case that only the dying, and not those gathered around the dying, see these otherworldly visitors. But are they really otherworldly visitors, or are they hallucinations? Is the patient, as we say, confused? The authors do not think this is always the case, and neither do I. In what follows, I will try to show you why. In every other context hallucinations are higgledy-piggledy. They are as wild and unrealistic as the craziest dream. A moose that charges at you in the middle of Fifth Avenue in New York, a boyhood home in Oregon gleaming nostalgically in a steamy Malaysian jungle—most hallucinators recognize their visions as delusional even as they are having them. But the hallucinations of the almost dead, if that's what they are, have sorted themselves out. With uncanny regularity only the dead show up. Why should that be? Why does the living Aunt Adelaide never show up? Why is it always the deceased Aunt Eleanor?

The materialist might answer that it would be *illogical* to hallucinate someone you thought was still alive. After all, a person can't be living on earth and living on the Other Side at the same time. If you had a vision of someone alive on this side of the veil, that would be *proof* you were hallucinating and would undercut the benefit you might derive from the hallucination. So the subconscious mind sorts out who's died and who hasn't. It keeps track. And when your time is up, it decks out a nice dead relative for you to hallucinate, a nice dead relative to take care of you when you finally die. Your fear of death vanishes. So the argument goes. But this argument is not as convincing as it might first appear. After all, how logical *are* hallucinations? Hallucinations are made of memory fragments, and those fragments are no more orderly as they come and go in the theater of the mind than the stuff of our daydreams. Zen masters compare the behavior of this mental detritus to a pack of drunken monkeys. And Aldous Huxley refers to them as "the bobbing scum of miscellaneous memories" and as "imbecilities—mere casual waste products of psycho-physiological activity."[8] The materialist's line of reasoning is plausible up to a point, but it overlooks the almost random nature of hallucinations.

But let us grant for the sake of argument that it does have force. I think I can show, and I try to show my students, that whatever force we grant it for the moment is not good enough in the face of the facts. In *Final Gifts* there is the following account:

> A dignified Chinese woman, Su was getting devoted care from her daughter, Lily. Both were Buddhists, and very accepting of the mother's terminal status.
>
> "I've had a good life for ninety-three years," she said. "And I've been on this earth long enough!" She dreamed often of her husband, who had died some years before.
>
> "I will join him soon," she said.
>
> But one day Su seemed very puzzled.
>
> "Why is my sister with my husband?" she asked. "They are both calling me to come."
>
> "Is your sister dead?" I asked.
>
> "No, she still lives in China," she said. "I have not seen her for many years."
>
> When I related this conversation to the daughter, she was astonished and tearful.
>
> "My aunt died two days ago in China," Lily said. "We decided not to tell Mother—her sister had the same kind of cancer."[9]

Coincidence? Did Su just happen to hallucinate her sister two days after her death, but never before? And if the materialist's explanation is correct, why did Su hallucinate a person she thought was alive in the first place?

A classic book by W. Barrett published eighty years ago collects cases like this one, and B. and J. Guggenheim devote a whole chapter to such cases in a more recent book.[10] Of course, there is always the possibility that Su could have known telepathically of her sister's death. But if Su had never had any powerful telepathic experiences before, isn't this explanation ad hoc? I think the most likely explanation for her sister's appearance alongside her husband in her dream vision is that the newly dead sister actually came (in spirit), along with her husband, to greet her and comfort her before her death. She was probably not a hallucination after all. She should be taken at face value.

Of course, there is plenty of room for differing interpretations, as my students make clear. But at least we are asking the big question, do we really live on after death? And we are answering it to the best of our ability, each in our own way. Not only are we answering it; we are answering it from a base of knowledge we never had before.

The Near-Death Experience

Although Callanan and Kelley are not primarily concerned with the near-death experience (NDE), they refer to it many times in *Final Gifts* and contrast it to the experience of the slowly dying. In the NDE, a person is jerked out of this life into another locale, then jerked back into this life from that locale. In between the jerks, the NDE unfolds. Most of us are familiar with the main features of a well-developed NDE: the sense of being out of the body, traveling down a tunnel, meeting deceased relatives, undergoing a life review, meeting and possibly merging with an intimately knowing, living Light, and so forth.[11] NDErs who merge with this Light tell us the main purpose of life is to grow in love, while a secondary one is to grow in knowledge and wisdom. They come out of their experience deeply changed, eager to accept the challenge, exhilarated by the second chance they've been given. And there's nothing "clubby" about NDErs. They don't talk like they're better than others, or more saved, or favored by God. They're just heralds of hope for a world that has lost its way, the modern equivalent of angels. They strike me not as proud but humble— like the saints of past ages whose close brushes with God made them permanently humble.

Between Life and Death is a well-crafted documentary that looks at the NDE.[12] It balances the sweeping, often rhapsodic claims made by NDErs, who sometimes claim they meet God, against the skeptical voice of science, which more often than not dismisses the NDE as a stupendous hallucination. In class, we consider both sides of the argument, beginning with the typical

NDEr's absolute certainty that what they experienced is real. Against this we pit science's claim that it can artificially create the experience by probing the right temporal lobe of the brain. (This claimed experience, it should be pointed out, falls far short of a well-developed NDE, with nothing remotely like changed lives or "merging with God" ever reported.) Back and forth the debate goes. I point out that NDErs witness events happening in our world while out of their "clinically dead" body—things later verified as really happening by witnesses. I mention recent research showing that NDErs blind from birth see our world for the first time when out of their body with its blind eyes. I summarize more recent research showing that some (and possibly most) NDEs occur when there is no measurable brain activity: exactly the opposite of what would be expected in the brain of a person having a uniquely rich and vivid hallucination.[13] And so forth.

On balance, NDEs point with considerable force to a continued life beyond death. For if a person is vividly alert and reports traveling to a different dimension while her body is clinically dead, with no blood moving through her brain and no heartbeat or respiration, then it follows that human consciousness is not dependent on a living body. Although free of it, personal consciousness continues. The person feels himself to be intact as the very being he felt himself to be before. He's just not attached to his physical body anymore. It's important to point out, though, that all this evidence by itself does not suggest eternal life. It suggests only a continuing life on the other side of the grave of indefinite and unknown duration.

Mediums

The experience of mediums, even reputable ones, is the least trustworthy evidence for life after death; it is also by far the most interesting, for it not only leads to the conclusion, if taken at face value, that there is life after death; it describes that life.

The reason we cannot bank on mediums' accounts of the next world is that there is always the possibility, some would say the likelihood, that even the best and most sincere medium might be describing material in her subconscious imagination rather than channeling material from a spirit on the Other Side working through her. The best mediums have always been aware of this possibility, but most are amazed by the material they produce, either by voice or by writing, while in trance or wide awake or somewhere in between. Those who write, moreover, often do so at a nonstop pace and in a handwriting not their own. One of the greatest mediums of the nineteenth century, Stainton Moses, could be fully absorbed in an abstruse philosophy book held in one hand while his other hand wrote "automatically" its message ostensibly from the Other Side. And Luis Gasparetto, a Brazilian physician who channels great painters, paints with eyes closed, with brush held by hand or between his toes, with the canvas right side up or turned upside down, and at tremendous speed. He has no trouble painting two pictures in totally different styles simultaneously, one hand to a canvas. He has been photographed and filmed many times and never accused of fraud. He takes no credit for his paintings, but claims they originate from painters on the Other Side who merely use his body as an instrument. I come from a family of artists and have watched Gasparetto work: in my opinion what he does is not humanly possible. There is some other factor at work.

That brings us to Helen Greaves and Frances Banks, the medium and the alleged after-death communicator whose account we read in its entirety in *Testimony of Light*. Both were esteemed British citizens whose spotless reputations are vouched for by persons of high standing in the Anglican Church. Canon J. D. Pearce-Higgins compares their collaboration to some of the great revelations of the past, Mother Julian of Norwich's *Revelations of Divine Love* in particular. *Testimony of Light* is in a completely different class from the works of some best-selling modern mediums like Sylvia Browne. If ever there was a book that succeeded in breaking through the barrier between our world of matter and that other world of light, it is this one. But there are no guarantees.

That aside, the themes of the book and the actual descriptions are remarkably rich. One of its most appealing features is Frances's descriptions of the people she meets, from the "great Beings" to the "stumblers," from the bicycle thief to Pierre Curie, from the twelve-year-old dancer stricken with polio and readying herself for another incarnation on earth to the Parisian painter of promise "reduced to the gutter" and now living in the "Shadow Lands," barely aware that he ever died. Her conversations with this great variety of people are fascinating, as are her descriptions of "Spheres of unimaginable joy and beauty" ranging all the way down to the "lower regions," where missionary spirits work to free "poor half-alive creatures in their self-darkness." Leslie Weatherhead wrote, "I think death is a tremendous adventure—a gateway into a new life, in which you have further powers, deeper joys, and wonderful horizons."[14] Frances describes just such a world—at least for those who live wisely in this one. Is Frances' world the world you and I will come to at death? I *hope* it is. So do many of my students.

Summing Up

I believe that a course on death sells itself short if it does not reach as high as it can. Even if the instructor is ill equipped by training to teach a course like the one I've described, he or she should try. Students are almost never introduced to the really big questions in college anymore, and they, and their world, suffer from this neglect.

We should be beacons of light to our students, holding up to them the greatest visions and highest hopes that the planet has so far seen. We don't do that by remaining respectable, safe social scientists and academicians. We should make it easier for our students to make an act of faith, if so inclined, in something worthy of them, something they can live out of and be constantly inspired by, something that only a great vision can awaken in them. I think that a course like mine provides such a vision, a reason to live nobly, a mandate to avoid becoming another Ivan Iliych. Mother Teresa said, "Let no one ever come to you without coming away better and happier." A pretty idea, but is it feasible for us to become like that? It is. But first we have to believe that it is *expected* of us. Every one of the books I've described here tells the student that it is, but none so powerfully as the last. And that is as it should be. *Testimony of Light* strikes me as authentic, as coming from a world that vibrates at a higher pitch than ours, and where truth is not as veiled. No wonder the course is popular. Who wouldn't want to steal a glimpse of life's meaning and purpose from a higher source? It's like taking wild honey from a forest hive after the bees have been smoked out. Let us enjoy the honey.

NOTES

1. L. Tolstoy, *The Kruetzer Sonata and Other Short Stories* (New York: Dover, 1993); M. Albom, *Tuesdays with Morrie: An Old Man, a Young Man, and Life's Greatest Lesson* (New York: Doubleday, 1997); H. Obayashi, ed., *Death and Afterlife: Perspectives on World Religions* (London: Praeger, 1992); C. S. Lewis, *A Grief Observed* (New York: Bantam, 1976); M. Callanan and P. Kelley, *Final Gifts* (New York: Bantam, 1992); and H. Greaves, *Testimony of Light* (Saffron Walden, UK: C. W. Daniel, 1969).

2. Albom, *Tuesdays with Morrie*, 1.

3. Ibid., 91.

4. G. Cummins, *The Road to Immortality* (London: Ivor Nicholson & Watson, 1932).

5. Ian Stevenson's many works include *Twenty Cases Suggestive of Reincarnation,* 2nd ed. (Charlottesville: University Press of Virginia, 1974), and *Where Reincarnation and Biology Intersect* (Westport, CT: Praeger, 1997).

6. T. Zito, "Scholar Maps, Codifies 'Reincarnations,'" *New York Times*, December 10, 1978, XI, 5.

7. I. Stevenson and S. Pasricha, "A Preliminary Report on an Unusual Case of the Reincarnation Type with Xenoglossy," *Journal of the American Society for Psychical Research* 74 (1980): 331–48.

8. A. Huxley, "Distractions—I," in *Vedanta for the Western World*, ed. C. Isherwood (Hollywood, CA: Vedanta, 1945), 126–27.

9. Callanan and Kelley, *Final Gifts*, 91.

10. See W. Barrett, *Death-Bed Visions* (London: Methuen, 1926); and B. and J. Guggenheim, *Hello from Heaven!* (New York: Bantam, 1995).

11. Raymond Moody is widely seen as responsible for the modern formulation and coinage of the term *near-death experience*. See his *Life After Life* (Atlanta: Mockingbird, 1975).

12. Roger James and Antony Thomas, producers, *Between Life and Death* (A Film for the Humanities & Sciences, Princeton, NJ, 1998).

13. W. Van Lommel, R. Van Wees, V. Meyers, and I. Elfferich, "Near-death Experience in Survivors of Cardiac Arrest: A Prospective Study in the Netherlands," *Lancet* 358 (2001): 2039–45.

14. Quoted in B. and J. Guggenheim, *Hello from Heaven!* 323.

BIBLIOGRAPHY

Albom, M. *Tuesdays with Morrie: An Old Man, a Young Man, and Life's Greatest Lesson.* New York: Doubleday, 1997.

Barrett, W. *Death-Bed Visions.* London: Methuen, 1926.

Callanan, M., and P. Kelley. *Final Gifts.* New York: Bantam, 1992.

Cummins, G. *The Road to Immortality.* London: Ivor Nicholson & Watson, 1932.

Greaves, H. *Testimony of Light.* Saffron Walden, UK: C. W. Daniel, 1969.

Guggenheim, B. and J. *Hello from Heaven!* New York: Bantam, 1995.

Huxley, A. "Distractions—I." in *Vedanta for the Western World*, edited by C. Isherwood, 125–29. Hollywood: Vedanta, 1945.

James, Roger, and Antony Thomas, producers. *Between Life and Death.* A Film for the Humanities & Sciences, Princeton, NJ, 1998.

Lewis, C. S. *A Grief Observed.* New York: Bantam, 1976.

Moody, Raymond. *Life After Life.* Atlanta: Mockingbird, 1975.

Obayashi, H., ed. *Death and Afterlife: Perspectives of World Religions.* London: Praeger, 1992.

Tolstoy, L. *The Kreutzer Sonata and Other Short Stories.* New York: Dover, 1993.

Stevenson, Ian. *Twenty Cases Suggestive of Reincarnation.* 2nd ed. Charlottesville: University Press of Virginia, 1974.

Stevenson, I. *Where Reincarnation and Biology Intersect.* Westport, CT: Praeger, 1997.

Stevenson, I., and S. Pasricha. "A Preliminary Report on an Unusual Case of the Reincarnation Type with Xenoglossy." *Journal of the American Society for Psychical Research* 74 (1980): 331–48.

Van Lommel, W., R. Van Wees, V. Meyers, and I. Elfferich. "Near-death Experience in Survivors of Cardiac Arrest: A Prospective Study in the Netherlands." *Lancet* 358 (2001): 2039–45.

Zito, T. "Scholar Maps, Codifies 'Reincarnations.'" *New York Times*, December 10, 1978, XI, 1, 5, 6.

Appendix

Alternative Media Resources

VIDEOS

Always, dir. Steven Spielberg (Universal City Studios, 1989).

Dead Man, dir. Jim Jarmusch (Pandora Filmproduktion, 1995).

Defending Your Life, dir. Albert Brooks (Geffen Pictures Productions, 1991; Warner Home Video, 1999).

Fight to Die (CNN Special Presentation, 1995).

The Fisher King, dir. Terry Gilliam (Columbia Pictures, 1991).

Four Weddings and a Funeral, dir. Mike Newell (Channel Four Films, 1994).

Hitting Sticks, Healing Hearts (River Tracks Productions, 1991).

Hurt (Johnny Cash) dir. Mark Romanek (2002).

Intensive Care: Who Decides? (*Dateline* NBC, nd).

In the Bedroom, dir. Todd Fields (Miramax, 2002).

Iris, dir. Robert Eyre (BBC, 2001).

Jesus of Montreal, dir. Denys Arcand (National Film Board of Canada, 1989).

La Ofrenda: The Days of the Dead, dir. Lourdes Portillo and Susana Muñoz (Direct Cinema, 1989).

Letting Go: The Hospice Journey, dirs. Deborah Dickson and Susan Frömke (Films for the Sciences and Humanities, 1996).

Living with Dying (Alfred Univesity School of Health Related Professions, 1976).

The Man Who Learned to Fall (Beitel/Lazar Productions, 2004).

Memory of the Camps (PBS Video, 1989).

Nuit et Brouillard, dir. Alain Resnais (Reel Images, [1955] 1978).

On Our Own Terms: Moyers on Dying (PBS, 2000).

Richard Cardinal: Cry from a Diary of a Métis Child, dir. Alanis Obomsawin (National Film Board of Canada, 1986).

Santitos, dir. Alejandro Springall (1998).

The Sixth Sense, dir. M. Night Shyamalan (Hollywood Pictures, 1999).

Steel Magnolias, dir. Herbert Ross (Rastar Films, 1989).

Strangers in Good Company, dir. Cynthia Scott (National Film Board of Canada, 1990).

Surviving Death: Stories of Grief, dir. Elizabeth Murray (National Film Board of Canada, 1998).

Tuesdays With Morrie, dir. Mick Jackson (Harpo Productions, 1999).

What Dreams May Come, dir. Vincent Ward (Universal Pictures, Polygram Films, 1998).

When Strangers Reunite, dirs. Florchita Bautista and Marie Boti (National Film Board of Canada, 1999).

Wit, dir. Mike Nichols (Avenue Pictures Productions, 2001).

SONGS

Kate Campbell, "Tupelo's Too Far" on *Moonpie Dreams* (Compass Records, 1997).

Johnny Cash, "Hurt" on *American IV: The Man Comes Around* (Lost Highway, 2002).

Everlast, "Graves to Dig" on *Eat at Whitey's* (Rhino, 2000).

Vince Gill, "The Key to Life" on *The Key* (MCA Nashville, 1998).

Vince Gill, "Go Rest High on That Mountain" on *When Love Finds You* (Geffen, 1994).

Ann Peebles, "I Can't Stand the Rain" on *I Can't Stand the Rain* (Hi Records, 1974).

Puff Daddy, Faith Evans, and 112, "I'll Be Missing you" on *No Way Out* (Bad Boy, 1997).

Lou Reed, "Magic and Loss" on *Magic and Loss* (Sire Records, 1992).

Ralph Stanley, "O Death" on *Oh Brother, Where Art Thou? Soundtrack* (Lost Highway, 2000).

Jim and Jean Strathdee, "Listen to the Dark" on *Stand for What Is Right* (2007)

Sir John Tavener, "Requiem."

Traditional, "Will the Circle Be Unbroken."

LITERATURE

Mitch Albom, *Tuesdays with Morrie: An Old Man, a Young Man, and Life's Greatest Lesson* (New York: Doubleday, 1997).

Pauline Chen, *Final Exam: A Surgeon's Reflection on Mortality* (New York: Random House, 2007).

Margaret Craven, *I Heard the Owl Call My Name* (New York: Dell, 1967/1973).

Vincent Lam, *Bloodletting and Miraculous Cures* (Toronto: Anchor Canada, 2005).

C. S. Lewis, *A Grief Observed* (New York: Bantam Books, 1976).

Elie Wiesel, *Night*, trans. Stella Rodway (New York: Bantam Books, 1982).

Leo Tolstoy, *The Death of Ivan Ilyich*, trans. Lynn Soltaroff (New York: Bantam, 1981).

Nicholas Wolterstorff, *Lament for a Son* (Grand Rapids, MI: Eedermans, 1987).

POEMS

W. H. Auden, "Funeral Blues."

Paul Celan, "Death Fugue."

Dylan Thomas, "Do Not Go Gentle into That Good Night."
Dylan Thomas, "A Refusal to Mourn the Death, by Fire, of a Child in London."

WEB SITES

Nan Chico, "Resources for Death and Dying Courses"
http://class.csueastbay.edu/faculty/NAN/dd/dd.htm
The Chicago Forum on Pedagogy and the Study of Religion
http://marty-center.uchicago.edu/fellows/chicagoforum.shtml
Cemetery Culture: City of the Silent
http://www.alsirat.com/silence/
Death in Art
http://www.lamortdanslart.com/main.htm
Dan Meinwald, "Memento Mori: Death and Photography in Nineteenth Century
    America"
http://www.cmp.ucr.edu/exhibitions/memento_mori/default.html
Journal of Religion and Film
http://www.unomaha.edu/jrf/
King's College Centre for Education about Grief and Bereavement, "Where to Study
    about Death, Dying, and Bereavement"
http://www.uwo.ca/kings/academic_programs/centres/deathed/courses-death.html
Kearl's Guide to Sociological Thanatology
http://www.trinity.edu/mkearl/death.html
Markers, Association of Gravestone Studies
http://www.gravestonestudies.org/markers.htm
Memorial Ecosystems, "Leaders in Conservation Burial"
http://www.memorialecosystems.com
National Funeral Directors Association
www.nfda.org
On Our Own Terms: Moyers on Dying
http://www.pbs.org/wnet/onourownterms/index.html

Index